DEADLOCK!

Ethnicity and Electoral Competition in Trinidad and Tobago 1995-2002

Selwyn Ryan

ISBN 976-618-033-4 (Soft Cover)

Printed by: Zenith Printing Services Limited
Fernandes Industrial Centre
Eastern Main Road Laventille
REPUBLIC OF TRINIDAD AND TOBAGO

Table of Contents

Preface

In the decades that followed the achievement of Independence, the appropriateness of the political model that was adopted throughout the Anglophone Caribbean was continuously debated by the region's political elites. Everywhere the system seemed incapable of meeting the material and security needs and expectations of the Caribbean people. The complaint was that the system tended to shut out the "people" and subaltern groups, and that effective power remained in the hands of those elites who had succeeded the colonial power. It was also widely believed that the latter had maintained effective economic control through those who had replaced them. What was achieved, according to this point of view, was "flag" or "symbolic" independence, and not real independence. Neo-colonialism was seen to be triumphant. A great deal of political energy was thus mobilised by post-independence out or anti-system elites to smash the edifices of the neo-colonial state. All sorts of dogmas and formulae were trotted out as antidotes to the virus of elitism, class exclusivism, patrimonialism or "doctor politics" (aka "doctatorship"). These ranged from one party systems which would harness the energies of the people in all their social and ethnic diversity, people's assemblies which would do the same thing from the bottom up, or vanguard parties that would energise and lead the masses.

In Trinidad and Tobago, there were proposals for a big "macco" Senate, or for a "party of parties" to harness the energies of the various "tribes" and corporate groups in the society (Best and Harris 1991). Every formula that was in vogue in Cuba and other countries in Latin America, Africa, China, Eastern Europe or the Soviet Union had an echo in the Caribbean as groups competed with each other to install some alternative to the Westminster model. Defenders of the latter, for their part, claimed that that model was as Caribbean as sugar cane or bananas despite its British origin, and, what is more, was better suited to the people's political temperament and historical experience.

While many of these movements articulated their perceptions of exclusion and marginalisation in class or populist terms, others did so in terms of ethnic diversity along a white-black or Indian-African continuum where the latter was relevant as in Guyana, Suriname or Trinidad and Tobago. For much of the period, however the lament of the Indo-Caribbean people was not seen to be particularly legitimate by the region's leading intellectual cohorts committed as most were to Marxian notions about class. In-so-far as they recognised the problem of ethnicity, socialism was seen to be the eventual solvent of "false consciousness" and other primitive attitudes. Had Stalin and Tito not solved the nationality question? Had Mao and the Chinese communists not found a formula to mobilise the energies of the very diverse peoples who occupied the China Mainland? Had Forbes Burnham and Cheddi Jagan not shown that Indians and Africans could unite for common political ends? Did Burnham not later show that he was able to co-opt Indian, Amerindian and Portuguese elites in his mission to construct a cooperative socialist Republic? Had Castro not defused the explosive black- white issue in Cuba by replacing it with class and other revolutionary alternatives (Moore 1988). The dominant assumption was that "East Indians" would in time become "West Indians" through a process of creolisation and assimilation, and that out of many peoples, one people and one Caribbean nation would emerge triumphant.

Lloyd Best has argued that this undervaluing of the fact of ethnicity was largely responsible for the collapse of Federation and Dr. Williams' nationalist party project. As he wrote:

> In conceptualising his party, Dr. Williams betrayed very much the same perceptions that were later to torpedo his strategy for the WI Federation. The consistent feature was the remarkably low recognition of ethnicity as the decisive factor. In the case of the Federation, the cardinal error was the failure to see that not only was ethnicity present and active, but also that island homeland was the defining basis for solidarity. This is

the most important single error being repeated in Caricom today. We continue to treat with "insularity" as if it is some aberration that would one day disappear if there were a sufficient exhortation to that end.

In the case of the party politics of Trinidad and Tobago, there has been a corresponding failure. We have treated racial bonding as if it were an exotic feature reflecting the shenanigans of a recalcitrant or intransigent minority. But the imperative of history was and still is clear. Either the WI party must provide copiously and explicitly for internal coalition to acknowledge the ethnic fact; or it must repudiate and reject it thereby condemning itself. (*Express*, January 25, 2002)

The ethnic problem did not go away as the socialist optimists and creole ideologists hoped. Indeed, it became more persistent as previously marginalised ethnic groups in the region – Indians, Javanese, African Maroons (aka "Bush Negroes"), Amerindians – became more geographically and socially mobile and mainstreamed. These subaltern groups demanded to be seen as a legitimate but distinctive part of the "creole" order, not as individual accretions *via* the assimilation\ integration route, but in terms that were more pluralist and group based. What they wanted was not token acceptance as deculturalised orientals, but to be regarded as authentic West Indians who nevertheless brought the distinctive fragrance of the lotus or some other oriental flower to the Caribbean bouquet. Above all, they wanted a secure space in the political kingdoms that dotted the Caribbean landscape.

Criticisms of the Westminster Model were even forthcoming in respect of societies that were not divided along racial lines. Looking at societies in West Africa, St. Lucian Nobel Laureate, Sir Arthur Lewis, argued that plural societies required a different model of governance. As Lewis (1965:55) wrote:

Britain and France are class societies, and their institutions and conventions are designed to cope with this fact. West Africa is not a class society; its problem is that it is a plural society. What is good for a class society is bad for a plural society. Hence to create good political institutions in West Africa one has to think their problem through from the foundations up... men who stand for elections represent groups with different interests, ideas and characteristics, and the real contest is between these groups. To exclude the losing groups from participation in decision making clearly violates the primary meaning of democracy.

As disenchantment deepened with the Westminster model, attention was focussed on various alternative models. Some found answers in systems of proportional representation, particularly the mixed version of that model that was in place in the western half of Germany. A Constitution Commission appointed by the Government of Trinidad and Tobago following the Black Power revolution of the early seventies (Ryan and Stewart 1995), chaired by Sir Hugh Wooding, recommended such a system for Trinidad and Tobago, but it was peremptorily rejected by the then Prime Minister, Dr. Eric Williams who recognised that it would decentre and disestablish the political order which he had created and which had enjoyed hegemony during the preceding 20 years. Williams believed that what was needed in plural societies such as those in Trinidad and Tobago was not more freedoms, but more discipline. As he wrote:

> In a period when Trinidad and Tobago is at the mercy of all sorts of unpredictable international influences which require immediate and firm action .... a Government of Trinidad and Tobago could not hope to survive if it is in the hands of an unstable coalition of proportional representation parties and individuals where a crucial issue might depend on the placation of the vote of some one or other of them .... Trinidad

and Tobago finds itself rather in the position emphasized by Professor Rupert Emerson, that the prime requirement of the new developing states is not for more freedoms but for discipline, and that in any country with tribal, racial and religious hostilities, the essential need is strong and unified management. (Williams 1973:245)

Williams turned his back quite resolutely on all proposals for proportional representation, which in his view meant racial or communal representation. He expressed himself quite opposed to any suggestion that minority groups be given special constitutional standing:

> There are those who would like the Trinidad and Tobago Independence Constitution to be patterned on that of Cyprus which means that the Constitution will emphasize, and in fact establish sharp lines of division between the various racial groups.... I would far prefer to have a government of Trinidad and Tobago accused of not dividing up the community into racial groups rather than have it accused of constitutional provisions which would establish a Negro President and an Indian Vice-President of a Republic, with a fixed proportion of seats or places to the various racial groups in the Cabinet, in Parliament, in the Judiciary, in the Police Service and in the Civil Service. As far as I am concerned, that way madness lies. (*Trinidad Guardian,* April 8, 1962)

In Guyana, where a virtual civil war was often in the making as persons of Indian and African descent fought for economic, political, and racial superiority and security (who was to be on top), Burnham thought he had found the answer in state socialism, classical proportional representation, rigged elections, and the establishment of a repressive militariat. His death, the collapse of the Soviet Union, and with it the cold war, and the rise of the third wave democratic movement, made that formula unsustainable for his successors. One had to find other ways to defang and dismount the ethnic tiger.

In neighbouring Suriname, another model, broadly termed the *Verbroedering*, (brotherhood) "consociational" or "consensus" model emerged prior to the achievement of independence in 1975. The political culture of Suriname was influenced by the political system in the Netherlands which encourages multipolar as opposed to the bipolar politics that characterises Westminster. The *verbroedering politiek* system however had its roots in the practical experience of Surinamese politicians who had to find a way to preempt ethnic conflict between the mulatto elites, the creoles of African provenience, the Hindustanis and the Javanese.

This study looks at contemporary politics in Trinidad and Tobago especially as it relates to the demands being made for inclusion and security by the constituent ethnic groups, especially the two that are numerically dominant. It also looks at the demand for "power sharing" or "shared governance" as a mechanism for resolving the parliamentary deadlock which occurred following the general elections of 2000 and 2002, and the general deadlock which obtained in the society at large.

The writing of contemporary history is fraught with difficulties for authors. One of the many disadvantages is that much of what "really happened" only becomes known long after the event when the protagonists and commentators feel free to stop the "spin cycle" and reveal what was really done or said, and why. There is also the advantage that comes from taking the "long view" that allows one to see with dispassion the connections that exist between the new, the old and the very old. Eras and events are never as discrete as authors often make them out to be.

There are however advantages to be had when narratives are written during or shortly after the events to which they refer. The contemporary analyst is sometimes better able to capture detail, nauances, and moods which might escape those who attempt to reconstruct events long after they occur, and therefore has to rely on sterile "documents" without being fully privy to the environment that surrounded and informed the events that are being analysed.

There is still a great deal of controversy about some of the political events which took place in the period under review. Opinion about who or what was right or wrong, or who did what and for what reason, are still sharply divided across ethnic lines. The author was himself a commentator and at times a participant in some of the events, and his biases, whether conscious or not, may well be evident in the comments made and the conclusions that are drawn. As George Bernard shaw wisely observed, "we cannot get away from the critics' tempers, his impatiences, his sorenesses, his friendships, his spites, his enthusiasms, nay his very politics and religion if they are touched by what he criticises. They are all hard at work." In writing this account, we have consciously adopted the strategy of allowing the main protagonists and commentators to articulate their views in the hope that by doing so, readers will be able to come to conclusions of their own where these differ from ours.

Acknowledgements

In the writing of this book, thanks are due to a number of people all of whom it would be invidious to identify. Some of the views expressed herein benefited from comments made by persons who were not aware that they were influencing my thought processes in any way. I also benefited from the many exchanges of views which were aired in the daily media, particularly the *Trinidad Express* and the *Trinidad and Tobago Review*. Some of the chapters in the book began as columns in the *Sunday Express* or as papers which were previously presented at academic conferences. Some of the material was also drawn from earlier publications of which this book forms part of a series.

In the preparation of the book for publication, I owe a particular debt to Mr. Roy McCree of the Institute of Social and Economic Studies who was largely responsible for editing the document, and to Ms. Gloria Lawrence who patiently typed, retyped, and formatted it. I am also grateful to other members of the ISES staff for the usual courtesies extended over the year that the book being produced. I also wish to thank Ms. Alice Besson of Paria for the artwork and Zenith Printing Services Ltd. for printing and binding services.

Chapter 1

BACKGROUND TO DEADLOCK

> The races are fearful of the other getting the upper hand in the politics of the country. The fear might be unjustified. But justified or not, it is a real fear, and we have to treat with it… We need a formula for power sharing, but we reject that power sharing means you pick one minister and I pick one. That is doomed to failure.
>
> *- Patrick Manning*
> *Guardian*, September 21, 2002

> In my house there are many mansions. Under the big tent of the UNC there is room for all.
>
> *- Basdeo Panday*
> *Newsday*, September 16, 2002

*T*his book sets out to give an account of and to analyze the political events and issues that were the subject of acute political controversy in Trinidad and Tobago in the years immediately preceding and following the birth of the new millennium. Four general elections were required to break the electoral deadlock that developed in the country as the 20th Century came to its historic close. Evidence of the impending deadlock was evident as early as 1995 when the Political Leader of the People's National Movement (PNM), Mr. Patrick Manning, indicated that he could not govern the country effectively with a one seat majority in the House of Representatives, and sought to resolve the issue by calling early elections. The election however ended in a 17-17 tie in Trinidad between the

PNM and the United National Congress (UNC), the former opposition party.

Prior to 1995, the Afro-based PNM had governed Trinidad and Tobago continuously for 30 years - 1956-1986. The PNM's dominance was decisively broken in 1986 when a grand "rainbow coalition" consisting of the opposition United Labour Front (ULF), the Organization For National Reconstruction (ONR), and dissident PNM forces came together with other groupings to form the NAR. The NAR coalition won 33 of the 36 seats in Parliament. The coalition was however politically unstable and collapsed within months of winning power as its various constituent wings struggled to regain, retain, or maintain political, social and economic power (Ryan 1989). Within months of being in office, the Indo element of the party, which was concentrated in the ULF, found itself once more in opposition. In 1988, the dissident ULF faction transformed itself into the United National Congress, a name which symbolized the party's effort to alter its image from that of an arm of the radical trade union movement to one that could appeal to the middle class in general and the Indian middle class in particular, many of whom had hitherto supported the PNM, the ONR, which had appeared on the scene in 1981 (Ryan 1989a) or the NAR in 1986.

The failure of the "rainbow coalition" led to the massive return to the PNM of those elements which had deserted it in 1986. Many Indo-Trinidadians also turned to the UNC which succeeded the ULF. The two major ethnic groups had concluded that the type of coalition movement represented by the NAR ideal would not work in the foreseeable future, and that the struggle for dominance would have to be fought on a "winner take all" basis.

The PNM won the first round in the elections of 1991, winning 21 of the 36 seats to the UNC's 13. Its victory was however only made possible because the NAR retained the support of 24.43 percent of the electorate even though it could only win the two seats in Tobago. In sum, the PNM won a 21 seat victory largely because the election was a three party event and the NAR took votes that might well have gone to the UNC. The UNC also claimed that the PNM won because of a flawed voters list and slow voting in certain polling divisions, a claim that had no foundation. It also claimed that it lost the election by a mere 7,000 votes in three closely contested constituencies, and that had it had a better understanding of the demography of the constituencies and the organizational capacity to mobilize its base, they could have brought out the vote required to give them at least 18 seats.

If the UNC's claim was correct, as might well have been the case, the deadlock would have occurred a decade earlier than it actually did. In any event, the UNC vowed that it would not make the same tactical and organizational errors as it had done in 1991, and that the party would restructure itself to win the 1995 election, a goal which it was certain was within its grasp. To do so, however, it needed money; but above all, it needed to project itself as a "national" as opposed to an Indian party based in central and south Trinidad where the sugar, rice and vegetable enclaves were to be found. Between 1991 and 1995, the UNC would sedulously seek to "break through" the sugar cane curtain.

The UNC leadership was fully aware of another reality *viz.,* that the demographics of the country were changing in its favour. The publication of the results of the 1990 census had revealed that Indians were the largest single ethnic group: 40.6 percent of the population were classified as Indian compared to 39.6 percent for Afro-Trinidadians, and 18 percent for the mixed grouping. The party leadership was convinced that population growth and internal migration was serving to undermine the iron grip which the PNM enjoyed in the sixties and which had allowed it to win and retain power for 30 years. Several seats that were hitherto "safe" for the PNM had now become competitive in that either party could win them.

As Panday himself gleefully chortled:

> That simple fact has put the PNM on the horns of a dilemma from which it seems unable to extricate itself. This dilemma

> arises from the history of the elite in the PNM, which has, for more than 30 years, ridden the backs of the African masses by appealing to race in order to win the elections. That strategy worked well for them as long as the African electorate was in the majority. Now that that is no longer so, Manning realizes that he cannot win the elections without substantial Indian votes, votes which the PNM has studiously alienated over the years in a long history of discrimination, vilification and humiliation. (*Trinidad Guardian*, October 11, 1993)

Panday's statement seemed to assume that Indians were an undifferentiated lot, and that all would support an Indian dominated party regardless of class or religion. Past voting trends however indicated that this did not occur. It also ignored the fact that a significant proportion of the mixed population and the minority elements, which together constituted some 20 percent of the population, were more likely to throw their electoral weight behind the PNM. Panday however expressed regret that Indians had not yet come to appreciate the power which the new demographic reality conferred on them. As he lamented:

> ...When in 1945, Indo-Trinbagonians celebrated the 100th anniversary of Indian Arrival Day, Indians constituted 27 percent of the total population. They accepted the fact that against a background of racial voting, they could not and would not participate in any meaningful way in the governance of the country. Today, Indians constitute the largest single ethnic group in the country, yet many of them are of the same view still. (*ibid.*)

Panday was however convinced that the age of PNM dominance was over, and that with the demise of the NAR, the rights of succession belonged to the UNC. After close to 150 years of being in the wilderness and of genuflecting to others on the question of national political leadership, the time had come to mobilize the Indian population to make a bid for political power. Those who opted not to be so mobilized thus had to be demonized and called *neemakharams,* people who were prepared to sell their souls and betray their ancestors for a mess of pottage from the new oligarchy. Panday denied that this was his strategy, and sought to mask his game plan by stigmatizing those in the Afro-Trinidadian community whom he called "pseudo racists," persons who pretended that they were ruling in the interest of the Africans when in fact they were governing in the interest of those whom he called the "parasitic clique."

It however seemed clear that while the main text of Panday's message articulated a cross racial appeal against the "parasitic oligarchy" and their spokes-persons, the sub-text represented an unambiguous communal appeal. In saying that Indians "were their worst enemy, willing to sell their birthright for a jacket and tie, a wig and a gown, a seat in the Senate, or a little contract here and there," Panday was clearly attacking elements within the Indian bourgeoisie who were forging links with the wider community in various ways and in the spaces that were being opened up as the state became more ethnically neutral. He was telling them that they had a "higher" responsibility to support their *jhat* in its quest for a turn at the crease. Panday also told the NAR that it had to purge itself of the French creole element in the party as a condition of any unity arrangement with the UNC. According to Panday:

> What is left of the party is dominated by the French creoles. It is the same group which dominates the PNM. The French creoles support both the PNM and the NAR. But they don't really want the PNM to lose the elections. They use the NAR as a counter-weight and tool to threaten the PNM that if it does not do so and so, then they will stay with the NAR. They don't want the NAR to join in any political party. But the NAR will have to make up its mind if it will continue to be used to win elections rather than a counter-weight. (*Express*, May 2, 1993)

Panday however did not formally shut the door on unity talks since, as he boasted, "the history of my political career is trying to forge unity. The opposition's position is that unity is critical and crucial.

What I have learnt from 1986 is that there must be mechanisms for the resolution of disputes." As was his wont, he indicated that the "people" would have to decide what the nature of the UNC-NAR relationship would be. The final judge of what the "people" would do of course would be Panday himself, and it may well be that he had concluded that the "people" had spoken loud and clear in a bye-election which had been held in May 1994 in Pointe-a-Pierre which indicated that the UNC had neutralized the NAR except among the white/off white "French creole" element.

Panday's comments served to amplify the anxieties of those in the non-Indian population who, for a variety of reasons, were fearful of the political ascendancy of the Indian community and who indicated that they would support the PNM or any other political party as an alternative to what they considered to be their more "immediate political enemy." Many who were pro-NAR in sympathy vowed to support the PNM instead of the party of their first choice if this was seen as being likely to ensure the defeat of the UNC. Many dissident PNM supporters also indicated that if an anti-PNM vote or abstention was seen to make a UNC victory likely, they would continue to support the PNM even though they were extremely unhappy with many of the economic and other policies which that party was pursuing.

The white and mixed business community which regarded Indian businessmen as fierce economic competitors and who also endorsed the basic structural adjustment policies being pursued by the PNM government, were prepared to support and finance the latter's electoral campaign and to denigrate the UNC whenever possible. They deeply resented being characterized as a "parasitic oligarchy" which, in conjunction with a black political elite, exploited the non-white elements in the society. As Panday had complained:

> It is becoming clearer to the masses in the East/West Corridor that they are being used by the parasitic oligarchy to win power which they use in their own interest. The poor, the hungry, the unemployed, the destitute and the desperate of Laventille, Belmont, Cocorite, Waterhole, Gonzales and

the rest of the corridor are slowly but surely coming around to the view that they are not the PNM, but the beasts of burden of the PNM, whose backs are ridden election after election by a small French creole clique supported by a black managerial elite. (*Trinidad Guardian,* October 11, 1993)

The UNC leadership was of the view that their best option for the election, which was due in 1996, was to seek to enter into some sort of formal or informal electoral arrangement with the NAR. Some elements in the NAR were also of the view that such an arrangement was the only way for the former governing party to revitalize itself. The NAR leadership in fact entered into a "common platform" agreement with the UNC to contest a bye-election in Caroni East in September 1994 as a prelude to a fuller alliance in time for the 1996 election. The then Political Leader of the NAR, Mr. Selby Wilson, noted that he was under pressure from UNC-NAR "floaters" to enter into the electoral entente with the UNC. To quote Mr. Wilson:

Because of the structure of the NAR and because the UNC, as it were, splintered off from the NAR, both parties have a significant number of people whom I call "floating voters" between the UNC and the NAR, people who are sympathetic towards the NAR and sympathetic towards the UNC as demonstrated in the Point-a-Pierre election where we saw the UNC's majority come by the movement of persons who voted for the NAR in the 1986 elections switching their allegiance to the UNC. And there are floating sympathizers of both parties. Indeed, some of the pressure for the movement toward joining up with the UNC came from these supporters in that they are always advocating that the parties must get together again and try to recreate 1986. (*Sunday Express,* October 2, 1994)

Many members of the NAR party, especially the white and mixed element, however, strongly objected to the *entente,* and forced the leadership to withdraw from the arrangement. The collapse of the *entente* also led Mr. Wilson to resign from the leadership of the NAR. Wilson however indicted that he too was suspicious of Panday's motives for joining the *entente*. Panday was described as being "fluid" and more concerned with electoral success than national unity.

The collapse of the "common platform" forced the UNC to adopt a "united front from below" strategy. That strategy was one that sought to attract as many of the NAR's Indian supporters as was possible. It also sought to appeal to the black underclass which was disenchanted with the PNM government which was pursuing policies that had given rise to increased unemployment and a reduction in welfare services which, given the dramatic reduction in available tax revenues, the economy could no longer afford. The strategy was given a "trial run" in the bye-elections held in May-July 1994 in the constituencies of Laventille and Pointe-a-Pierre. The results in the latter constituency indicated that the UNC did in fact capture the bulk of the Indian vote which had gone to the NAR in 1991. It however failed in its bid to win over the support of the black underclass in Laventille. The UNC received a mere 340 votes in the latter constituency compared to the 3,854 won by the PNM.

Looking for Indians

Despite persistent complaints by some Indian spokesmen about underrepresentation in the political system, Indians were well represented in the 1991-1996 Parliament. Seventeen of the 36 Members of that Parliament were Indian (47 percent), while in the 31 member nominated Senate, 17 or 55 percent were Indian. In the 1986-1991 Parliament, there were only 10 Indians out of the 36. The Indian community was however not proportionally represented in the governing party or in the government itself. The Political Leader of the PNM indeed expressed concern about this and indicated a wish to redress the imbalance. The party had sought to achieve this goal by including more Indians on its slate of candidates. Of those who did contest, only 4 were however elected. Three of these were appointed to the cabinet. The Prime Minister publicly expressed regret that more Indian PNM candidates did not win seats and indicated that he was anxious to compensate for this by appointing Indians to the Senate and making them ministers thereafter. Only 1 Indian, the Chairman of the party, was however made a minister *via* an appointment to the Senate. Another, who was invited to join the Cabinet, declined out of concern that he might be viewed as a "token" Indian, and perhaps even a *neemakharam.*

Indians accused the Prime Minister of "patronizing" the Indian community, but the Prime Minister was genuinely committed to the policy of incorporating Indians in positions of executive responsibility within the PNM. While the policy was informed by the goal of continued PNM dominance, it was also seen as being essential if future ethnic conflict was to be avoided.

There were those who believed that the only way to avoid conflict arising from the intensification of ethnic competition was to reconstitute the National Alliance For Reconstruction or some such combination or to find some formula to ensure that political power was shared between the two equally balanced ethnic communities. The experience of the NAR between 1986 and 1991 had however made the recreation of such experiments unlikely for several years to come. That experience had in fact led to a hardening of political tensions between the two major communities. Ethnically based political competition became sharper and more shrill, and threatened to escalate even further as the general election grew closer. There was in fact a growing fear in the Afro-Trinidadian community that Indians, who were dominant in the commercial sector and were gaining ascendancy in the bureaucracy, would also win political power, thus concentrating in their hands all the critical levers of power. A Report entitled *Ethnicity and Employment Practices in the Public Sector* (Ryan and La Guerre 1994:25) had in fact concluded that while Indo-Trinidadians were underrepresented at the higher end of the Central Public Service for historical and other reasons, they were well represented in the clerical, legal, medical and other professional sectors where merit and criteria prevailed. It also went on to indicate that it was not "inconceivable that the Public Service may eventually become dominated by Indo-Trinidadians." The only areas which remained outside its grasp was the state-owned corporations and the security services.[1]

It was of course true, as we noted above, that the Indo-Trinidadian community, like its Afro-Trinidadian counterpart, was differentiated along cultural, class and denominational lines, and that as was the case in the past, it may not have voted as a solid bloc. Survey data had however indicated that the UNC had however begun to enjoy considerable support among Presbyterians, Indian Catholics and Muslims. Given the right set of circumstances, it was possible that more upwardly mobile Indians who had in the past supported the NAR or the PNM could be induced to support a restructured UNC. As we shall see, this is precisely what occurred in 1995.

The UNC leadership however formally endorsed power sharing and was seeking to force the PNM to concede it. Mr. Panday called for the creation of a government of national unity, and promised that when he won control of the Government, he would put such a united front in place. Having experimented unsuccessfully in the past with a number of strategies designed to force pre-election accommodations, formal alliances or coalitions, Panday believed that a post-election power sharing strategy would provide the mechanism needed for effective governance in Trinidad and Tobago since, in his view, neither the PNM nor the UNC had the legitimacy to govern on their own. One thus had to be concerned not only with how to win elections, but how to govern after winning. Only a national government, he argued, would have the moral authority to govern Trinidad and Tobago effectively. The Guyana experience had fortified Panday's thinking on this issue (Ryan 1992: 47-49).

Panday's refusal to cooperate with the PNM to enact fundamental legislation which required a qualitative majority was thus designed to force the latter party to concede that it could not govern Trinidad and Tobago effectively without UNC concurrence given the fact that the two dominant parties represented two entrenched clusters which not only had rough numerical parity, but which also had effective veto power over the other in many spheres of national life. In his view, Trinidad and Tobago's political system was bi-polar rather than uni-polar, and as such, its political system and culture should reflect this reality.

The Elections of 1995

The outcome of the Trinidad and Tobago General Elections of November 1995 constituted a veritable social revolution in that what emerged was not merely an alternation of elite or a changing of the guards, but a fundamental change in the ethnic composition of that ruling elite. The People's National Movement (PNM), which had its centre of gravity in the Afro-Trinidadian population, and which had been in power since 1956 with a brief 5-year interregnum, secured 254,159 or 48.74 percent of the votes cast and 17 of the 36 seats; the United National Congress (UNC), which drew its support largely from the Indo-Trinidadian population, amassed 240,372 votes or 45.74 percent of those cast and also won 17 seats, while the National Alliance for Reconstruction, (NAR) the cross-ethnic coalition which had governed the country between 1986 and 1991, obtained 24,933 votes, a mere 4.76 percent of the votes cast and 2 seats, both in Tobago. Neither of the Trinidad based national parties could thus govern without the support of the two Tobago based members of Parliament.

The election was called some 17 months before they were constitutionally due. The then Prime Minister advised Parliament that his decision to have the President dissolve Parliament and call elections was informed by his belief that he could not govern effectively. The PNM, which had won 21 seats in the 1991 election, had lost one of them in a bye-election in May 1994. The party's majority was further reduced when another of its parliamentarians, the former Minister of Foreign Affairs, resigned his seat after a highly emotional break with the Prime Minister. The Government's decision to remove the Speaker of the House and replace her with the Deputy Speaker who was an elected PNM member of Parliament, also effectively meant that the Government could only count on the routine support of 18 of the 36 members of Parliament. The Government's claim meant that no elected parliamentarian or minister could fall sick or travel on private or official business for any extended period without running the risk that the Government's legislative schedule would be seriously affected. The Government also argued that it ran the risk of being overthrown following a successful vote of no confidence. This was hardly likely however, since a specific resolution dealing with confidence would have had to be introduced and the Speaker would have been able to exercise his right to cast the deciding vote. A vote of no confidence required the Opposition to persuade a majority of all the members to support the motion and the UNC simply did not have the 19 votes required.

As important as were some of the reasons formally given, the ruling party's decision to call a general rather than a bye-election to fill the seat vacated by the resignation of the member for San Fernando West was prompted by concern that it could lose the seat because of low turnout among its support base. The UNC had been boasting that they had organized San Fernando West with "military precision," and that the constituency was theirs for the taking. The Party was also aware that, for much the same reason, it might not do as well as it wished in the local government elections which were then due and for which it was preparing. If either or both of these developments occurred, it was feared that it would provide a major boost for the opposition which could serve to generate a bandwagon effect which it might have been difficult to reverse in 1996, a year in which the government was also expecting to have tough negotiations with public sector unions. The decision to call a general election was thus seen as a way to circumvent all of these difficulties.

Following the elections, the former Prime Minister let it be known that the party leadership feared that if the elections had not been called when they were, the PNM might have lost at least two more seats, a claim that was hotly disputed within PNM circles by elements who felt that if the election was scheduled when they were due, both the party and the Government would have been better prepared. Those who subscribed to this latter view believe that the Government would have been better advised to present a populist budget, which was already substantially prepared, before calling the election. They also believed that the Government would have been the beneficiary of the numerous job creation projects which were in the pipeline and which were scheduled to come on stream in 1996.

The Prime Minister however calculated that the PNM faithful and the floating vote were more likely to rally to the party in a general confrontation with the UNC which he was advised was in a state of organizational disarray. He firmly believed that the PNM could not possibly lose a general election; it indeed stood a very good chance to win the 2 seats which it claimed it required to govern effectively.

It is of course now "history" that instead of winning the election with an increased majority, the PNM won only 17 seats in Trinidad, the same number as the UNC, which left the two NAR members of Parliament from the sister isle of Tobago effectively holding the balance between the two major parties. This was exactly the result which the NAR had hoped to achieve. The NAR in fact did not expect to win the election, and had contested only 19 seats. The party in fact hoped that the result in Trinidad would be a stalemate and that the NAR would thus "make the difference."

Despite its loss of power, the PNM's overall voting support actually increased from 233,950 in 1991 to 255,855 in 1995. The party increased its vote in all but three constituencies, Arima, Laventille West, and Tobago East. This increase in support came from new voters, 43,255 of whom were added to the 1995 electoral list, as well as from upscale elements who previously supported the NAR. Of the 102,397 votes which the NAR lost in the election, approximately 21,935 or 13 percent went to the PNM. The other 88, 770 (87 percent) went mainly to the UNC. The split was largely along ethnic lines as was foreshadowed by the results of the two bye-elections which were held in 1994.

There were several reasons for the outcome of the election. Some had to do with failures of the ruling party and its leader; others had to do with the general state of the economy, while yet others had to do with what the opposition parties were able to achieve. Also important was the state of race relations which had been dramatically transformed in the period following the 1991 election and more particularly in 1995, the year in which the Indian community marked the 150th anniversary of its arrival in Trinidad and Tobago. The burden of our argument however, is that while several factors contributed to the outcome of the election, the ethnic factor is by far the one with the greatest explanatory significance. For Indo-Trinidadians, the capture of political power was the jewel, the crowning achievement for which many had laboured and dreamt.

This claim was challenged by some observers who argued that claims about the salience of the race factor are asserted and not proved and that race is used as a "loose description of a number of variables." The argument is that "issues" were far more important and fundamental in the election as was the fact that the UNC had managed to transform itself into a party that seemed able, for the first time, to function as an effective alternative to the PNM government. It was also better financed than it had previously been. In sum, the UNC had an organizational weapon that was more vital than race. It was argued further that culture, religion, and geographical location were also important determinants of voting behaviour, all of which, is of course true. These can however all be subsumed under the broad concept of ethnicity which is a first order issue which informs one's cosmology and how one constructs and perceives "reality" and the issues.

It is true that in contemporary Trinidad, there is a great deal of fluidity and that individuals are cross pressured and straddle a variety of overlapping ethnicities. For many, ethnicity is only symbolic, cosmetic, or nostalgic, and does not express itself in everyday behaviour. For others however, it is more than symbolic. The context often determines which orientation is relevant. Our argument is that in 1995, ethnic pride was the dominant factor that drove many Indo-Trinidadians, many of whom had voted PNM, ONR or NAR before going into the UNC fold, even though many had reservations about how well that party might perform in terms of addressing certain policy issues, especially those relating to the economy. To most of them, the overriding view was that the time had come for Trinidad and Tobago to have an Indian Prime Minister. The dramatic swing in voter allegiance among Indians of all classes and creeds to the UNC cannot possibly be explained otherwise.

Those who challenge the view that race was the critical variable also argue that the PNM had lost its appeal to many voters of all ethnicities and that the party was rejected on grounds other than race. The Party, they assert, had shown that it was incapable of solving the many critical problems facing the country-spiralling crime rates, high unemployment, persistent poverty and dispossession, the drug trade, a growing coarseness in the society and a general decline in its institutional fabric and in the standard of governance, and that many had come to believe that it was time to ignore the race factor and give the UNC the chance for which it was asking. It is also argued that the UNC had succeeded in restructuring and re-imaging itself and was now attractive to the Indian middle class as well as to others who were not Indian. While it is true that the UNC had been able to re-engineer itself, the fact is that it failed to attract much support from the Afro-Trinidadian community though it appears that some at the pedestrian level switched for opportunistic reasons. What happened, in the main, was that Indo-Trinidadian voters of all confessional allegiances and classes who in the past had split their votes among several competing parties – the PNM, the ONR and the NAR – solidified behind the "new" UNC. In their view, the election promised to provide them with an unprecedented opportunity to deal with the problem of political peripheralisation about which they had long complained. As one put it, "we just wanted people to treat us like we are part of the country."

Afro-Trinidadians who were disenchanted with the PNM for the reasons given above, as well as for other reasons, either continued to support that Party out of fear for what a UNC victory might mean in terms of the reallocation of material and symbolic resources – the so called "fear factor" – or withheld their support from all parties. Some abstained in the belief that the PNM would win anyway. While it is true that none of this can be proved conclusively, the correlation between voting behaviour and the ethnic composition of polling divisions clearly points to the conclusion that most Indo-Trinidadians voted for the UNC and most Afro-Trinidadians voted for the PNM. One understands why some resisted this conclusion. For ideological reasons it was important to establish that race and/or ethnicity had ceased to be a major factor in the politics of Trinidad and Tobago. The evidence however suggests that both parties used and were beneficiaries of the race factor. It is also interesting to note that most of the commentators who asserted in public that race was not a factor in the election were Indo-Trinidadian rather than Afro-Trinidadian.

Reactions to the 1995 Election

The results of the 1995 election benchmarked a significant shift in the balance of ethnic forces in the society. The results were greeted with great jubilation by the Indian community which felt that it had finally arrived politically after having been marginalised for 150 years. This was so even though the UNC did not win a clear majority and had to share power with the NAR. As one Indian put it, "we have reached.... For the first time, Indians in Trinidad have put their differences aside and rallied together. We have been ruled by others all our lives; [now] we are in a different time. We have given ourselves a chance with Panday at the helm" (*Mirror,* January 16, 1996).

The Sanatan Dharma Maha Sabha well articulated the manner in which the election campaign and the results were viewed by the Hindu community. As it declared:

> The year 1995 saw at least 50,000 "Indians" assembled at Skinner Park to commemorate, and to commiserate; to succour dreams of grandeur and to brood on the anguish of remembered humiliations. It was a celebration of citizenship, the joy of triumph. It was a claim on the land and an affirmation of citizenship. It was a sharing of love with "African" school children and Orisha worshippers and Shouter Baptists. It was a call to national unity in every sphere of existence...
>
> We felt the beauty of achievement. We felt the force of pride in our achievements which none can deny; and we know that in this our Land, the land of our birth, our Janam Bhomi, we can become the President of our Republic, the

Prime Minister, the Attorney General or anything that we choose to be. The year 1995 is indeed the one of arrival. (*Express*, November 18, 1995)

Indo-Trinidadians had always resented the assumption of Afro-Trinidadians that they had a prescriptive right to succeed the British, and that any attempt on the part of the Indo-Trinidadians to become more fully incorporated in the political system was subversive of the order and equilibrium which obtained in the society. As former MP Hulsie Bhaggan puts it:

There appeared to be a sentiment among some Afro-Trinidadians which suggested that they had the divine right to political office. Most Indo-Trinidadians felt that it was their time now and they should be given a chance. (*Guardian*, March 17, 1996)

The Afro-Trinidadian community, for its part, was stunned, tearful and traumatized. As the calypsonian Cro Cro put it in his prize winning calypso, *They Look For Dat*, "November 7th, "I see Black Man Cry; Look blood still running from Black People Eye." Few assumed that such an unbearable and unforgivable "trespass" would ever have taken place in their lifetime or at least in the near future. To most, it was neither desirable nor sustainable.

The PNM Political Leader was disinclined to entertain any suggestion that he should seek to enter a coalition with the NAR since he had openly stated that the PNM would "fight alone, win alone or lose alone" (*Guardian*, November 7, 1995). The General Council of the party however authorized the leadership to open negotiations with Mr. Robinson. While Manning ruled out any prospect that the Prime Ministership would be offered to Mr. Robinson, he agreed to entertain discussions with the former Prime Minister on the ground that the PNM did not really lose the elections.

The UNC-NAR Coalition

Efforts were made to persuade Mr. ANR Robinson, the Political Leader of the NAR to work with the PNM rather than with the UNC. These efforts came from many quarters. Some businessmen who were either sympathetic to the PNM or concerned that the change of government would lead to a loss of business confidence, sought to persuade Robinson and the NAR to enter into a coalition arrangement with the PNM instead of the UNC, as a holding arrangement until such time as new elections could be scheduled. This arrangement would have had the advantage of leaving the PNM in a position to determine the date for new elections. Some elements in or close to the PNM likewise felt that "any means necessary" should be used to persuade Robinson not to be the instrument by which a Hinduraj was established in Trinidad and Tobago. Robinson was accused of "betraying" his race. The calypsonian Cro Cro, for example, felt that Robinson had plunged the "sword in his hands" into the breast of the African man.

Robinson however resisted the appeal to form a partnership with the PNM, preferring instead to form a coalition with the UNC. This move was clearly dictated by his belief that he could get a better deal, both for himself and Tobago, from the UNC than he could from the PNM. The heated exchanges during the campaign between Robinson and Manning over the Tobago self-government issue, the events of 1990 (Robinson had accused Manning of being a co-conspirator with the Jamaat when it sought to effect a seizure of state power in 1990), and Robinson's own experiences with the PNM dating back to 1969-1970 had clearly made it difficult for the two men to work together. Robinson may well have welcomed the opportunity to humiliate the PNM as Dr. Williams had humiliated him.[2] It is also possible that even though the UNC and the NAR were seemingly at "war" during the election, the NAR *entente* did not materialize immediately following the election and that there had in fact been signalling in advance to the effect that if no party won a clear majority, the UNC and the NAR would have to work together.

Robinson has insisted that his decision to work with the UNC was driven by principle and concern for the national interest. The NAR, he told the 9th Annual NAR Convention in April 1996, was placed in a position of highest responsibility. Experienced statesman as he was, he chose not to exploit the position for any selfish purpose which might have had catastrophic consequences for the country, both politically and economically. This might have happened, for example, if he had attempted to follow the strategy used in St. Vincent by James "Son" Mitchell who demanded and got the Prime Ministership as the price for his tie breaking cooperation with the People's Political Party in 1972.

In Robinson's view, the electorate had rejected the appeal of both the PNM and the UNC for a mandate to rule. Robinson however claimed that the electorate's rejection of the PNM's demand was politically and sociologically more compelling, even though the PNM got more votes in Trinidad than the UNC. One is not clear how that judgement was arrived at. Were there forces at work which suggested to Robinson that the "zeitgeist" was moving in favour of the Indians and that he had to recognise the "necessity" of moving with it? What indeed would have happened if Robinson had decided to embrace Manning and re-unite the PNM? Would the Indian community have swallowed it as they had done in 1981 when George Chambers was chosen by the President before Errol Mahabir or Kamaludin Mohammed following Dr. Williams death in office? (cf. Ryan 1989a). Would there have been a renewed refugee phenomenon, such as occurred in 1987, both psychically and physically? (Ryan 1989b). Would there have been open protests on the streets as there were in St. Kitts and Guyana in 1992?

We of course have no answers to these questions. Nor do we know whether they ever entered Robinson's mind. According to Robinson, the PNM's record in power over the past 35 years was there for all to see. In the last year of its most recent term, its record was particularly dismal. To quote Mr. Robinson:

The ruling party, the PNM, had chalked up a dismal record, particularly in its fourth year of governance. It had adopted a confrontational stance with almost every major institution in the country; Police Service Commission, Public Service Commission, Teaching Service Commission, Police Commissioner, the Court of Appeal and even the Privy Council. It incarcerated the Speaker of the House of Representatives under a state of emergency and its leader thereupon declared himself to be father of the nation.... In its final year, 1995, the leadership in the party exhibited precipitate and alarming deterioration. (*Express*, April 23, 1996)

In Mr. Robinson's view, there were also serious concerns about the Opposition UNC, in general and Mr. Maharaj in particular. On balance, however, he felt he had to give the nod to Mr. Panday since there was no question of re-installing Mr. Manning as Head of Government after his call for a "renewed mandate had been rejected by the electorate." Robinson also tells us that he "rejected out of hand" the appeal to race to resolve the tie in favour of the PNM. His claim was that his own political history and his contemporary involvement in attempts to set up an International Tribunal which was seeking, *inter alia*, to try individuals for heinous crimes against humanity such as genocide, would have made such an act "politically incorrect."

One is however not entirely certain that Robinson's decision to work with the UNC was driven solely by concern for the national interest and that "selfish" considerations were also not operative. It is clear that Robinson sensed that he could work more easily with Mr. Panday than with Mr. Manning. Mr. Robinson must also have calculated that his political interests in Tobago would have been better served by an arrangement with the UNC which had no base in Tobago, than with the PNM which was still a viable party in Tobago.

Interestingly, the NAR Council had initially decided to avoid forming a formal coalition with any party and that it had decided instead to give the UNC "critical support," i.e., judge the latter on the basis of what it sought to do in Parliament. Those who were anxious to share in the allocation of spoils or who felt that the Indian community should not be frustrated, however opposed that decision. Mr. Robinson and the Council went along with this change of position and advised the President that he, and the other elected MP from Tobago, would give their support to Mr. Panday for the post of Prime Minister. The country was on the edge, and Robinson felt that he had to act decisively:

> We could have dillied; we could have dallied; we could have, as some adamantly held we should, negotiated - if necessary with both sides - in order to extract the best deal - in senatorial and ministerial appointments and settled quotas, not omitting the Prime Ministership. As a former Finance Minister, I had no doubt that the interest of the country required a clean break out of the deadlock and in the direction of stability in order to avoid deepening tension, uncertainty, economic deterioration and possible violence and a free fall of the Trinidad and Tobago dollar. (*Express*, April 23, 1996)

During the days preceding the decision to form a "co-partnership," there were numerous reports that in seeking to "make the difference," some members of the NAR sought to force the UNC to appoint several of its key members to positions in the Cabinet, the Senate, boards of statutory authorities, and state enterprises as the price for its cooperation. The names of several high profile persons from both Tobago and Trinidad were bruited about. Mr. Robinson however insisted that neither he, nor the other Tobago MP, Miss Nicholson, were ever party to those negotiations. As he reports:

> I want to make it abundantly clear... that while I made proposals to Mr. Panday on behalf of the NAR, I never at any time bargained or negotiated or sought to impose terms and conditions. All such allegations are completely false and absolutely without foundation. Miss Nicholson's hands and mine, and by extension the NAR's, are free of any such arrangements. I consider that the electoral and parliamentary statistics would speak for themselves and the Prime Minister would think fit to be guided accordingly. (*ibid.*)

Many NAR members were angry with Mr. Robinson for not insisting that NAR stalwarts be given key offices as the price of cooperation. Mr. Robinson tells us that he chose not to do so, since he was anxious to avoid any confrontation that might prove divisive:

> It is tempting for members of parties in a coalition government to feel that the role of the parties is to share between their members the fruits and benefits of power. The PNM did it among its own members with a vengeance. And there are members of both the UNC and NAR who feel "is we time now." They want to be the flip side of the PNM coinage. But if it was wrong under the PNM, it is wrong also under the UNC/NAR coalition. If it was wrong for the PNM to engage in acts of corruption, then it is wrong for the UNC/NAR to do the same. Do not ask me to support you in that line of conduct. Do not tell me because X did it before me, that is reason or justification for me to do it. If it was wrong for X, it is wrong for me, and no justification for me to do it. (*ibid.*)

A party, he insisted, is not a trade union seeking to realize the "unrealistic welfare expectations" of its members. A proper party is one that has a vision that encompasses the fundamentals of the entire society. More importantly, plural societies, more than others, require leaders to act responsibly rather than confrontationally:

> In multi-cultural societies that are divided on ethnic and racial lines, confidence building is a necessary process to the resolution of conflict situations. A high degree of patience, skillful and sensitive management and understanding are all required for long-term success. (*ibid.*)

Mr. Robinson, who was given the post of "Minister Extraordinaire" in the new regime with ministerial responsibility for Tobago, has since told us that his experience in the 1986-1991 regime had chastened him, and made him recognize the importance of settling differences internally, rather than to resort to public posturing as Panday *et. al.* were minded to do in 1987-1991 (Ryan 1989b). He was equally aware that there were forces which were anxious to pry open every crack that appeared in the coalition. More importantly, he felt that it was necessary to let all and sundry - both nationally and internationally - know that Trinidad and Tobago had one, and not two Prime Ministers. Apologizing for his caution and silence, he assured his listeners who thought his actions "foolish," that they would in time discover that his actions were in fact wise.

Robinson's statement was clearly an important one, not only for what it said in the text, but in the sub-text as well. Robinson was speaking to his supporters and detractors in Trinidad, those in Tobago, to Mr. Panday and the UNC, to people like calypsonian Cro Cro who accused him of selling out, and for the historical record. To his supporters who were very angry with him for playing Pontius Pilate by not seeking to ensure that the NAR got a fairer share of the disposable spoils, he was telling them that in the context of Trinidad, if not in Tobago, he was not a machine politician who would soil his hands in the pork barrel.

Mr. Robinson was also telling Mr. Panday and the rest of the UNC team that he should not be taken for granted and that he should be properly consulted before key and potentially far reaching decisions and statements were made. He also warned the UNC that no race should seek to construct an hegemonic edifice. That way lay disaster. Mr. Robinson was however clearly aware that while he had some leverage which could be used in this evenly balanced political game, he had to act with restraint. If he overplayed his hand and his bluff was called, the coalition could collapse, and with it all his hopes for settling the Tobago question and perhaps inheriting the Presidency, which some believe was the ultimate spoil to which he aspired.

The leaders of the coalition parties were aware of the mistakes which had been made in the 1986-1991 period of NAR rule and were determined that these should not be repeated. They had thus agreed on a code of conduct that would govern relationships between them. The *Heads of Agreement* provided, *inter alia*, that the two parties would work together to broaden and deepen the process of unity throughout the country, and that they would seek to include in this process all groups and individuals comprising the national community, including the Members of Parliament. The parties also agreed to ensure that the decision-making process with respect to the governance of the country embraced the principles of the rule of law, transparency in public affairs, and morality and integrity in public office. They also agreed to establish and sustain a code of conduct for cabinet ministers (see Box).

The parties likewise agreed to "review the existing political and legislative framework with the objective of integrating the unity process into existing structures and to establish appropriate mechanisms to initiate and foster dialogue and programmes to make the best use of the energy, talents, skills, and enterprise of the entire population in the nation-building process." There was also agreement to utilize existing mechanisms of conflict resolution and to develop new ones on a consensual basis.

The partners in the coalition which some had deemed improbable because of the "compulsions of the culture," were aware that there was a widespread belief that the new government would collapse under the pressures that would be brought to bear on it by place seekers, contract hunters and by those who, having been long in the wilderness, wanted to advance ethnic and community concerns which could only be secured at the expense of incumbents and current consumers of available resources. As Panday himself puts it:

> By becoming Prime Minister, I have evoked all kinds of feelings and released many pent-up seated hopes and aspirations; but unfortunately it has exposed many trepidations as well. That is to be expected in a society such as ours. (*Guardian*, December 4, 1996)

Mr. Panday's way of addressing this problem was to signal that he was not a "Caroni Prime Minister," and to urge his followers to cease displaying signs of vengeance, arrogance and triumphalism, and to accept their victory with dignity, humility and a sense of responsibility.

HEADS OF AGREEMENT

Whereas the United National congress and the National Alliance for Reconstruction held discussions with the view of forming the Government of Trinidad and Tobago following the general elections held on the 6ᵗʰ November, 1995 the parties hereby agree as follows:

1. To take measures progressively for the purpose of confidence building between the United National Congress and the National Alliance for Reconstruction with a view to facilitating, promoting and strengthening collaboration between the two parties. Towards this end the parties will place emphasis on decision-making by consensus, particularly at the level of the Parliamentary caucus.

2. To work together to broaden and deepen the process of unity throughout the country including in this process all groups and individuals in the national community as well as Members of Parliament. The parties will expeditiously introduce legislation to implement the national consensus agreement on Tobago contained in House Paper No. 6 of 1978 with appropriate constitutional and other legislative safeguards.

3. To utilize and where necessary view the existing political and legislative framework with the objective of integrating the unity process.

4. To take immediate initiatives to utilize the Human Resources of the United National Congress and the National Alliance for Reconstruction in the formation and continuance of the new government of Trinidad and Tobago.

5. To establish the legislative provisions and/or mechanisms to ensure that the decision-making

process with respect to the governance of the country embraces and gives effect to the principles of Truth, the Rule of Law, Transparency in Public Affairs and Morality and integrity in Public Office. The parties will establish and maintain codes of conduct for Cabinet Ministers, Parliamentarians, Members of The Tobago House of Assembly and local government representatives.

6. To restructure the political system to afford representation to sections of the electorate who by reason of non-alignment with major political groupings are denied participation in the governance of the Country.

7. To strengthen and deepen the decentralization process at all levels of Government.

8. To establish appropriate mechanisms and institutions to initiate and foster dialogue and programmes designed to harness the energy, talents, skills and enterprise of the entire population in the nation-building process.

9. To utilize existing mechanisms and to create appropriate ones for conflict resolution between the affected parties.

"Be careful what you do and say," he warned. Panday advised his supporters that his success as Prime Minister would be determined by how they behaved (*Express*, November 20, 1995; see also *Guardian*, March 28, 1996).

The new Prime Minister also called for the establishment of a "government of national unity," arguing that the society was "difficult to rule" and could not be governed effectively or productively without it. Interestingly, former UNC Member of Parliament, Hulsie Bhaggan, felt constrained to make the point that "those most vociferous for racial unity are in fact rabid, closet racists, [whilst] those who speak out in an open manner and call a spade a spade are likely to have worked through their prejudices" (*Guardian*, March 17, 1996).

In pursuit of the unity goal, Panday invited the PNM to collaborate with the UNC in forming an all party government, perhaps knowing full well that the PNM would refuse. As he put it:

> Because of the highly plural, divisive and fragmented nature of our society, no single group can run Trinidad and Tobago successfully to the exclusion of other groups. And based on that analysis, I have always argued on the need for national coalition government. But God disposes and what you want may not be what you get and so those who do not want unity, unity will be forced on them. (*Guardian*, November 7, 1996)

He also urged the creation of a consensual decision making process which would enable Government, labour and capital to participate as partners in the resolution of critical policy issues affecting the economy.[3] The UNC likewise signalled to the community that it did not propose to change everything overnight, including the memberships of statutory boards and the executives of state enterprises, as the NAR did in 1986, and, much to the chagrin of some of its supporters, stressed that it would maintain most of the economic policies that the PNM had put in place between 1991 and 1995 in the interest of continuity.

In his choice of Cabinet, Mr. Panday was sensitive to the anxieties of the non-Indian community who were not used to seeing cabinets which consisted mainly of persons of Indian ancestry. Seeing that there were only 4 elected members in the coalition who were not of that extraction, others were brought in via the Senate. The cabinet of 21 thus contained 8 non-Indians and 13 Indians, which was not an unreasonable balance having regard to the ethnic basis of the UNC and the need to tie all the elected parliamentarians to the Government in the interest of survival. Four of the Ministers were Hindus, as were two parliamentary secretaries. Three were Muslims while the remainder were Christians.

The PNM welcomed the UNC's initial endorsement of its policies, many of which had been criticized during the election campaign. It however rejected the invitation to form a national government which it viewed as being contrary to the Constitution and its conventions which require an active Opposition. The PNM was aware that the UNC was in fact using the unity formula to conceal its weakness or to perpetuate itself in power. It thus argued that while the PNM believed in unity, such unity would have to take place within the framework of the political parties. In Mr. Manning's view, both parties should re-engineer themselves so that they become more attractive to people of all ethnicities. To quote Manning, who described the PNM as the "alternative government":

> What is emerging from all of these things is that the government appears to be systematically seeking to undermine the position of the Opposition and therefore it is not the Opposition that suffers but the public. I have the responsibility to resist these attempts. Everything the government has done is to subvert the role of the Opposition under the guise of national unity. The population ought to watch very carefully what is happening, the net effect of which is to divide the society. It is for that reason we have not joined a government of national unity. The approach is dangerous.... Since 1987 when I became Political Leader, I said we need to bring the whole country together. We believe

the way to do it is at the level of the political party. All parties should be broad based reflecting the composition of the society in which we operate. It is in fact a coalition of interests. In this way the integrity of the Westminster system as we have it in Trinidad and Tobago is maintained. (*Guardian*, November 10, 1995)

The Jamaat and the Parties

The perceived closeness of the Jamaat al Muslimeen to the regime, a perception that remained for a long while inspite of the efforts which were being made by the new Government to put some distance between itself and the Jamaat provoked great concern.[4] Shortly after the new government took office, the Jamaat sought and received an audience with the Prime Minister at which it presented a five point agenda. They requested that

- the 8.8 acres of land granted by Dr. Eric Williams to construct an Islamic Cultural complex at 1 Mucurapo Road be regularised by a deed to the Jamaat al Muslimeen

- the $2.1 million offered by the State's lawyer as compensation for the destroyed Jamaat buildings be paid without further complications as an act of good faith, the remainder of the assessment to be completed by arbitration

- Muslim women and men who have been debarred from employment and schools for wearing the garment which covers the head and shoulders will face no further discrimination

- the Jamaat al Muslimeen be considered for state assistance in the construction of schools at 1 Mucurapo Road and that their teachers be admitted to teachers' training colleges and be paid by the State as is done with other denominational schools

- skilled and qualified members of the Jamaat al Muslimeen are not discriminated against for employment (*Express,* December 6, 1995).

Following the meeting, Bakr expressed optimism that their demands would be heeded. "There is a change in the atmosphere," he opined. "I have no reason to doubt Mr. Panday at this time. Down the road … we don't know" (*Express,* December 6, 1995). Bakr later indicated that the UNC had given them the assurance that the court award would be paid (*Guardian,* July 28, 1996). The general public however made it very clear to the UNC that it would strongly oppose any effort on its part to legitimize the Jamaat al Muslimeen. The UNC thus sought to distance itself from the Jamaat. The general public however remained convinced that a clandestine link existed. It was noted, for example, that the brother of a key Jamaat activist, had been the manager of the UNC campaign in the Tunapuna constituency and was made a supervisor on the Unemployment Relief Programme.

Comments made by the Jamaat in March 1996 however suggest that the group had lost patience with the Government which was accused of stonewalling on its commitments. To quote Bakr:

> I have my problems with the UNC. I am giving them a little chance, but time is running out. Before the election, Panday said he was going to obey the rule of law. And the court has ruled that the Jamaat should be paid compensation for buildings and property which were damaged by the State. But we are not hearing anything about it. (*Express,* March 3, 1996)

Bakr was angry with the Attorney General, the Jamaat's former attorney, for failing to appoint a team to meet with the Jamaat as promised, and chided Mr. Maharaj for being the only person to have benefitted financially from the crisis in that he had received millions of dollars in legal fees from the Muslimeen. "Meanwhile, we have no schools and our children can't go to other schools. When a government does not obey the rule of law, anarchy steps in because nobody is under compulsion to obey it" (*Mirror*, March 3, 1996).

Clearly, the pressure of public opinion had made the Government in general, and Messrs. Panday and Maharaj in particular, politically uncomfortable. The Government was clearly caught between the proverbial rock and a hard place. It wanted to placate the Muslimeen and eliminate the threat which it posed to social peace, the constitutional order, and perhaps to themselves. It however feared that doing so could be politically expensive since majority opinion was opposed to the payment of compensatory damages to those who had attempted to seize control of the state unconstitutionally, destroying many lives and much public and private property in the process.

The UNC was clearly concerned about the Jamaat, and was taking steps to forestall a coup attempt. There was in fact a report that the leaders of the UNC and the NAR had entered into a secret side deal to the one which had been made public on November 11th when the coalition was being formed. According to that report (*Mirror*, June 2, 1996), Clause 4 of the Agreement reads as follows:

> The United National Congress hereby acknowledges that it is not now, nor shall it during the pendency of his agreement, become engaged in any association or arrangement with Abu Bakr and the Jamaat al Muslimeen of any nature whatever.

There had been earlier concern in NAR circles about links between the UNC and the Jamaat, and this alleged link was one of the reasons given for the fracturing of the common platform that elements from both parties had sought to put in place for the Caroni by-election in August 1994. Having regard to the fact that the 1990 coup effort was directed against an NAR government led by Mr. Robinson, it was plausible to believe that the latter would have inserted such a provision in the Heads of Agreement. Mr. Robinson however denied ever seeing such a provision. Nor did he know anything about it. He however indicated that "several people, on their own tried to put forward something on behalf of one party or another, and that might have been one of them. But it was never put up" (*Mirror*, June 2, 1996).

Despite his quarrel with the UNC, Abu Bakr refused to have any dealings with the PNM and he continued to insist that the PNM's Political Leader and the MP for La Brea had met with one of their members at his home 5 weeks after the election to try and get the Jamaat to break with the UNC. Bakr however insisted that he would not allow the Jamaat to be used by the PNM to create any disharmony between itself and the UNC. That posture also included relationships between the Syrian and Indian communities who were known to be fierce economic competitors. To quote Bakr:

> Under the PNM, the Syrians benefitted. But now that the Indians are in power, the old colonials feel threatened. The Indians have all the infrastructure in place to get lucrative contracts. The only people who did not benefit from all this were the Africans. The Syrians are hoping that media hysteria will scare the UNC, and so they will not obey the law and pay us the money. They hope to be able to benefit from a NAR and UNC conflict. But we have practical experience now, and that scheme will not work again. They are hoping to drive a wedge between us, but we are the last of the Mohicans. The last of the resistance. (*Sunday Mirror*, March 10, 1996)

Bakr also recalled his pre-election criticisms of the PNM and its leaders and predicted that the "African people would wander in the wilderness for 40 years until a new leader comes forward from amongst the people, cross them over the River Jordan, and liberate them for the first time (*ibid.*).

Endnotes

1. The thrust by Indians for full incorporation in public sector job markets was greeted with much anxiety by Afro-Trinidadians. This concern was dramatically articulated by a former Public Service Commissioner, James Alva Bain who felt that social balance required that their rate of entry into the Public Service should be slowed down. To quote Bain:

> With the introduction of compulsory primary education, the East Indians have increasingly acquired education and have been increasingly invading the fields of the Civil Service, the professions and government. As their numbers must now reach parity with the people of African descent, there is a real possibility that, in the not too distant future, they will get control of the Government. Should this time come when the East Indian sectors own most of the property, business and wealth of the country as well as control of the Government, an imbalance could develop in our society that would not be good for the nation. It is an urgent necessity, therefore that all of us give serious thought to these matters and like sensible people make a conscious effort to counter any undesirable consequences that could develop from such a possible situation. (*Express*, April 26, 1976)

The *Report on Employment Practices in the Public Sector* (1994:25) also commented on the reactions of Afro-Trinidadians:

> That the Public Service might one day become dominated by Indians is not in itself a problem. The real problem is the possible response of Afro-Trinidadians to the increasing Indo-Trinidadian presence in what has traditionally been the preserve of the Afro-Trinidadian population. Already there are signs of tension and disquiet. In any Department or Ministry presided over by an Indo-Trinidadian, there is talk of discrimination against Afro-Trinidadians. The Afro-Trinidadian public servant feels particularly insecure in the knowledge that the current Chairman of the Public and Police Services Commissions is an Indo-Trinidadian. These

feelings of insecurity stem from the perception - nay, belief - that once an Indo-Trinidadian is put into a position of authority, he/she will naturally, automatically, instinctively, without really thinking about it and not necessarily with any malicious intent, favour his/her own kind in all matters. This perception is very strong, and can be discerned widely among Afro-Trinidadian public servants. Indians are characterized as "cliquish," "clannish" and "openly racist; and non-Indo-Trinidadians genuinely fear what might happen if an Indo-Trinidadian were to become head of their department.

2. Mr. Manning accused Mr. Robinson of acting out of spite in his dealings with the PNM and Trinidad. To quote Manning: "It may well be that the people of Trinidad are being victimised for the way they voted in 1991 when he was given no seat in Trinidad. We have always known it; vindictiveness and spite stare us in the face again.... That coalition is in power today because of the actions of the Minister Extraordinaire. All things that you feel could be brought to an end in this country could easily be brought to an end if the honourable gentleman acts responsibility; but vindictiveness is the order of the day" (*Express*, June 15, 1996).

3. To quote Panday further: "Trinidad and Tobago is the most difficult land to rule because of its highly plural nature. This, however was not the problem. In Trinidad people are forced to live in conditions where we cannot avoid one another. We are forced to interface with each other every day, whether we like it or not." This, he said was "nobody's fault" but the result of the country's history. "No matter how we have tried to paper over the cracks over the years, it takes situations like this election and the result of this election to expose the cracks for what they really are. That kind of division and divisiveness in our society, have been, in my humble view, the singular most debilitating factor in this society. It has been the underlying cause of all our problems" (*Express*, December 4, 1995).

4.   The Jamaat was aware that a large segment of the population was hostile to it and that such hostility would make it difficult for the UNC to embrace it. One week following the election, the Jamaat, in a full page paid advertisement, sought to appease those elements. The statement was full of praise for Mr. ANR Robinson whose "cultured upbringing," "high level of statesmanship and nationalism" and whose international reputation they recognized and acknowledged. Bakr openly apologised to Mr. Robinson and his family:

> The time had come to shed the events of the past. We acknowledge the pain experienced over the past five years, and hope that we can work together, following the example of Mr. deKlerk and President Nelson Mandela, between whom much more blood was shed.

The statement also appealed to the business community to be charitable to the poor. Businessmen were told that they had the Jamaat's support "in recognition of your role in the creation of jobs and wealth." Appeals for support for the new government also went out to the Christian leadership, civil servants and to the PNM as well. The latter were asked to join the UNC in creating a government of national unity. The Jamaat likewise took the opportunity to thank all those residents of the East West Corridor, San Fernando and Ortoire/Mayaro who listened to what they said during the campaign and whom they claim helped to determine the outcome of the election in the marginal seats. The African element in the community were also urged to "embrace their Asiatic brothers and sisters of India' and to resist the attempts of those who seek to promote disunity and conflict or frustrate the goal of creating national Unity (*Sunday Mirror*, November 12, 1995).

The statement also came close to making an apology for the events of June 1990. To quote Bakr, "to those whom we have offended, we simply ask you to understand the circumstances of the day, and to join with us in bringing into reality the words of our National Anthem, "every creed and race find our equal place." All of this was clearly done in the hope that the public would not hobble the UNC when it sought to deal with the compensation issue.

The "honeymoon" between the Jamaat and Robinson did not last long, however. In response to the latter's appeal to have July 27, 1990 recognized as an important day in the history of the country, Bakr replied that it was already so recognized. According to Bakr, "for people like Robinson, July 27, 1990 is a "nemesis." Anytime they plan to oppress poor people, they remember July 20." Bakr claims he was an "instrument of God" in 1990. "Whatever God use me for, he done use me.… One thing they will never do again is put the police and army on people's land again. They can't do [any] more wickedness to poor people again. I will rise up again. That's my nature." The Jamaat's Head of Security, Hassan Anyabile denied that Robinson was treated worse than any other hostage. He was treated under the circumstances of war. For that's what it was. War! (*Sunday Mirror*, July 14, 1996).

One of the reasons why Bakr *et al* find it difficult to apologise for what they did had to do with the nature of the religious ideology which they espouse. As far as they were concerned in 1990, they had embarked on a "jihad," a religious war against the "kuffir state" which, in their view, was determined to oppress and crush them The aim of the oppression was genocidal; the target group was the African Muslim community. In their view, there was a "mortal threat" to their existence and they were thus forced to act in self-defense, which their "law" and their religion enjoined them to do.

Bilaal Abdullah in fact argued that all major religions recognised the concept of "just war." The Bible, he says, recognizes that "there is a time for peace and a time for war." Muslims also recognize that one has to fight against evil. According to Bilaal, "Allah instructs us in the Quoran to neither oppress others, nor to allow ourselves to be oppressed. The fight of good against evil, which is waged perpetually on the spiritual plane, sometimes requires a physical manifestation." Hinduism too is clear on this point, argues Bilaal. "The Gita speaks of Krishna urging Arjun to do his moral duty at the Battle of Kuruksetra" (*Mirror,* August 11, 1991).

Given their belief that what they did was justified, the Muslimeen found it difficult to apologise, even though they expressed regret for whatever collateral damage their actions caused to innocents. To quote Bilaal, "unless I change my understanding of the mortal threat that I felt that I and others was under, it is difficult to talk about apologizing for what, in my mind, was self-defence. The point being made is that this group of Muslims believes that there is one law for true believers and one for "kuffirs." As Hasan Anyabile put it while commenting on the state's refusals to compensate them in spite of what the Court had enjoined, "we are following our laws. They are breaking their own again" (*Mirror,* July 14, 1996).

Bakr, who described the Jamaat as "king makers" warned the UNC that problems could arise if compensation was not paid. As he said on the sixth anniversary of the attempted coup, "we have been victorious over all our enemies to date. The NAR lost all its seats in 1991 and the PNM lost in 1995. If the [UNC] kick up and become our enemy, they [will] lose too" (*Sunday Guardian,* July 28, 1996).

Chapter 2

THE MILLENNIUM ELECTIONS

*T*he general elections of 2000, the first in the new millennium, took place amidst charges that the UNC had stolen the election by systematically padding the voters' list in five swing constituencies where victories were won by narrow majorities. The UNC for its part, denied this was so. Its aim was to break the deadlock which had occurred in the 1995 election which ended in a 17-17 tie in Trinidad, and which had required the party to make *ad hoc* coalition arrangements first with the Tobago based National Alliance For Reconstruction, and when that failed, two members of the PNM crossed over in response to offers of ministerial office and other inducements (Ryan 1996,1999).

The UNC achieved its goal of winning an absolute majority, both in Parliament and in the country at large. In terms of the popular vote, the UNC secured 307,791 votes and 51.74 percent of the 594,875 votes that were validly cast, while the PNM received 276,334 or 46.45 percent. The NAR secured 7,409 or 1.25 percent, while the Tobago based People's Empowerment Party won 2,071 or 0.35 percent of the votes cast. Unlike what obtained in the 1995 elections, the UNC won 19 seats in Trinidad and the PNM 15. The PNM picked up one additional seat in Tobago, with the National Alliance for Reconstruction (NAR) taking the remaining Tobago seat. The UNC thus had a clear majority (19-17) in Trinidad and Tobago.

The UNC was justifiably enthusiastic about its performance. It had not only increased its support over that obtained in 1995 by 67,419 votes, but had secured an absolute majority. In 1995 it had obtained 45.74 percent of the votes cast. The UNC boasted that it had received the highest number of votes ever cast in an election in Trinidad and Tobago, and was now the "natural" party of government. It was in fact an extraordinary performance, given all that had been said during the campaign about the party's involvement in sleaze, corruption and election fraud, and all that Mr. Panday had done to rattle sacred icons in the society. The results of the elections seemed to formalise what appeared to be evident at the time, namely, that the Afro-creole political hegemony which had been institutionalised in 1956 with the first electoral triumph of the PNM, had now been replaced by an Indo-creole *jahajibhai* hegemony, attempts to disguise it by talk of national unity and inclusiveness, notwithstanding.

Issues in the Campaign

Performance vs. Corruption

The election was a referendum on the performance of the UNC administration since it came to power in 1995. There were several issues on the electoral table relating to how the UNC had dealt with the economy and procurement process, the administrative system, the machinery for elections, the issue of diversity, and its style of governance system generally.

The central focus of the UNC's campaign was on its "performance." The UNC's boast was that under its management, the economy had grown by some 5 percent, annually, and that unemployment had been reduced from 18 percent to 11.5 percent. It had also reduced personal income tax generally, and had improved the water production and distribution system so that 80 percent of the population was now said to be in receipt of a 24-hour supply. Areas which had never received a pipe borne supply or only an intermittent one, were now regularly on line. This applied especially to rural areas in the South of the country. The UNC also boasted that old age pensions had been increased from TT$820 to TT$1000.00 and that coverage of the school-feeding programme had been expanded. Most importantly, the party claimed that educational opportunities had been expanded to the point where secondary school entry had now become universally available to all who sought it, and not only for those who had "passed" the dreaded Common Entrance Examination which the PNM had introduced in 1960 and which the UNC had abolished. Under the latter system, some 10,000 children were denied entry to a secondary school each year. The UNC had also pledged to match, "dollar for dollar," all expenses which students and parents had incurred in pursuit of tertiary education, a pledge which was welcomed by many who would probably have voted PNM, but who assumed that the pledge would be available to all tertiary educational institutions, whether at the University of West Indies, other tertiary institutions in Trinidad and Tobago, or all other approved tertiary institutions abroad.

The PNM's critique of the UNC's proposal for universal secondary education was that this had always been part of the PNM's vision from as early as 1960, but had to be planned and phased properly. The PNM indicated that its aim was to introduce universal secondary education by the year 2005 and that its school-building programme was geared towards this date. There simply was not enough places to accommodate all who wished to be admitted. Schools were thus grossly overcrowded. Buildings were however only one of the prerequisites for achieving viability. The UNC, in its view, was rushing indecently to accelerate the target date without ensuring that all the supportive systems were in place. The PNM noted that under the UNC system, children with scores of less than 30 percent on the Secondary Education Assessment (SEA) which replaced the Common Entrance Examination were now to be admitted to secondary schools with no provision being made for remedial training.[1]

The Teachers Union (TTUTA) was also critical of what it described as the "madness" that was being pursued for political gain. The Union warned that students who were reading at frustration levels in the primary schools would not be able to cope when they were "promoted to secondary schools unless remedial programmes were put in place." Also critical of the UNC programme was the Inter American Development Bank (IADB) which had provided funding for the building of 20 schools to absorb the increased student intake as part of the Secondary Education Modernization Programme (SEMP). The IADB complained that in its haste to complete all 20 schools, enormous cost overruns had developed. The cost of the first 10 schools jumped from TT$136 million to TT$255 million, an increase of 87 percent. The IADB questioned the advisability of these large over budget expenditures, and there was a hint that all was not well in the state of Denmark. It was also felt that the new price tag for the schools would unnecessarily inflate the recurrent losses of the secondary education system and soak up funds needed for other aspects of the modernization programme, including the improvement of the quality of what was offered in the school spaces *(Newsday,* March 8, *2002).*

The PNM claimed that corruption was a major reason for the cost overruns, and that the UNC was seeking to gain political mileage with its promise of instant universal education without seeking to ensure that the system was sustainable. It was said that in its haste to complete the schools, two had to be abandoned with resultant losses of over TT$60 million.

On the question of the management of the administrative system, the UNC claimed that its aim was to introduce a results oriented administrative style that would underscore performance rather than slavish adherence to outmoded rules. This, and not anxiety to facilitate bureaucratic corruption, was what informed their management style. In terms of the latter allegation, the UNC's response was that the PNM was making complaints about corruption merely to delegitimise the UNC's performance record which they envied and could not match. The PNM insisted that the UNC's penchant for by-passing all the established rules and protocols for dealing with public procurement was intended to disguise the fact that the Treasury was being milked with impunity.

On the issue of diversity and inclusiveness, Panday claimed that the UNC's big *ashram* gave welcome and shelter to persons of all ethnicities, and that its management of diversity was "a model to the world." In his Father's House, there were mansions enough for all who wished entry. Those who did not want unity would have unity forced upon them. The allusion was to the PNM's policy of "fighting alone, and either winning or losing alone," and of refusing all calls for power sharing in a government of national unity. Panday insisted that he did not want to be a "Caroni Prime Minister," but a Prime Minister for the whole nation, including the parasitic oligarchy which he used to lampoon during his years as Leader of the Opposition. The PNM responses on all these questions, which would be elaborated upon in subsequent chapters, was to assert that the UNC's claims were hollow and opportunistic, and that the UNC's style of governance was ruining the country financially.

Surveys by St. Augustine Research Associates (SARA) in March 2000 indicated that the Afro- and Indo- populations were fundamentally divided in their assessment of the UNC and Mr. Panday's performance while in office. The population was divided almost equally in terms of whether or not it was time for a change of government. Forty-three (43) percent of the population believed that the UNC should be given another term, while 42 percent said it was time for a change. Nine (9) percent were uncertain about the need for change while six (6) percent refused to record their opinion. When responses to this question were disaggregated in terms of ethnicity, there was a positive correlation between ethnicity and disposition to change. Eighty-one (81) percent of the Indo-Trinidadians were opposed to change, while 12 percent were in favour of it. Sixty-nine (69) percent of those who were Afro-Trinidadians were keen on change, while 14 percent were willing to give the UNC another term. In terms of the mixed population, 56 percent wanted political change, while 22 percent supported another term for the UNC administration. The *dougla* element (Mixed-Indo and Afro-Trinidadians) were more equivocal. Forty-eight (48) percent wanted change while 32 percent felt that the UNC deserved another chance (Table 1).

Table 1
Do you think it is time for a change of Government,
or should the UNC be given another 5 years?

Response	Afro-Trinidad-ian	Indo-Trinidad-ian	Dougla	Other Mixed	National
Time for Change	69	12	48	56	42
UNC Next 5 Years	14	81	32	22	43
Do not know	9	5	15	11	9
Refuse to say	8	2	5	11	6

When asked to indicate which party they preferred to see in control of the government, forty-three (43) percent said UNC, while 27 percent said the PNM, a lead for the UNC of 16 percent. Ten (10) percent wanted neither, another 10 percent wanted a new party and three (3) percent the NAR. Six (6) percent refused to record an option (Table 2).

Table 2
Which party would you prefer to see in control of the
next Government of Trinidad and Tobago?

Response	Afro-Trinidad-ian	Indo-Trinidad-ian	Dougla	Other Mixed	National
UNC	14	81	31	16	43
PNM	46	5	43	21	27
NAR	4	1	2	7	3
None of the Above	13	4	9	23	10
New Party	12	4	13	25	10
Refuse to Say	11	5	2	8	6

When disaggregated in terms of ethnicity, 81 percent of the Indo-Trinidadians plumped for the UNC while only five (5) percent gave the PNM the nod. Of the Afro-Trinidadians, 46 percent preferred the PNM, 14 percent the UNC, 13 percent wanted none of the existing parties, while 12 percent said they would support a new party (Table 2). The survey clearly indicated that the Indo-Trinidadian population was solidly behind the UNC while the Afro-Trinidadians were not solid in their support for the PNM.

When those who indicated that they intended to vote were asked a more direct and intrusive question, "which party would you vote for if elections were held soon?," 91 percent of the Indo-Trinidadians said they would vote for the UNC, five (5) percent for the PNM and four (4) percent for some new party (if one were to come forward). The view held by some persons that Indo-Trinidadians felt betrayed by the UNC, and that they would stay away from the polls or even vote for the PNM as a way of demonstrating their disaffection with the UNC was not supported by the findings of the survey. Many were of the view that they were either better off materially or were likely to be some time in the future. We can also assume that they enjoyed the psychological externalities that came from seeing their coethnics in office. The Afro-Trinidadians were more divided in their responses. Sixty-seven (67) percent said they would vote for the PNM, 15 percent for the UNC, 5 percent for the NAR and 13 percent for a new party. The mixed group were also very divided. Forty-two (42) percent endorsed the PNM, 16 percent the UNC, 15 percent the NAR and 26 percent some new party. The *dougla* element was the most equivocal of all. Thirty-six (36) percent said they would vote for the UNC, 46 percent would give their franchise to the PNM, while 14 percent said they would opt for a new party (Table 3).

Table 3
(If planning to vote)
If an election were called soon, for which party would you vote?

Response	African	Indian	Dougla	Other Mixed	National
UNC	15	91	36	16	50
PNM	67	5	46	42	36
NAR	5	0	4	15	3
Some new Party	13	4	14	26	10

Taken together, the above figures indicated that the UNC was doing better at attracting the non-Indian population than the PNM was in terms of winning over Indo-Trinidadians. The net swing in favour of the UNC was in the vicinity of 10 percent among Afro-Trinidadians. While more of the mixed population was supportive of the PNM, a very significant minority (16 percent) said that they would vote for the UNC. What the data indicated was that the UNC stood a better than even chance of being returned to power. The UNC had clearly made good use of the advantages of incumbency, especially by increasing the availability of water and other public goods, and by increasing the minimum wage.

Mr. Panday and the UNC waged a brilliant political campaign which the PNM, try as it might, was unable to match. The UNC's operations strategists and media specialists targetted their audience and out-manoeuvered the PNM team. Its advertising strategy was cleverly aimed at the PNM core constituency, and while some of the negative advertisements annoyed a majority of blacks, they clearly helped to soften up the edges of the PNM base, already disenchanted with the PNM leader, Patrick Manning. This effect was particularly telling in the marginal constituencies where money was lavished as if it were an inexhaustible resource. One particular advertisement, "we come too far to turn back now," while appearing on the surface to be a universal message directed to all who wanted economic progress, was aimed at the UNC base which it was feared might have been turned off from the UNC leadership for reasons having to do with perceptions of constituency and ethnic group neglect, and allegations of electoral and other kinds of sleaze. What the descendants of the *Jahajibhais* were being told was that they had begun a journey in 1845 when the ship, the Fatal Rozack came with the first group of indentured workers, and had come too far to turn back. Some substituted "black" for "black." Political power, recently acquired, must be maintained by any means necessary.

The PNM and its supporters were traumatised by the outcome of the election as they had been in 1995, and insisted that it was stolen. Defeat was never conceded, and the results in two constituencies, Ortoire - Mayaro and Pointe-a-Pierre, were challenged in the courts. The claim was that two candidates who won their seats were citizens of the United States and Canada respectively when they filed their nomination papers, and were therefore not legally entitled to contest the election. The two MPs were accused of having perjured themselves when they filed their nomination papers, but the charges against them had to be dismissed by the Director of Public Prosecutions (DPP) because the State was unable to prove the matters without the cooperation of the United States and Canadian immigration authorities. Canada's strict privacy laws were cited as reason why information about the MP for Pointe-a-Pierre could not be disclosed. The United States Embassy also indicated it could not help the prosecution to determine whether the candidate for Ortorie-Mayaro had sworn an oath before taking up his US citizenship in 1996.

The PNM also insisted that the incidence of voter padding was far more serious and widespread than the Elections and Boundaries Commission (EBC) admitted. The EBC conceded that the UNC had in fact attempted to subvert the system, but that their efforts had been nipped in the but (see Chapter 7).

Elections to the House of Representative, 2000
Analysis of Votes Received by Political Party and Rejected Ballots

Electoral	Total Number of Votes Cast	Rejected Ballots	Valid Votes Polled	P.N.M. No. of Votes	P.N.M. %	U.N.C. No. of Votes	U.N.C. %
Arima	17,478	83	17,395	10,942	62.90	6,453	37.10
Arouca North	18,196	41	18,152	11,804	65.03	6,348	34.97
Arouca South	18,037	57	17,980	13,373	74.38	4,607	25.62
Barataria/San Juan	16,270	51	16,219	7,121	43.91	9,098	56.09
Caroni Central	19,526	72	19,454	6,278	32.27	13,176	67.73
Caroni East	19,111	101	19,010	4,714	24.80	14,296	75.20
Chaguanas	19,562	72	19,491	3,712	19.04	15,779	80.96
Couva North	18,193	90	18,103	3,720	20.55	14,383	79.45
Couva South	18,185	67	18,118	5,087	28.08	12,889	71.14
Diego Martin Central	14,420	43	14,377	10,322	71.80	4,055	28.20
Digeo Martin East	13,464	42	13,422	9,246	68.89	4,176	31.11
Diego Martin West	14,917	50	14,867	10,846	72.95	4,021	27.05
Fyzabad	19,617	97	19,520	7.132	36.54	11,896	60.94

Elections to the House of Representative, 2000
Analysis of Votes Received by Political Party and Rejected Ballots - Cont'd

Electoral	Total Number of Votes Cast	Rejected Ballots	Valid Votes Polled	P.N.M.		U.N.C.	
				No. of Votes	%	No. of Votes	%
La Brea	16,331	80	16,251	9,188	56.54	7,063	43.46
Laventille East/Morvant	13,984	65	13,919	11,335	81.44	2,584	18.56
Laventile West	12,266	40	12,226	10,733	87.79	1,493	12.21
Naparima	16,750	54	16,696	2,845	17.04	13,738	82.28
Narvia	19,456	91	19,365	6,379	32.94	12,844	66.33
Oropouche	17,185	76	17,110	2,572	15.03	14,538	84.97
Ortoire / Mayaro	20,343	117	20,226	9,303	46.00	10,923	54.00
Point Fortin	17,028	86	16,942	9,926	58.59	7,016	41.41
Pointe-a-Pierre	18,036	65	17,971	6,847	38.10	11,124	61.90
POS North / St. Anns West	12,726	54	12,672	10,099	79.70	2,573	20.30
Port of Spain South	12,309	52	12,257	9,101	74.25	3,'56	25.75
Princes Town	18,982	100	18,882	6,454	34.18	12,428	65.82
San Fernando East	17,052	87	16,965	10,339	60.94	6,626	39.06

Elections to the House of Representative, 2000
Analysis of Votes Received by Political Party and Rejected Ballots - Concluded

Electoral District	Total Number of Votes Cast	Rejected Ballots	Valid Votes Polled	P.N.M.		U.N.C.	
				No. of Votes	%	No. of Votes	%
San Fernando West	17,474	65	17,409	8,233	47.29	9,176	52.71
Siparia	18,188	85	18,103	2,833	15.65	15,270	84.35
St. Ann's East	15,537	76	15,461	11,129	71.98	4,332	28.02
St. Augustine	17,257	52	17205	5,618	32.65	11,587	67.35
St. Joseph	17,218	78	17,140	7,387	43.10	9,753	56.90
Tabaquite	17,754	62	17,692	4,029	2.77	13,282	75.07
Tobago East	8,311	38	8,273	3,632	43.90	-	-
Tobago West	9,935	56	9,879	5,040	51.02	-	-
Toco/Manzanilla	18,444	109	18,335	10,289	56.12	8,046	43.88
Tunapuna	17,985	197	17,788	8,726	49.06	9,062	50.94
Total	**597,525**	**2,650**	**594,875**	**276,334**	**46.45**	**307,791**	**51.74**

Following the elections, a constitutional impasse developed as a result of President Robinson's refusal to accept Prime Minister Panday's advice to appoint as many as seven defeated UNC candidates to the Senate and also as junior ministers. Prior to this, the practice was to refrain from appointing defeated candidates to the upper house. Mr. Panday sought to break with that tradition which the PNM had institutionalised. There was much controversy as to whether the President had the constitutional power to refuse the Prime Minister's advice (Ghany 2000: 23-40). My own view was that the President did not have the constitutional authority to refuse the Prime Minister's advice, and had gone out on a limb. The President perhaps recognized that he was on shaky legal grounds and asked for legal as opposed to emotional advice.

In response to the President's request, the UNC asked four eminent legal minds to provide an opinion which would help the President. The persons, who were defined as men of "Olympian legal competence," were Justice Telford Georges, former judge of the Appeal Court, Queen's Counsel Tajmool Hosein, and two former Presidents of the Republic, Messrs. Noor Hassanali and Ellis Clarke. Opinions were also solicited from several senior British jurists, including Sir William Wade whose book the President had cited in support of his stand. All advised that the President had to act on the advice of the Prime Minister in this matter, and that he was not empowered to introduce a new category of disqualification, i.e., defeat in an election. Some analysts also noted that the appointment to the upper house of persons who lost elections took place routinely in several Caribbean States, Grenada being a case in point, as well as in the United Kingdom where persons who were retired by the electorate were appointed to the House of Lords and given ministerial though not Cabinet status.

The President's response to the UNC's efforts to convince him that he was acting unconstitutionally was to accuse the Government of being "engaged in a campaign to harass the Head of State in the hope of driving him out of office in disgust." The UNC was however right in claiming that the President was acting unconstitutionally and that the Government had an obligation to challenge his actions (*Guardian*, January 30, 2001). The President's dilemma was however a genuine one. In his letter to Mr. Panday, the President declared that he found "it impossible to accept the principle, not expressed or denied in the Constitution, that persons who have been rejected by the electorate can constitute a substantial part of the Cabinet, even the majority, and consequently the effective Executive in our democratic state."

Mr. Robinson's *cri de coeur* brought into full focus some of the patterns of behaviour of the Panday regime that had been causing concern to many since it came to power in 1995. Mr. Panday clearly enjoyed breaking with political tradition, especially those departures which upset the political establishment. Some of these initiatives, such as having a defeated UNC candidate occupy the post of Speaker, seducing two PNM MPs to cross the floor, and seeking to suborn or pick off others by dangling inducements, all served to foster the 'anything goes' political culture which had been characteristic of the 1946-1956 era in Trinidad and Tobago. They also established precedents which threatened to change the chemistry of Trinidad's political culture.

Mr. Panday's manoeuver was a cynical and very clever attempt to create patronage for those who came aboard his political ship, either by crossing the floor, or agreeing to serve as candidates in constituencies that the UNC did not expect to win. Mr. Panday was also aware of the value of billeting such persons as ministers in potentially winnable constituencies. His plan was to channel resources through them to help the UNC win those constituencies in future elections. Mr. Robinson was however painfully aware that if that initiative was to become part of tradition, it could lead to further abuse. What, for example, would prevent a Prime Minister from insisting that all those who faced the polls on behalf of his party be rewarded with invitations to join the government, whether they won or lost their seats by a single vote or several thousands? What then would be the point of having constituency based elections? What would a future President do if President Robinson capitulated? Mr. Robinson obviously believed that

Mr. Panday's formula constituted a caricature of the Westminster system which Trinidad tries to mimic, however imperfectly.

There were two dimensions to the historic and controversial political discourse which President Robinson gave to the nation in his broadcast on January 5, 2001. One was his stirring call to the citizenry to take a stand to ensure that their hard won political gains were not stolen while they slept as had happened in so many other parts of the world where leaders constructed edifices of personalised power by stealth, all in the name of a majority of the people. Robinson told the nation that "there have been newly independent countries where numbers have counted, but it is one person who determined the course of events. Dictatorships have arisen on the basis of the influence or power of a single man.... Over our years of existence, we have managed to preserve our democratic system of government, but that is no guarantee for the future" (*Express*, January 6, 2001).

In language that reminded one of Thomas Jefferson in the American Declaration of Independence, Robinson reminded the nation of the "long train of abuses" [Jefferson's term] that had characterised government over the past five years, all of which, in his view, amounted to a betrayal of the trust that the people had invested in Mr. Panday's government. Jefferson, one recalls, argued that a people were entitled to resist their governors if their trust was continuously betrayed. In this case, Robinson chose to stand up for the people since "the electorate does not always have an opportunity to act until it is too late. Sometimes, by the time the electorate gets to know what is happening, it does not have a chance. Things creep up on them." Robinson shared his mother's folk wisdom with the population – wisdom that reminded them that "bad habits grow by slow degrees, streams run into rivers, and rivers run into the sea" (*ibid.*).

The second part of Robinson's discourse raised challenging questions as to who was to be the ultimate guardian or guarantor of the Constitution and the democratic order, the individual who was elected tribune of the people or the individual who personified the state? Could the latter refuse in the name of a higher law to heed the advice of the former if he deemed that advice not to be in the public interest? What would a President do if he were asked by a crazy Prime Minister to make a failed insurrectionist (Bakr, for example) a Senator and Minister of National Security? Would the President have to rubber stamp that advice? Most people would probably say no. This implied that the President had some discretion to disagree when he believed he had to.

Robinson's argument was that statutory power was a trust which should only be used for the purposes for which it was given, and in a manner that was 'proper and right.' It could never be absolute. But what happens when a society is in transition and the philosophical foundations are interpreted in a different way by a new hegemon with a different set of values and different notions of good and evil or wrong and right? Who arbitrates between the votaries of the rising hegemon and the declining hegemon? What if the President finds himself on the 'wrong' side of history, defending values that have flown away in the dusk like the 'owl of minerva'? What is the role of the 'people' in its diverse manifestations?

Some advocates of a broad construction approach to the analysis of a statute, whether a constitution or otherwise, argued that it should be looked at holistically, including what is in the preamble. If that is done, so it is claimed, one would agree that in terms of our Constitution, the President had residual powers which allowed him to refuse advice in certain contexts. Those who adopted a "black letter approach" to statutory interpretation argued otherwise. The literalists held that one only turned to the preamble and the notes of interpretation when the meaning of the words were unclear. But who determines when the words are clear? The President indicated that he needed to be convinced by legal argument. But was there any legal argument that was unchallengeably right or wrong? One recalls that in the United States Supreme Court and in the Privy Council, much that was once deemed right was now considered wrong and *vice versa*.

It is however important that we understand the crisis for what it was. It was not merely a struggle between two willful and stubborn personalities, as important as that dimension of the crisis was. The two gladiators merely embodied the crisis. It was also not a constitutional crisis or impasse in the way in which those terms are conventionally understood. It was really a collision of visions, epistemologies and political cultures. Robinson personified the old hybrid Afro-Saxon, Anglo-Creole political value system that was transplanted from Victorian England into the manured soils of the colonies. That value system had mutated into something different in form and content from the parent variety, but nevertheless remained recognizable.

Panday personified the Indo-Saxon or Indo-Creole variant. That variant also employs some of the forms of the Victorian model, but infuses it with an unmistakable neopatrimonial esthetic which has a seemingly different approach to leadership and followership. This collision of political cultures was bound to occur as the society shifted its centre of gravity from the hills to the groves, or as Lloyd Best puts it, from 'port' to 'plantation' (see Chapter 10).

Interestingly, Best argues that "Indos" and "Afros" share the same "Afro-Saxon" culture, and that there is no such thing as an "Indo-Saxon." "Afros" and "Indos," he contends, not only share the same space and many similar historical experiences, but more importantly, were shaped by the same schools and the Anglo-centric attitudes learnt therein. The socialisation derived from this common schooling (as opposed to knowledge and education) served to distort and even erase such distinctiveness as might have been generated as a result of values acquired in the home, places of worship, or the work place. Epistemologically, we have all become Afro-Saxons without much by way of ancestral memories. As Best writes:

> Indos came into WI society long after the Afro-Saxon character of the culture and civilisation had already been established. It goes without saying that, much like any new

> tributary to the stream of history, Indos did add their quota.
> However, for all kinds of reasons, including those we in
> Trinidad and Tobago can only at our peril fail to explore,
> the stream of history has rolled relentlessly on. This remains
> true not only for territories where Indos were comparatively
> numerous, but for the whole region. It is hard not to regard
> Afro-Saxon culture as the solvent which makes a unity of
> the "repeating island," while also making of the region one
> integrated whole. (*Sunday Express*, November 10, 2002)

Best however seems to be mesmerized by his dated QRC model
of schooling and may not be aware that schooling in south and central
Trinidad was informed by the Canadian missionary experience and thus
differed from those in the north which drew on English patterns.
Moreover, home, confessional space, and other agents of primary
socialisation count for as much or much more than school, and the
differences of culture and attitude that are generated thereby are not
as insignificant as Best argues, though there are surface similarities that
derive from the fact that large sections of both ethnic groups have
achieved middle class status and are consumers of American culture. It
is also important to note that people have multiple personalities and
masks which they wear as the situation warrants. The differences in
the masks worn express themselves most clearly in the field of culture
and politics. Best concedes that there might be genuine cultural
differences of perception and posture between the two groups, but
these he sees as "minor." Quixotically, he argues that "the thing that
joins the two [groups] is the readiness to complain, protest and
exaggerate to the point that it amounts to a shared culture of victim-
hood" (*ibid.*).

It really took a Panday to lay bare the absurdities of the Westminster
model which he caricatured in a grotesque way. Dr. Williams had of
course begun the process. What Panday did was to make it even clearer
that constitutions cannot always restrain those who would not be
restrained. Kings make constitutions and not the other way around.
Traditional constitution reform cannot therefore be the only answer.

There was also need to rebuild moral capital faster than it was now being consumed – assuming of course that it was not too late.

Some argued that Trinidad and Tobago did not practice Westminster style politics, and that what one had was a plebiscitary neo-patrimonial dictatorship in which the Prime Minister is not *primus inter pares* as myth has it. This is true, though it is equally so of what obtains at Westminster. In our version of the model, the Prime Minister is the boss, and most of his Ministers are courtiers who do his bidding. The fact that some of them 'won' their seats disguised the fact that most people voted for the leader and/or the party and not for them. In a real sense, then, one could say that it mattered little whether they were appointed to the Executive *via* the Senate, won their seats, or lost. While much of this was true, myths, conventions, and fictions are important in politics. They help give flesh and blood to the barebones of the constitutional parchment, and serve to restrain arbitrary and aggressive behaviour on the part of political elites who abhor such restraints. Sometimes they override what is inscribed in the written document.

In the end, Mr. Robinson capitulated and made the appointments though he indicated that he still had reservations. As he told Panday, 55 days after he first received his advice, "my course is clear, though not without reservations. I will now act in accordance with the advice contained in your letter of January 2, 2001 and appoint persons named therein at Senators." While many were relieved, as many were disappointed that the President did not stay the course. He however had no constitutional basis for so doing. He had however invented a new constitutional precedent, *viz.,* that the President had a power of delay which when exercised, gave him the opportunity to mobilise public opinion against an advice which he felt he ought not to take.

Endnote

1.   The PNM had forgotten or perhaps was not aware that free secondary education had been introduced in 1960 in much the same cavalier fashion. Dodderidge Alleyne, Permanent Secondary to Dr. Williams recollected as follows:

Dr. Williams is having a meeting with Pat Robinson, Borrell and Scotty Lewis. They had torn up his draft Budget Speech and they had recast it, all of them. And then he asked them a question, very important question. "What do we now tell the people?" So they said, but you have the Budget Speech. He said "No." "What do I tell the people?" And somebody, I think it was Pat, said, "Well, what about free secondary education?" And he slapped his thigh, at the same time John Donaldson, not the young one, entered the door, and he said, "John, John, come, come, come, we have just decided to have free secondary education."

There was no preparation for the training of teachers. But you see there are some things in history which if they are not done when they are done, they are not done at all. So they started building schools. Hugh Harris started building schools. He was turning sods every week or so and Dr. Williams and Mr. Romain for whom QRC was the Alumni, set about to remove all the good teachers from Queens Royal College in order to fill these other schools. It was a good thing, because of what it has done, although the period during when this thing was being done was very difficult for teachers, and for students.

Tranquillity, for example, where it was insisted upon that there should be twelve hundred, sixteen hundred, eighteen hundred children. The Principal hid himself in his office, locked in, and when they said, but we can't take any more, they said call Education. Education called the Prime Minister. He said, "You have to take them." And when the Principal asked, "but where do we put them?," he said, "Put them in the corridor, put them anywhere, but don't trouble me." But we got over that period and we now produce more 'A' level students than any other country in the Caribbean, some would say more than all of them put together (Alleyne 1999).

Chapter 3

THE UNC PARTY ELECTIONS OF 2001

*O*n June 1, 2001, the UNC held elections to fill a number of posts in the party hierarchy. Particular attention was focussed on the post of Deputy Political Leader, an office that hitherto was not deemed important. The assumption was that given Mr. Panday's then age (68), and the state of his health (he had recently had a heart by-pass operation), the victor would either succeed Mr. Panday as Political Leader of the Party or at least enhance his chances of doing so whenever Panday retired or assumed the Presidency of the Republic as he hinted he might wish to do some day.

Three slates contested the election, the "All Inclusives," Team Unity, and the Women's Platform. The positions taken by the three slates reflected a conflict of visions about the future of the UNC. The view taken by the All Inclusives was that the UNC had its base in the Indian community of South and Central Trinidad, and its victory in the general elections of 2000 was only made possible because of the input made by its Afro-creole wing. The party's goal must not merely be to defend its gains, but to become entrenched as the natural party of government and also win the twenty-four seats that were required to amend entrenched provisions of the Constitution. To consolidate its power, the UNC had to seek new blood and new sinews from wherever possible. Status as foundation members, while important, could not be decisive in choosing leaders. One needed balance between ethnicities, geography and generational status. The UNC had to become a cosmopolitan "party of parties," or an ethnically confederate party.[1]

Mr. Panday's brother, Subhas, and 11 other Members of Parliament took the view that political new comer, Mr. Carlos John, the then Minister of Infrastructure, could best perform the bridging role between Afro-creoles and Indo-creoles. "I begged Carlos because I saw him as a bridge that will take us across the Caroni River to bring our people together. We are supporting Carlos to help the Prime Minister expand the horizons of the party" (*Mirror,* May 20, 2001). "Whether John was a 'Johnny-come-lately,' or was once a member of the PNM, was irrelevant. He is a hard worker and unquestionably loyal to the leader," something Mr. Panday said he had difficulty saying about "some people" on the other slate. Panday pointedly accused the leader of Team Unity, Ramesh Lawrence Maharaj, of "walking with knife against the Prime Minister for President" campaign (*Express,* May 19, 2001). John was thus the "African" horse that the UNC had to ride if it was to enter the "new Jerusalem." *Power had to be shared with African elements if it was to be augmented and sustained.* In sum, Indo-Trinidadian ethnic security and survival could only be secured if all the other groups felt that their interests were also secure in a non-zero sum political process.

Subhas Panday went so far as to accuse Maharaj of being a power hungry dictator and a greedy megalomaniac who could not wait for the leader to die. "We on the other hand have an all inclusive vision for all the people of the nation, and we are not turning back." Members of John's slate also charged that the Team Unity faction was "racist," and wanted to take the UNC back to "the old days of Bhadase Sagan Maraj's Peoples Democratic Party (PDP) and the Democratic Labour Party (DLP)" (Ryan 1972). Their own goal was to make the UNC relevant to the 21st century. John in fact argued that the UNC could not function as Indian parties did traditionally. Political realities had changed, and parties had to function like modern dynamic corporations which head-hunt for CEOs rather than look to persons who had been working with the company for 30 or 40 years. "The days of length of service are really over. Leadership was about vision and not about who came first ... The dynamics have changed" (*Newsday,* May 20, 2001). John also believed that being African and being from the private sector meant that he could add more value to the UNC than Indian

MPs, a remark that did not endear him to some of the latter. "My perception is that the party is still anchored centrally," a euphemism for being based on Indians who were heavily concentrated in Central Trinidad. "I believe my race could have a favourable impact in realising that dream of expanding the party's core support" (*Sunday Express,* May 20, 2001). Boasted John: "Being the only African in the running will be my greatest asset in this battle.... I think if I win, it would add value to the party" (*Express,* April 30, 2001). While John was clearly overstating the assets which he brought to the table, there was a certain plausibility to his argument, other things being equal.

The Team Unity faction led by Attorney General Ramesh Maharaj, Minister of Food Production, Trevor Sudama and Minister of Foreign Affairs Ralph Maraj was seen as representing the party's communal base. Team Unity however denied that they were motivated by considerations of race or communalism. They claimed to be merely anxious to ensure that the people who built the party continued to have the critical say about how it was shaped, and the direction it took. The ethnic fundamentalists among them argued that Indians had an essential and unique interest and identity which only Indians could understand and properly protect. As one activist moaned:

> The door is open now, and anybody, I mean anybody, could simply walk in and take over the party.... It is not about race. People who want high office must deserve it. They must be prepared to work in the trenches, to pay their dues and work their way up. You can't just come along with a fistful of dollars, a pinstripe suit, and get a government in your lap.... This is not a business you are buying over; *the next leader must understand the political culture of the people he or she represents.* (*Sunday Mirror,* May 20, 2001)

Those who considered themselves to be the "old guard" argued that while new blood was welcomed, commitment and understanding of the Indian community were also important. The "creole" faction which had previously been associated with the Organisation For National Reconstruction (ONR) and the National Alliance For

National Reconstruction (ONR) and the National Alliance For Reconstruction (NAR) and which had entered the party just prior to the 1995 elections should not be allowed to take over the UNC which was now only beginning to enjoy the fruits of office after its long soujourn in the wilderness. As Trevor Sudama put it:

> When you look at some of the key figures who came in recently, they came from the NAR/ONR. The UNC is for inclusion, but its up to members to decide what position they occupy in the party. We have a right to make our claims for longevity, loyalty and commitment. We put our lives on the line for this party. We want to have everyone involved when it comes to the political leadership, but we need people who have a vision for society, who can understand its ethnic and cultural diversity, and how to manage it. That requires a much larger vision than what we're seeing from some of the aspirants. The new members being brought in aren't being screened as our constitution demands they should be by a membership screening team. Anybody coming in off the street is being given membership automatically. Nobody's asking if they subscribe to UNC principles. We welcome everyone, but our concern is the dominance of any one particular interest in the party and, given where John has come from – a conglomerate, [and the PNM] - it's a matter of concern if he brings in that influence as a dominant one. Members must decide on it. (*Guardian,* May 20, 2001)

Sudama sneered about those who boasted about their competence, "even if their only competence is to pave roads," a pointed reference to John's role as the Minister of Infrastructure. Sudama conceded that the House of the Rising Sun had many rooms and a place for everyone. *"Everyone must [however] know their place"* (*Express*, May 17, 2001). MP for Naparima, Ralph Maraj, likewise complained that all over the world, "high financiers were gaining control of political parties." According to Maraj, "a political party is not a sports car that you buy and discard. It is an inheritance." Maraj warned about political predators who took the cynical view that those who had "more corn would feed more fowl. That is insulting you," he told party activists (*Express*, May 17, 2001).

The third faction was led by the then Minister of Education, Kamla Persad-Bissessar. Bissessar's campaign was gender based, a fact that counted against her in a society that is still very patriarchal. None of her parliamentary colleagues endorsed her slate. She was also seen as being a "jeannie-come-lately" since she had run on a NAR ticket in 1991 and had been savagely critical of Basdeo Panday and the UNC during that campaign. She however insisted that she joined the UNC before Mr. Panday became Prime Minister in 1995. Like John, she warned the old guard that the UNC could no longer rely on its old 'soul' to survive; all sections of the party needed to feel assured of access to its decision making processes (*Newsday*, May 15, 2001). Nor could the party allow itself to be constructed as "Indian." "I am not an "Indian," she insisted. "I am of Indian origin. Trinidad and Tobago is my land" (*Express*, May 28, 2001). Interestingly, Persad-Bissessar felt the need to make clear that she only chose to run after she had satisfied herself that her "beloved leader" had not anointed any successor. "If I thought Panday had anointed anyone, I would not have entered" (*Express*, May 25, 2001).

The elections, which were supposed to be an exercise in "one love," was a "mudfest" which at times turned violent. The party was in fact a microcosm of the larger society and party financier, FIFA Vice President Jack Warner, warned John that "dem fellas would be racial and kill [you]" (*Sunday Mirror*, May 20, 2001). John in fact confessed that had he known before hand that the contest would have been so bitter, he would "never have thrown [his] hat in the ring."

> I thought this was going to be an exercise in democracy; but it has taken a real twist and gone down a different road. The campaign has become characterised by a display of obscenity, gutter politics, vulgarity, and a lot of hanging of dirty linen in public where one's achievements are now being twisted to work against them... Yesterday I was their colleague. Today I am their foe. The "sharks" smile with

me in the day and stab me in the back at night. They are changing right before my very eyes. (*Express*, May 20, 2001)

Racial slurs were also hurled at John who complained that the contest was taking an emotional toll on him and his family. John disclaimed any interest in the Prime Ministership, which he was accused of secretly coveting, and claimed he merely wanted to do party work. He also indicated his belief that given the diversity in the society, the UNC should have three deputy leaders rather than one, so that the deputy was not seen as the heir apparent to the Prime Minister.

A trenchant attack on Team Unity was also launched by the then Minister of Enterprise, Development, Tourism, and Foreign Affairs, Mervyn Assam, who characterised the Team as a group of persons who had been "rejected" by the Prime Minister. Assam accused the old guard of riding on the backs of the "johnny come latelys" in the 2000 election:

> A lot of my colleagues got their seats on a platter, but are talking about being in the trenches; but while they were there, we could only get 14 seats. In 2000, the East West Corridor again made the difference. San Juan, St. Joseph and Tunapuna got us into government without the need for a coalition. It wasn't Couva South (Maharaj's seat), Oropouche (Sudama's seat) or Naparima (Ralph Maraj). The dinosaurs want to lead this party back; but it was the East West Corridor that gave new life and new possibilities to the UNC. It is here where we will get the 24 seats. (*Express*, May 30, 2001)

Hinducentric fundamentalists were unhappy that Mr. Panday seemed to support the All Inclusives by giving his tacit approval those whom he had once called the "parasitic oligarchy." Panday was in fact viewed as an arch *neemakharam* [ingrate] by radical "Indian rights" groups. As one such group, the Indian Review Committee, complained:

> The UNC is already a national party. Mr. Panday uses terms "inclusion" and "national party" as a façade. He is also being ungrateful towards his supporters.... It seems

Trinidadians of Indian descent are in danger in the UNC, a party they have strongly supported since its formation in 1988. Probably Indians need to seriously reconsider their position in the UNC in the light of what is occurring in recent years. The UNC elite, in pursuit of a policy of "national unity" and "inclusion," really noble policies, are engaged in reverse discrimination against Indian supporters. Indians must consider whether they are just political beasts of burden to be ridden by "Indian" politicians, and now that office and government have been acquired, are being discarded and betrayed. (*Express,* May 11, 2001)

Elements in that group in fact called for the creation of a new "all Indian" party to rise from central Trinidad to wrest control from the UNC leadership which, in their view, was pursuing a policy of appeasement of African voters and every "Tom, Jack and Carlos," and stigmatising all that was Indian (*Newsday,* May 22, 2001). A similar view was expressed by Kamal Persad, a weekly columnist for the *Sunday Express.* Persad argued that the UNC was a "creole" party headed by Indians…. The UNC in all its symbols, cultural projections, and ethos is anti-Indian. Politically it had Indian support, but just like the PNM, it has never really defined national unity in fullness…. These are tendencies that will create a backlash from Indians" (*Express,* May 28, 2001).

In what was clearly meant to be a major statement, the Secretary General of the Sanatan Dharma Maha Sabha, Mr. Sat Maharaj, who himself had a reputation for articulating Hinducentric views, disassociated himself from the call for an "Indian party." Indeed, he argued that the founder of the People's Democratic Party (PDP) and the Maha Sabha, Bhadase Sagan Maraj, was more politically advanced than "many of the UNC members now demanding a return to tradition." He noted that Maraj had made strategic and tactical alliances with other elements in the society in the 50s. "Bhadase," he said, "recognised the need for multiethnic strategic alliances to promote the welfare of all citizens, regardless of ethnicity, religion, ancestral origin or local geography" (*Guardian,* May 26, 2001). Maharaj argued that

Maraj and Panday were in fact in the same political tradition even though they had been political "enemies":

> Both Bhadase and Basdeo Panday realised that in a multi-ethnic society, it is politically fatal to win power with the support of only one group. Secession, domestic strife and disunity always follow political success by one tribe or ethnic group which failed to form alliances with others. (*Guardian*, May 26, 2001)

Maharaj observed that the PNM had also sought to make strategic alliances with Presbyterians, Muslims, local whites and business elites. Panday had now deepened and institutionalized those links to the point where "the UNC is a real multi-ethnic party." Maharaj chided those who would have the UNC become an exclusively Indian party. "The UNC election is exposing the political narrowness of those who can only see the past." Maharaj observed that the fastest growing ethnic bloc in the population were the *douglas*, who are often marginalised in the Hindu community since they are seen as "bastards". "There is no POPPG or NAR for them to join. The UNC has to provide a comfortable home for them" (*Guardian*, May 26, 2001).

It is important to note that notwithstanding their postures, all the slates were multi-ethnic in composition. Team Unity included high profile Afro-Trinidadians, some of whom were themselves relative newcomers. These included a former Commissioner of Police, a former Chief of Defense Staff, a Shouter Baptist Archbishop, a former trade union leader, the Junior Minister of Education, and the Minister of Information and Telecommunication, who was once a PNM Minister. The All Inclusives featured several stalwart Indians. Ironically, more "creoles" were on the Team Unity slate. Team Unity however had its centre of gravity in the traditional Indian constituency which felt it was losing influence, while the All Inclusive drew its energy and inspiration from that politically and socially mobile element which had come into the UNC following the collapse of the NAR in 1988, and which had sought to transform it from a sugar worker based party into a modern political party that was attractive to the Indian middle class.

It is perhaps worth noting that Team Unity sought to compound the dilemma of Indians by alleging that Panday's game plan was to make John Prime Minister when the Presidency became vacant and assume that office himself. As Sudama charged, "the ultimate goal was for Basdeo Panday to be Head of State. He wanted to make [John] Prime Minister in the year 2002 after President Robinson's term expires. Carlos John will be Prime Minister and Basdeo Panday will be President. That for Panday will be inclusion." But Indians were folks too, argued Sudama. Sudama felt that Panday's refusal to endorse an Indian as his successor was evidence of his "self-hatred." If this allegation was true and had come to pass, it would have meant that Panday would wear the "crown" while CL Financial, the conglomerate with which John was associated, would take possession of the "crown jewels." This was an unlikely scenario, but many were prepared to believe that the claim had merit.

Panday later admitted that he silently gave John his support in the party election, but denied that he had anointed him as his successor. As he told a UNC gathering, "let me state for the record that there is no Panday slate that can lay claim to my endorsement. This does not mean that I do not have a defined team for our national executive" (*Express,* April 9, 2001).[2] In Panday's view, however, the deputy leader of the UNC did not automatically become Prime Minister if the incumbent died or became incapacitated. That was something which the President had to determine. Maharaj felt otherwise, and argued that the Constitution of the party assumed that the deputy leader would succeed as Prime Minister if a vacancy arose. The Party had to prepare for successorship:

> When a Prime Minister has to be appointed, it has to be the leader of a political party. So where in the constitution it says that the deputy political leader performs the function of the political leader in the absence of the political leader, one sees the connection between government and the political party. So what the membership is saying is, if we have voted for a deputy political leader and that (person) is in the Parliament, he is the leader of the House, he is an

AG, there is nothing in the constitution that prevents him
from acting as PM. Why it is that you don't want him to
act? That is what the members are asking. (*Guardian,*
September 2, 2001)

This basically was the Maharaj's *cheval de la bataille.* Panday was
however resolutely opposed to having Maharaj as his successor, but
also refused to endorse Persad-Bissessar as an alternative. Patriarchy
triumphed over ethnicity. Panday would claim that his historic mission
was to smash the paradigm that says a party with an Indian base could
only be successfully led by an Indian, and complained that Team Unity
wanted to go back to the days when the UNC was seen as "the Indian"
or "Caroni Party" (*Guardian,* September 11, 2001). He, on the other
hand, had become very sensitive to the problem of managing diversity
in a plural society, a "challenge made infinitely more difficult by the
obsession of certain elements that are bent on divisiveness, separatism
and group domination. These elements are found across the political
spectrum. I acknowledge that" (*Express,* April 19, 2001).

Panday and the Election Campaign

Mr. Panday's reactions as he observed the leadership struggle
were very contradictory. He first boasted that the "one man one vote"
election was a "tremendous exercise in democracy" which could stand
comparison with that which took place in the United Kingdom, the
United States, and anywhere else in the Caribbean. He also claimed
that the behaviour of the UNC membership was not less civilised than
that of English or American voters. Contrary to what was assumed,
the unfolding events did not sadden him at all. He felt certain that
party voters would make intelligent choices and would not be bought
for a "mess of pottage" or a "ten days" job as alleged by those opposed
to John's slate. The party, he advised, had to grow up and deal with the
"trauma of change" (*Newsday,* May 15, 2001). Mr. Panday however let
it be known that the behaviour of some of the candidates was making
them "inelectable" as future leaders of the UNC. As he remarked:

I am extremely happy and pleased that some people are exposing themselves in such a way that they will never be leaders of this party. The people will have an opportunity to look at them and see those who are willing to sacrifice the party and the government and everybody in order to gain power. It is upon this basis that the party will choose its leadership. (*Guardian*, May 22, 2001)

Panday however refused to intervene to heal the rift in the party. He preferred instead to have would be leaders "make fools of themselves" and let the people judge who among them was fit or unfit to lead. Mr. Panday did not name the fools, but the reference to Messrs. Maharaj, Maraj and Sudama was clear.

A few things now seem clear about the struggle. One was that the fight was between those who felt that the UNC was at bottom an Indian party and that Indians had an unique interest which could best be protected by co-ethnics, and those who believed that having achieved political power, Indians were no longer "alienated " or had an ethnic agenda which required that their leader be an Indian. The struggle was also one for succession to Basdeo Panday. Ramesh Lawrence Maharaj was determined to succeed Panday, and it was clear that he was prepared to do whatever was necessary to achieve that ambition. Maharaj did not however have the support of a majority of UNC MPs as the successor to Mr. Panday. They saw him as an ambitious and ruthless autocrat who lacked personal integrity. MPs saw Maharaj's tactics and his attempt to dictate their choice as a "sign of things to come."

Election Outcome

The outcome of the elections came as a surprise to many. Turnout was very low, especially in the non-traditional UNC areas. Despite all the hoopla and money, only 26,344 persons, a little over a third (36 percent) of the registered membership bothered to vote. Forty-three thousand (43,000) persons had been registered and paid for during the campaign by the respective slates, and turn out was expected to be higher. It may well be that the facilities were not conveniently located to make it easy for members to vote. The infighting also clearly turned off many would be voters.

The Team Unity candidate for the post of deputy political leader emerged victorious. He however received only 10,983 or 42 percent of the votes cast. Much to the surprise of many, second place went not to John but to Persad-Bissessar. The latter got 7,995 or 30 percent of the votes cast and Mr. John 6,775 or 26 percent of the votes cast. The pattern of voting however revealed that Maharaj got most of his support in four UNC heartland constituencies. Voter turnout was higher in these areas. John's support was more widely dispersed along the East-West-Corridor and in Tobago. It is hard to resist the conclusion that John was defeated by the Indian vote despite the presence of several Indian MPs on his campaign wagon and the suspicion that he had the blessing of the Political Leader. Fear of an Afro-creole resumption of power and tribal solidarity triumphed over hope that Afro-creole support would help to ensure the continued growth of the party.

The bitter campaign left stretchmarks which scarred the party and the UNC Government permanently. One minister confessed that "camaraderie does not exist anymore" (*Guardian*, June 4, 2001). Another stalwart opined prophetically that the party's survival would be the "Ninth Wonder of the World." While all the combatants professed that they would not allow personal feelings of hurt or pique to endanger the long term interests of the party, it was clear that there was a residue of bitterness which expressed itself in the Cabinet which split along pro and anti-Panday lines.

There was much speculation as to why Panday decided to alter the instructions which he had given in 1998 that members of the cabinet should not hold office in the Party. The argument given then was that the two offices were onerous and that ministers should concentrate on their official responsibilities. It was however clear that Panday wanted to prevent ambitious persons in the cabinet, especially the then Attorney General, from combining ministerial power with that which comes from holding party office. Panday's decision to reverse that decision was made during his visit to England for a medical check up that was related to his heart condition. He in fact confessed that he had erred in making the decision to debar ministers from standing for office, and had decided to revoke it (*Express*, April 9, 2000). Panday may have had intimations of his mortality and wanted to leave behind a stable political party as an enduring monument. He was not "smoking out" his rivals as Eric Williams had allegedly done in 1973 in respect to the PNM. As he himself explained:

> If I have to leave any legacy to the country, it has to be the political party which I now belong to, and which will struggle and fight for the rights of people. I have seen many parties die with their founders, including the PNM. I do not wish my party to die with me; I, therefore, must prepare the party for my demise. I don't want to die in the party, because if I die in the party, I fear the party will die with me and I would have left no legacy in the struggle. You are wrong. I am not trying any "shot" like Eric Williams. I am merely preparing the party for choosing its leader because I cannot put that upon my successor. The people have to choose a successor, not me, and that is what I'm doing. (*Sunday Mirror*, May 27, 2001)

The election however did have serious unintended consequences for Mr. Panday and the UNC. Key members of the party had stood up to him and had tarnished his image as its unchallengeable leader. Prior to the election, the UNC was seen as Panday's personal party. This was no longer quite so. As Raffique Shah, a former political colleague of Panday, well put it:

> [Panday] is no longer the infallible never-to-be-challenged Pope of the UNC. Panday's past misdeeds have caught up with him. The all-Indian party that he opted for in 1977/78 has returned to haunt him. The ULF supporters whom he told then that Africans were "trying to take over the party," are the ones who are ensuring that Africans never come to power, not in the UNC. And it was he who knowingly foisted Ramesh on the party, that after planting his boots on Kelvin

Ramnath's behind. Ramesh has turned out to be his biggest
nightmare, not Patrick Manning. (*Sunday Express,* June 10,
2001)

As we shall see, reports of Panday's political death were somewhat
premature, even if substantively correct. The party elections also set
the stage for the fracturing of the UNC and its collapse while in office.

Endnotes

1. The term "party of parties" was coined by Lloyd Best.

2. Subhas Panday told a party meeting that "if members vote for John, it would make the leader happy" (*Guardian,* May 21, 2001), a remark for which he was rebuked by the Prime Minister who diplomatically disowned it, though only after the election. The signals were clear that Mr. Panday was quietly backing the All Inclusives. John was known to be socially close to the Panday family and was called upon in June 2003 to explain why he had wired £20,000 to an account in the name of Oma Panday, Mr. Panday's wife.

Chapter 4

THE COLLAPSE OF THE UNC

> We are looking at the perennial problem of
> *neemakharamism*, that is, people riding the party's back to
> get into office, and having got there, they turn their backs,
> scorning the base degrees by which they did ascend.

- Basdeo Panday

*O*ne of the unintended consequences of the inner party
election was the splitting apart of the UNC and its dramatic
collapse in office after just one year. The postures adopted,
and the statements made by the protagonists of the respective slates
and by Mr. Panday himself, had made reconciliation difficult. Following
the party election, the members of Team Unity and Mr. Panday became
engaged in an orgy of name calling and mutual recrimination which
eventually led to the expulsion of the three Team Unity ministers from
the Cabinet and the UNC. The dissidents were banned for three
months by the Party's National Assembly, and had their portfolios
truncated. They were eventually expelled after having been angrily
advised by Mr. Panday that "who want to resign could resign."

Much of the name calling was initiated by Mr. Panday who labelled
the dissidents "treacherous triplets" and *neemakharams* who had betrayed
their leader.[1] Panday complained that in Caribbean parties, there was
always "some jackass who would challenge the leader," and that it was
a phenomenon with which Eric Williams, George Chambers, ANR
Robinson, and others had to deal. Panday however noted that unlike
what happened in Communist countries where people were shot for
so doing, the "lil cussout" that had taken place within the UNC was a

"normal part of the dialectic of the democratic process. Once people competed for power, there was going to be conflict." But while it was "natural for people to aspire to leadership," it was his duty as the incumbent "to ensure that they were kept out." Panday accused Maharaj, whom he likened to Cerberus, the "monstrous three headed dog which in Greek mythology guarded the gates of Hades," of foolishly conspiring to hand over power to the PNM because he had not been anointed as his successor. "Hell hath no fury like a politician who believes he had been spurned" (*Guardian*, October 22, 2001).

Maharaj was deemed an "imposter," a "pretender," a "jackass," a "Judas," a "terrorist" and a modern day "Rawan." Bemoaned Panday: "over the years, the rising sun had come to be regarded as my shining and beloved political wife; but recently, a political Rawan tried to steal her from me …. In the process, the political Rawan will be destroyed." Panday's reference was to the story in the Hindu epic, the *Ramayana*, of Ram and Rawan who were locked in battle for Ram's wife, Seeta. Rawan was destroyed by Ram in battle, and Seeta returned to him. Panday's metaphor of Ram and Rawan was an allusion to the battle within the party between himself and Maharaj for use of the UNC's symbol in the impending general election (*Express*, November 10, 2001). Panday also argued that whereas Jesus had one betrayer, Judas, he had three. "No political leader will allow a Judas to remain on board" (*Guardian*, October 22, 2001).

The Team Unity Challenge

Obviously hurt by Panday's accusations that he had betrayed him, Maharaj denied that he was a *neemakharam,* an ingrate. He reminded Panday that when he was kicked out of the cabinet by ANR Robinson in 1988 following the break up of the NAR government coalition (Ryan 1989a), and was impecunious, he had provided him with rent free office in his chambers, secretarial services, briefs, and spending money since he had little of his own. He had also raised funds and provided legal expertise which, according to Maharaj, kept Mr. Panday out of jail following his arrest on charges of sexual misbehaviour involving three female employees in the offices of the All Trinidad Sugar Workers and Factory Employees Union. Maharaj clearly hinted that Panday was guilty in that matter, and that were it not for his efforts, he would have ended up in jail.[2] Maharaj "tearfully" noted that he was a loyal and devoted chela [disciple] to Mr. Panday. "Nobody loved Mr. Panday more than [I]. Nobody has been closer to Mr. Panday more than [I]. This has been the most agonising experience in my life. The Prime Minister is a person I have built a strong attachment to over the years. We have been both lawyers in practice together, we have been in political struggle together from about 1979. I have respect for him as my leader." He however felt that standing up to and exposing Panday was the correct thing for him to do. That act allowed him to live with his conscience and face his family (*Newsday,* November 4, 2001). He also claimed that he felt he had an obligation to save the UNC from Panday and the "parasitic oligarchy" which had him in thrall, and return it to its founding principles, regardless of the consequences for himself personally or politically.

Maharaj insisted that corruption and not his ambition to succeed Panday was at the root of the crisis between himself, his other two cabinet colleagues, and Mr. Panday. The dissidents claim that they had come to the conclusion that corruption was getting out of hand, and that they could no longer turn a blind eye to it. They complained that when they talked about it to Panday, they were treated with contempt (*Express,* January 3, 2001). Maharaj complained that on many a morning, he awoke feeling that he "smelled of corruption." "Many a time I wanted to leave, but stayed on to look after the interests of the people" (*Guardian,* October 21, 2001). Maharaj also claimed that he was not planning to contest the 2001 election and was only persuaded to do so by Panday. Maharaj in fact expected to be passed over as a candidate, and was known to be seeking career opportunities abroad.

According to Maharaj, it was "totally frustrating to sit in Cabinet and witness the amount of corruption that was taking place in the country. The problem got worse when Robinson, who was "Minister Extraordinaire" in the [1995] Cabinet, left to take up the position of

President of Trinidad and Tobago in [1997]" (*Express,* December 9, 2001). Maharaj claimed that "most of the ministers in government did not seem to know the difference between the public interest and their own interests. The Prime Minister knew who the culprits were, but chose to condone their behaviour" (*Express,* December 3, 2001). He accused the latter of preferring to break up the party and have his government collapse rather than deal with corruption. Mr. Maharaj's clear message was that the Prime Minister did not act and could not act because he himself was deeply involved.

Panday's Response

In his responses to the Team Unity challenge, Panday was particularly harsh on his "friend" Trevor Sudama whom he accused of sending "a dagger through my heart." Sudama was asked to explain how he could "join" with the PNM (see below) when his "mother and father, grandmother and grandfather and the thousands of people in Oropouche had given their sweat and blood to walk in the corridors of power? How could he forget the sweat and tears that were involved in removing the PNM?" Sudama was asked whether he was "drunk, insane, or suffering from "tabanca" (a colloquialism for the sense of loss suffered by jilted lovers) when he did so, and urged to "lie if he had to" in giving his explanation. Sudama was called upon to genuflect and apologize to the people of Oropouche for his treachery, or "face oblivion for the rest of [his] life" (*Newsday,* November 28, 2001). It was an obvious attempt to humiliate his "errant" colleague and project him as an ethnic villain and an apostate who deserved to be ostracised. Sudama refused to beg forgiveness or to withdraw from contesting the elections, saying that he would only return to the UNC fold if Panday himself left it. In Sudama's view, Panday was the "biggest betrayer," the *maha neemakharam* of the UNC in general, and the sugar workers in particular. Panday was accused of having ridden the backs of the sugar workers and then abandoning them for the "parasitic oligarchy" (*Guardian,* November 5, 2001).

Panday denied all the allegations about corruption, claiming that they were just that. As such, he refused to mount any "public lynching just to satisfy blood thirsty politicians" (*Express*, October 29, 2001). He observed that no evidence had been brought to incriminate any minister. Complained Panday, with mock incredulity: "they are asking you to change a government with mere allegations." He observed that allegations about corruption were standard fare in elections the world over, and boasted that his regime had addressed the issue of corruption as no other had done in Trinidad and Tobago before. He was however aware that many in the public believed otherwise, and promised that if the UNC was returned to power, he would introduce a strict ethical code for MPs and Ministers. He also promised to introduce a revised Prevention of Corruption Bill which would protect whistle blowers, and that within 90 days, he would appoint a Commission of Inquiry into all the government related issues which were the subject of allegations (*Newsday*, December 9, 2001).

Panday claimed, with some element of truth, that Maharaj's allegations about corruption were not based on principle, and were only forthcoming when he refused to anoint him as his successor. He also went on to "explain" that in a small place such as Trinidad and Tobago, it was difficult to avoid nepotism and cronyism. As he shrugged, "Trinidad and Tobago is a small place. Everyone is trying to get ahead. Everybody knows everybody else. A minister making a recommendation will know the persons involved, so he may as well also include in that recommendation his family firm, so that the firm will have the opportunity to play on a level playing field." This was by way of defending his Minister of Energy and Enterprise who had brought a matter to Cabinet in which recommendations were made which involved his family owned firm. The Minister did not excuse himself from the meeting to avoid the charge that a conflict of interest was involved in his refusal to do so.

Panday also sought to defend another top UNC official charged with public mismanagement with the cute observation that "if everyone in Trinidad and Tobago were to be prosecuted for mismanagement, everyone in Trinidad and Tobago will be jailed" (*Newsday*, November 28, 2001). Mrs. Kamla Bissessar-Persad, who replaced Maharaj as the new Attorney General, defended Mr. Panday and her other ministerial colleagues from allegations of corruption. "I know my Prime Minister and my political leader. His hands are clean and his heart is clean. The one sin my Prime Minister committed was not to put Ramesh Lawrence Maharaj to ride in PM 1," the Prime Minister's official car (*Newsday*, November 9, 2001).

Also defending Mr. Panday was Mr. Gerald Yetming, the UNC's Minister of Finance, who described the allegations against Mr. Panday as "propaganda crap" which he was not going to take on board until they were proven by the state authorities who had the resources and the responsibility to address the questions. Yetming too remained convinced that the anticorruption campaign mounted by Ramesh Maharaj was not driven by his concern about corruption. The issue was succession to Panday. The Minister made it clear, when asked whether he would welcome Mr. Maharaj back into the UNC fold, that the two of them could never again be on the same slate (*Guardian*, September 8, 2002).

The Strategic Alliance

The expulsion from the UNC of Maharaj, Maraj, and Sudama, who were dubbed "the gang of three" and the "three musketeers," was followed by the forging of a "strategic alliance" between themselves and the PNM. According to the Leader of the Opposition, Mr. Manning, the aim of the alliance was to "eradicate corruption in the public life of the country in the shortest possible time and to set the conditions that would guarantee the conduct of free and fair elections in the country" (*Guardian*, October 5, 2001). Some PNM stalwarts however had reservations about working with individuals whom they had previously criticised. PNM MPs were generally willing to use them to engineer a return to power. As one senior PNM MP asked supporters, "why shouldn't we use their votes when they used ours in the last term?" The reference was to the two PNM MPs who had crossed the floor to work with the UNC in 1995. "If they can be of use to us, we'll make use of the situation. Thief from thief make God laugh" (*Guardian*, October 14, 2001). These remarks were not well received in the Indian community and helped to delegitimise the alliance. Mr. Manning, it was said, had found the Indians he was looking for in 1991 to make his cabinet look less exclusively Afro-creole (Ryan 1999b: 231).

The members of Team Unity were sensitive to the charge that they had sold out to the dreaded and demonised PNM. Thus Mr. Maraj's explanation:

> We are joining hands with the PNM because we want to avoid the rising of a tyrant in this country. I have worked with the political leader of UNC for six years. He has all the makings of a dictator, a tyrant. Basdeo Panday, with too much power, can be a dangerous individual, dangerous to you and to your children. A good leader will ensure [that] in Cabinet there can be the airing of different views. We do not want a reign of terror in Trinidad and Tobago.... We will ensure democracy prevails. (*Express*, October 9, 2001)

Maraj insisted that they were not being disloyal to the UNC. They were trying to redeem it, and in the process save Trinidad and Tobago from the depredations of "Ali Baba and the Forty thieves."

The strategy of the Alliance involved advising the President that the two groups together constituted a majority in the House of Representatives. Mr. Manning in fact publicly indicated that this was what would be done. He also let it be known that the PNM had abandoned the policy, enunciated in 1995, of "winning or losing alone." "If the circumstances of the country have changed, and if new approaches and new arrangements and new alignments are called for in the context of a rescue mission, then the PNM is prepared to modify its policies and adopt approaches that are relevant to the circumstances of the day" (*Guardian*, October 7, 2001).

Elements sympathetic to Team Unity were correspondingly unhappy about the PNM's embrace of the dissidents. In their view, the alliance was not politically cost effective. As Indira Maharaj opined:

The three Musketeers, left alone, would have been far more disastrous to the UNC. The accommodation with the PNM, a symbol of racism and injustice for Indians, more so Hindus, would have made the trio look like political opportunists more than persons interested in the fight for morality and justice. And the act, now perceived as an act of betrayal by Indos, would have galvanised Indo support, which Panday and the UNC were losing quite rapidly, back into their fold. (*Express*, October 12, 2001)

The Prime Minister described what was afoot as a "conspiracy to effect a constitutional coup" which he preempted by advising the President to dissolve Parliament to allow him to go to the polls to get a renewed mandate. The people had to decide the matter, insisted Mr. Panday, who argued that the President had no option but to take his advice, a view that was endorsed by most of the country's legal minds and constitutional analysts. The President agreed with the Prime Minister, and so advised the Leader of the Opposition who had argued that the President did have a discretion as to whether to dissolve or invite the leader of the PNM to form a new administration (*Express*, October 5, 2001).

Some commentators argued that the President had an option to call on Mr. Manning to form a government. It was known that there were precedents in Canada and Australia where Governor Generals had refused to heed the advise to dissolve and had instead called upon the leader of the Opposition to form an alternative government. Lloyd Best argued that the President would have made the "right mistake' if he had so acted. As he put it:

The challenge was to fix the paramountcy of Parliament over Government and of Legislature over Executive. The reason the President waffled is that he was fully aware that even without the assistance of a vote against the Appropriations Bill by the three defecting members of Team Unity, he should have appointed the Accommodation. That would far and away have been the right mistake. Instead,

President Robinson has perpetrated by far the "wrong error."
(*Express,* April 9, 2002)

The Constitution was however consciously constructed to prevent palace coups of the sort. Even if one was able to pass a vote of no-confidence in the Government, the Prime Minister had the option, within 7 days of such a vote, of either resigning or advising the President to dissolve the Legislature (Section 77). The Constitution also enabled the Prime Minister to advise the President to prorogue or to dissolve the Legislature "at anytime." (Section 68(1)). The net effect of Mr. Panday's advice to the President was to preempt the plans of the "conspirators." Mr. Panday boasted that he had caught the PNM "with its pants down" (*Express,* October 10, 2001). He also implicitly threatened the members of Team Unity by asking them rhetorically whether they proposed "living in the sky." He likewise warned them that in challenging him, they were "playing with fire." The UNC had to make certain that Team Unity was comprehensively demonised and destroyed lest it draw away critical votes which the party needed to hold on to the marginal seats.

Public Opinion and the "Collapse"

How did the public view the Alliance and the roles played by the President and some of the various characters in the crisis? When asked whether the Alliance was deserving of support, 39 percent of those sampled agreed that it was, 41 percent disagreed, while 17 percent were uncertain. Afro-Trinidadians were more inclined to support the *entente* than were Indo-Trinidadians.[3] Forty-eight percent of the former did so compared to 30 percent of the latter. Hindus were less inclined to support it than were any other confessional group. Only 26 percent of them did, compared to 40 percent of those who were Muslim, 46 percent who were Catholics and 54 percent who were Anglicans. Sixty-two percent of the Hindus felt that an Alliance with the PNM was a bad idea (Table 4).

Table 4
Strategic Alliance Deserving of Public Support
(%)

Re-sponse	Nation-al	Indian	Afro	Hindu	Islam	Catho-lic	Angli-can
Agree	39	30	48	26	40	46	54
Disagree	41	54	28	62	46	31	25
Uncertain	17	14	21	11	13	20	20
Refuse to say	2	2	2	1	2	3	2

It was widely believed that the attempt on the part of the dissident MPs to forge an Alliance with the PNM cost them a great deal of support within the Indian community and that they would have fared better electorally had they not done so. It was said that the embrace of the PNM served to delegitimise and give credence to the charge that they were *neemakharams*. Forty-six percent of the general sample agreed that the political chances of Team Unity were hurt by the Alliance. Indians were more inclined to feel this way. Sixty-three percent of them did so, compared to 30 percent of the Afros (Table 5).

Table 5
Dissident MPs Hurt Political Chances by Entering
Strategic Alliance with PNM
(%)

Response	National	Indo	Afro
Agree	46	63	30
Disagree	30	9	48
Uncertain	23	26	21
Refuse to Say	1	1	2

A majority of the population took the view that the President did not have the constitutional authority to call upon Manning *et. al.* to form a new government to replace Mr. Panday's government. Only twenty-one percent of those sampled felt that he had, while 53 percent disagreed. Twenty-four percent were uncertain. Few Indos agreed that he had such power. Only 7 percent did, compared to 35 percent of the Afros. Sixty-eight percent of them disagreed that the President had the power (Table 6).

Table 6
Constitution Gave President Power to
Remove Panday as PM and Appoint Mr. Manning
(%)

Response	National	Indo	Afro
Agree	21	7	35
Disagree	53	68	40
Uncertain	24	23	23
Refuse to Say	2	2	2

There was also much controversy as to whether Mr. Panday did the right thing by advising the President to dissolve Parliament and to schedule fresh elections. Some felt he should have resigned rather than put the country through the agony of fresh elections, especially since the results of the 2000 elections were being challenged in the courts. The elections, it was said, were "unfinished." Seventy-seven percent of the sample felt Mr. Panday was right to let the people decide the matter while 14 percent disagreed. Indos were more inclined to agree than did Afros by a margin of 17 (88 to 71) (Table 7).

Table 7
Panday Did the Right Thing to Call Election
(%)

Response	National	Indo	Afro
Agree	77	88	71
Disagree	14	7	22
Uncertain	7	8	6
Refuse to Say	2	2	2

President Robinson's vacillation in dealing with the various matters that he had to address in the crisis gave rise to a great deal of comment as to whether he was competent or partisan, or whether he was simply using the power of delay to allow the public to have a say as to what were the merits and demerits of the various positions which were being taken. Interestingly, and perhaps surprisingly, a substantial majority of those sampled - 72 percent - gave President Robinson a "thumbs up" signal for his handling of the crisis. Indos were even more inclined to give him their support than were Afros by a margin of 17 points.

Table 8
President Handled Political Crisis Quite Well
(%)

Response	National	Indo	Afro
Agree	77	88	71
Disagree	14	7	22
Uncertain	7	8	6
Refuse to Say	2	2	2

Indians and the Panday Phenomenon

In the run up to the 2001 general elections, the question as to whether Indians should violate the culture of silence and speak out against the public misbehaviour that was evident in UNC ranks was feverishly debated within tribal spaces. *Express* columnist Indira Maharaj gave voice to the intra-ethnic debate that was taking place within the Indian community when she publicly chastised those who advocated silence on the ground that the community was too vulnerable to allow criticism and dissent. She argued that the silence of Indian and Hindu religious leaders and academics had contributed mightily to the creation of the Frankenstein phenomenon that Panday had become. Panday had not only ignored the cultural and other concerns of the Indian community, but was also guilty of all sorts of political transgressions. As she complained:

> Silence! Silence! Silence! The Hindu community in Trinidad and Tobago has adopted this as its present theme. We hear it everywhere. We see it everywhere. We speak it everywhere. We feel it everywhere. It is the destructive fire that is burning at the fibre of the Hindu community. It is the plague that is damning the Hindu community. We remain silent in the name of ethnic loyalty while our leaders perpetuate injustices on us. We remain silent in the absence of a culture policy. We remain silent in the face of an erring minister.
>
> We remain silent in our temples as leaders practise a *laissez-faire* morality. We remain silent in face of Maha Sabha transgressions on the Hindu community in the name of Hindu unity. Raviji remains silent in the midst of injustices to the Hindu community in the name of Hindu solidarity. Hindu academics cling to their silence. Hindu women remain silent in the midst of their degradation. Women remain silent even in the midst of their own inequality. We remain silent in the face of chutney singers singing bhajans as chutney. We Hindus, remain silent in the midst of our own degradation. It is a silence born of trauma. It is the silence born of the experience of colonialism. It is the silence born

of oppression of the post-colonial history. It is the silence born out of being invisible in the national landscape for many years. It is a silence born out of the perception of our own impotence.

Maharaj likened Indo-Caribbean leaders to Afro-Trinidadians whom she claimed had also failed to criticize Williams. Indos, she argued, must heed the lesson of Williams:

> Indos should note and learn from the fact that the African community is still harvesting the very bitter fruits of its own silence and mindless support of God, Eric Williams and the PNM two decades after Williams' death. We must be grateful ultimately that Basdeo Panday did not get the time and hence the opportunity to do unto the Indo community what Williams and the PNM did unto their own community. (*Express*, May 3, 2001)

Maharaj argued further that silence would put democracy at risk. Criticism on the other hand served to keep the leadership in harness and disabuse them of the belief that they were gods:

> We must divest our "gods" of their undeserved halos. We must acknowledge that the Hindu and Indo communities, like the national community, have suffered under their maximum leaders, and a new leadership paradigm is a necessity. We must acknowledge that we have created our own *Hiranyakashipus*, Frankensteins, and we have suffered and continue to suffer. *(ibid.)*

Maharaj conceded that Panday had performed an important historical function, but argued that he had outlived his purpose and had to be retired from his godship:

> The ascension of the UNC was ... one of the best things that could have happened to this country and particularly for Indos. It was a psychological necessity for Indos, for they had been too long excluded from the corridors of power,

and they needed the taste of political power to recover from the alienation, the invisibility, a diminished sense of pride in self, which were the results of the policies of successive PNM administrations. The six years of UNC power ... taught Indos unforgettable lessons. It was to reveal Basdeo Panday as a concrete manifestation of moral revulsion and *neemakharamism*. It does not matter who are the wielders of power, whether Indos or Afros. The arrogance and dominance of the greed principle in Basdeo Panday's UNC fast forwarded the political maturity of Indos, and led to the dispensing [sic] of the God, Basdeo Panday. They also put race in politics in proper perspective. (*Express*, February 15, 2002)

Maharaj believed that Panday's morally revolting behaviour had laid permanently to rest claims to a moral high ground by Indos which they held in the PNM era. "Indos and Afros now stand on the same ground, as it were" (*Express*, November 30, 2001). She likewise believed that in time to come, Panday would be "treated worse than Rawan, a symbol of absolute evil in Tulsidaos popular Ramcharitmanas who is burnt at the end of the Ramleela celebration" (*Express*, October 5, 2001). Ramesh Maharaj, on the other hand, was now "being seen as being on the side of morality on the battlefield of Kurukshetra."

Also critical of Panday was *Express* columnist, Kamal Persad, arch critic of the PNM, who described the Panday regime as an "oriental despotism." Persad noted that in the past, "kuchoor" (confusion) in the Indian party played itself out in the periphery of the society. Now the problem had become mainstream. "What was marginal had now become the centre, and even in Government, the Indian based party continues to splinter, thus destabilising the entire country" (*Express*, September 9, 2001). It could no longer be said that the perpetual splintering of Indian parties was due to the fact that the parties were in perpetual opposition and had nothing to induce them to hold together. Persad was also prophetic in his projection that the PNM would return to power:

Indians are at a political juncture. Mr. Panday referred to
the possibility of losing the next general election. The hour
of decision is primarily for Indians. The Indian Spectre, it
seems, has returned to haunt Indians. It is only Indians who
are being abused and insulted in the internal UNC crisis. It
is Basdeo Panday and not Team Unity who is paving the
path for the PNM's return to power. *(ibid.)*

Similar assertions about the immorality of the group around Panday
were made by the late Professor Syam Roopnarinesingh, who described
Panday as a "cynical Indian":

As the electoral flames blaze around him, the Indian has
found himself with an inner conflict in choosing between
inherent values of honesty and probity on the one hand,
and blind ethnic loyalty, on the other. He is in mental turmoil.
He can conform to the expectations of his group or follow
his conscience and be labelled a *neemakharam*. He can worship
honesty and integrity, or despise them; he can forget his
religious teachings and foster ethnic discrimination or take
the honourable stand that I cherish, that human values are
independent of the colour of the skin or the shape of the
nose.

Most people, especially the canefield grassroots, who never
shared in the economic bounty of the country, even under
Panday, are not aware that these conflicts exist and do not
resolve them by any rational decision. More often, they do
not know where they stand; they contradict themselves and
their innate beliefs without knowing it. They piously light
dozens of deyas or observe the rules of Ramadhan in
consonance with the philosophy that good triumphs
over evil, honesty over dishonesty, morality over corruption,
and yet let themselves be swayed by the effrontery of wily
scheming politicians.

Against their own set of moral values and beliefs, they allow
themselves to be deceived by empty promises as
parliamentarians wallow in self pity and say "is we time" or

"my hands clean." Is it feasible that our oriental tenets are so superficial that they are not strong enough to serve as a guiding principle in making decisions? Have we abandoned our adopted beliefs to satisfy a baser instinct? Do we not have the inner strength and independence of mind to make the right decision in a plural society? Or are we sycophants and hangers-on who stand to lose personally from the downfall of corrupt governance? (*Newsday,* January 14, 2002)

Another harsh rebuke of Mr. Panday and the UNC came from retired Appeal Court Judge, Lennox Deyalsingh, whose anguished *cri de coeur* resonated with many of his co-ethics, especially those in the middle class. Deyalsingh was angry at Panday for having pitched forked UNC members and supporters into a mix of political quicksand from which they felt they could only escape by either holding their noses and voting for the UNC, withholding their franchise, or voting for the PNM. Panday was accused of several political crimes. According to Deyalsingh, he failed to realise that the days of the maximum leader were over, and that change in the way in which citizens relate to leaders was an irreversible process. Leaders must be transparent, accountable and should above all not disgrace their followers. In his attempt to reverse or derail the process of democratic change, Panday was said to have brought about the ruin of the UNC and himself. Deyalsingh found this willingness on Panday's part to commit political suicide sad and ironic, since he had a genuine opportunity to leave behind a great legacy - a party which the country desperately needed if it was ever to be blessed with good governance. "What a pity!", moaned Deyalsingh. "What a great loss to the country. The UNC, the only present alternative to the PNM, is as surely as the sun rises tomorrow, witnessing the setting of its own sun at the hands of its Leader. And this, at a time when the country needs both parties to ensure that our democratic system prevails" (*Newsday,* October 21, November 4, December 2, 2001).

Deyalsingh was equally harsh on Panday for not dealing seriously with the question of corruption and for not heeding the warning that the cancer of corruption had metastasized and was destroying the fabric of the party, the society and the government. Deyalsingh in fact absolved the dissidents in Team Unity from the imperatives of collective responsibility since, in his view, they had to make a choice either "for corruption" or "against corruption." They chose the latter, in the process precipitating an "ugly war" between the two factions which would destroy the UNC. Deyalsingh wondered aloud as to why Panday chose to remain deaf to the demands for a Commission of Inquiry into the incidence of corruption, and why he did not "hang the jacks of the corrupters." The question was rhetorical. "Many of us understand why the Government did not launch effective investigations into corruption. We still hesitate, and would hate to go on to draw the inferences to which the situation points. We are reluctant to believe (even against our better judgement) that corruption has taken on such a grip on the government that it has now become a captive to corrupt forces, and is helpless to do anything about corruption" (*ibid.*).

Panday's errant behaviour cross pressured many UNC members and supporters, forcing them to make choices which they would rather not make. As Deyalsingh agonised: "should they vote for the UNC and be inwardly smeared with the brush of corruption, or should they take a stand for their country and vote against corruption by voting for the PNM?" Deyalsingh was realistic enough to admit that Indians would still prefer an "Indian" Prime Minister, even if they had to choose one that appears to condone corruption or who might even be involved in it himself. But he was clear that win or lose, Panday had lost the mandate of heaven. As he said by way of *obiter,* "he may hold office, but he will no longer hold our hearts. He may say, "as long as I have the power, your hearts mean nothing to me." But he should walk softly, because it is the heart of a disenchanted people which topples a king from his throne in good time." Deyalsingh felt that the outcome of the election would be determined by the votes of the honest middle class, "we of all races who go out and vote for the party which we believe can do the best job of governing the country (*Newsday,* November 4, 2001).

The leaders of Team Unity for their part declared themselves proud of the stance they had taken to expose UNC corruption. They felt that if they had not taken such a stance, the general population would have been entitled to believe that all Indians were "fowl thieves," as one businessman contemptuously described them. As Ramesh Maharaj put it, "a lot of people are feeling shamed to have voted for the UNC government. The issue is not whether performance beats old talk; its whether the performance includes corruption" (*Express*, December 3, 2001).

As we shall see in Chapter 5 the crisis within the party impacted negatively on the Government and ultimately led to its collapse and loss of political power.

Endnotes

1. See Chapter 14 (315-318) for an analysis of this concept.

2. These offenses allegedly occurred in 1994. Maharaj mounted a muscular public campaign to project Panday as someone who was a victim of a smear campaign orchestrated by the PNM and an erstwhile member of his party who had broken away. Panday was later cleared of the charges but many remained convinced that he was guilty.

3. Forty-eight percent of the sample of 992 persons was Indo-Trinidadian, 50 percent were Afro-Trinidadian or Mixed while 2 percent were Other. The survey was conducted by the author's St. Augustine Research Associates (SARA) in October 2001.

Chapter 5

THE ELECTIONS OF 2001

*A*s expected, ethnicity featured very prominently in the 2001 election, both as text and sub-text. The Afro-creole population was broadly convinced that the UNC was the most corrupt regime that Trinidad and Tobago had ever seen, and many even argued that there was a relationship between sleaze and ethnicity. The UNC and its supporters countered with the charge that the PNM had also been corrupt during its multiple terms in office, but particularly in the boom years 1973 to 1983. Did not one PNM minister say "all ah we thief"? (Ryan 1989:71). The PNM's counter comment was that UNC corruption was more spectacular, more unapologetic and more "in your face" than anything seen during the PNM era. There was no stealth or pretense that what was being done was morally wrong. They had seemingly adopted wholesale the "Indian theory of relativity - everything for relatives" as Salman Rushdie had defined it in his novel, the *Moor's Last Sigh*.

The elections were however not merely a clash of ethnicities. It was also a clash of oligarchies, classes, governance paradigms, and political cultures. The accusation that the political leader of the UNC and the party itself had been captured by a "parasitic oligarchy," key members of which had migrated from the PNM in 1995 and thereafter, was frequently made during the campaign. It was alleged that this oligarchic group was conspiring to capture prized state companies for a mess of pottage, and that all of this was to be achieved at the expense of the workers in these industries and the state which was the ultimate owner. Panday was said to have sold out to this parasitic ruling class. The financial conglomerate, Colonial Life [CL] Financial, challenged these claims, and argued that it was in fact committed to ensure the well being of the workers in the industries concerned and the people in general. What was good for CL Financial was good for the national interest. Panday justifying his ideological retreat, likewise argued that it would have been foolish for him "to alienate the business community since they were the ones to bring in the jobs and the investment" (*Guardian*, September 11, 2001).

The PNM, for its part, sought to recapture the support of elements within the business oligarchy and the resources which were so critical to the winning and retention of political power. One PNM activist was quoted as telling businessmen that "the PNM [was] the place for them to put their money. Business people know that they can't put money in a sinking ship." The boast was that big and small business were quietly switching to the PNM. The PNM's answer to suggestions that a PNM government would also be beholden to oligarchs was that the PNM's track record spoke for itself, and that no financier or group of financiers had ever enjoyed the kind of undue influence on the PNM as that which obtained in respect of the UNC.

There was also a "silent" class struggle taking place in the country, though few people framed the issues in these terms. The increase in the minimum wage promised by the UNC was clearly a class issue. The non-unionised working class welcomed the promised increase which they saw as overdue, while the business class claimed that the increases would affect the competitiveness of Trinidad products in regional and international markets. Team Unity also claimed that a proposal to sell the assets of the Agricultural Development Bank to the commercial banks was an "attack by the parasitic oligarchy on the small people of Trinidad and Tobago." The party likewise accused the UNC of having sold out the sugar workers. Complained MP Trevor Sudama: "You got into power by riding the backs of sugar workers. Today, workers in Caroni cannot get their pensions and you have turned a deaf ear."

The elections also involved a clash of paradigms as to what constituted good governance. The PNM and its supporters charged the UNC with corrupt governance, sleaze, and state plunder. They also accused it of breaking all the established rules of state procurement, of chronic cronyism, and generally of undermining all the critical institutions of the state and the procedures which were put in place over the years to try and effect good governance. The PNM's argument was that Trinidad and Tobago was collapsing under the weight of corruption, misgovernance, and needed to be saved. The UNC's style was said to be more oriental than occidental, and more patrimonial than bureaucratised in a Weberian sense. The PNM's promise was to defelonise the state and return the country to the "standards and principles of honourable behaviour in public life." As they saw it, they were "moral crusaders" in pursuit of good governance. They wanted to effect a new governance paradigm, a new physics of politics.

Team Unity said much the same thing. Sudama claimed that he left the UNC because he could not "stand the stench of corruption." Maharaj said likewise. "Most of the ministers in government are involved in corruption. Mr. Panday saw himself as being above the law and the prevailing conventions of the system as it were, rather than being constrained by it." Ironically, Mr. Panday set tongues wagging when he told former President Bill Clinton at a conference held in Trinidad that unlike what occurs in the United States where Presidents could not serve more than two consecutive terms, there were only two ways out of the vortex of the Westminster system of government, death or disgrace, and that he was not sure which would come first for him. Wags replied that he should consider the alternative of resignation (*Guardian,* October 23, 2001).

In response to PNM allegations that the UNC had transgressed all the established rules of good governance, the UNC elite claimed that its style was a "doing style." They got the job done; they performed even if they had to bend the rules, rules which were created at a different time for a different type of economy. They in fact seemed to be saying that corruption was not bad if there was a product to show at the end of the process. The two paradigms were thus in conflict. The one stressed "performance" while the other argued that performance without concern for transparency, accountability and proper standards of public morality and behaviour led to cynicism, a gross waste of resources, a precipitous decline of social capital, and ultimately, to the type of social and economic collapse that was typical of other benighted countries elsewhere in the "third" world.

The competing governance paradigms were located in different political cultures which were in turn informed by differences in general cultural styles. The culture clash as one between Afro-Saxon and Indo-Saxon epistemologies. The former was more eurocentric and more public interest focussed while the latter still retained dimensions of the oriental with its emphasis on family, kin, and pseudo - kin (see Ryan 1999a:189-214 for a fuller statement of this argument). These may well be stereotypes and urban myths, but there was clearly a view among Afro-creoles, the mixed element, and some middle class Indians that a cultural gulf existed between the worlds of the "cane field Indian," and those in the vegetable and rice fields, and that of the creoles of the urban corridors. The former, it was alleged, was tolerant of corruption if it enhanced the well being of the tribe. Their moral standards were more "flexible." Corruption was only bad if "others" were involved.

Indians however denied that Indians in general and Hindus in particular had a bifurcated morality, a higher tolerance threshold for corruption than did Afro-creoles, and claimed that they too were ashamed of their political leaders. They could not however bring themselves to vote for the PNM, which, over the years, had systematically marginalised Indians. Corruption notwithstanding, the UNC was still the best available vehicle for the empowerment of the group (*Express*, February 15, 2001) (see Chapter 9).

Another cleavage was that relating to "exclusion" and "inclusion." The Prime Minister claimed that he was committed to a policy of inclusion and national unity. "Some people want to destroy me for that," he complained. Panday was referring to Team Unity and the

PNM, both of which he claimed were seeking to divide the country along ethnic lines. The former however challenged Panday's characterisation of what was involved. According to Maharaj, "national unity does not come from taking a Syrian, a Chinese, and an Afro-Trinidadian from the business sector and appointing them to the Cabinet." Team Unity and the PNM both acknowledged that politics and society in Trinidad and Tobago were in a state of transition, and that the politics of hybridity and coalition was and would continue to be the order of the day. Whether or not one accepted inclusion in principle or not, there really was no alternative to the politics of inclusion in practice. All parties had to reinvent themselves to take account of this new reality, though all claimed to be doing it more meaningfully than the other.

The UNC's Response

The UNC's answer to the crusade against corruption was that the charges were not proven, and that in any event people were more exercised by "performance" issues - jobs, enhanced educational opportunity, enhanced old age pensions, the provision of improved infrastructure, including better roads, an improved supply of water and electricity, and the general management of the economy. As Mr. Panday whinged contemptuously, "Corruption, Corruption, Corruption! All yuh could see corruption? You can't see corruption because they won't bring any evidence against anybody! But you could see airport." Referring to former PNM administrations, Panday noted they were corrupt, but the country had realised little from the oil boom. "They were corrupt and you did not see anything. But everything you do, they cry corruption." Panday's seeming message was that while both regimes were guilty of corruption, the physical evidence of what the UNC did, its performance, was apparent for all to see. One was "bad" corruption while the other was of the variety that some describe as "good" corruption.

The Government highlighted the steps it had taken to co-finance tertiary education at institutions in Trinidad and Tobago by way of the so called "dollar for dollar" programme and the campaign promises which it had made to provide each secondary school child with $1,000 each year for text books, and free textbooks for children in primary schools. The UNC also boasted that it had paid off the debt owed to the University of the West Indies, that it had built 25 new primary schools and 17 new secondary schools, and had plans to build 27 more primary schools and 18 secondary schools. It also promised to create 150,000 jobs over the next 5 years. On the eve of the election, the UNC Political Leader boasted that his party had abolished the dreaded Common Entrance Examination. "We introduced universal free secondary education, leaving no child behind. We introduced the "Dollar for Dollar" Education Plan on the path to pushing tertiary enrollment to 20 percent" (*Sunday Express*, December 9, 2001).

Mr. Panday told voters that in assessing the parties, there was no need to look beyond the respective records of the parties in managing the economy, creating jobs, bringing relief to the poor, encouraging groups that traditionally suffered discrimination such as the Baptists and devotees of Orisha, and education. In his view, the population would reject allegations of corruption as a basis for removing a government that had delivered unprecedented benefits to the population (*ibid.*).

The PNM's Response

The PNM's retort was that it could not do as much as it would have wished during the 1991-1995 period when it returned to power since it was committed to pursuing conditionalities dictated by multilateral lending agencies which involved reducing the public debt, downsizing the public sector, and laying the foundation for renewed growth. The policies were just beginning to pay-off when the UNC came to power. The latter inherited rising oil prices, and benefitted from the increased investments in the energy sector and much else which the PNM had negotiated. The UNC was accused of having wasted a great deal of these resources, and what is worse, of having increased the public debt enormously. The general claim of the PNM was that it had done more in the boom years of the seventies than the UNC had done in the boom years of the late nineties.

The PNM for its part produced an Action Plan that sought to match or outbid the UNC, recognising that it had failed to do so successfully in the 2000 election. The PNM was in fact determined not to be out promised by the UNC on pocket book issues; it insisted that the election had to be fought on the themes of corruption and good governance. To this end, it promised, *inter alia*, to reduce taxes on individuals and companies; to satisfy public servants arrears of income with an immediate grant of one month's salary as a guarantee of good faith; to create 20,000 jobs per year; to build 10,000 homes each year; to provide free school books for all primary schools and pay a $1,000 book grant per student to all secondary school students; to reduce the air fare between Tobago and Trinidad by $100; to abolish the Health Surcharge; to increase old age pensions and National Insurance benefits to $1,000; to remove taxes on the first $5,000 of monthly pension income; and to appoint Commissions of Inquiry into corruption and a Commission to review the Constitution of Trinidad and Tobago (*Express*, December 5, 2001). The party likewise promised enhanced performance (doubling the dollar) without the attendant grand corruption that it alleged had characterised six and a half years of UNC rule. Its promise was to "charge, handcuff, successfully prosecute, and jail all those in the UNC who had betrayed the public trust."

In reply to the UNC's claims that it had out-performed the PNM, the latter argued that in its heyday (1956-1986), it had a more impressive school building and maintenance record than the UNC was conceding. It had pioneered free secondary and university education, and had also introduced a school feeding programme and sustained the Youth Training and Employment Partnership Programmes (YTEPP). The UNC had closed down the latter and had also abolished the Civilian Conservation Corps which trained youths. The PNM also noted that under the UNC, the costs of building 10 schools had skyrocketed from TT$100m in 1998 to TT$500m in 2001. The imputation was that the main beneficiaries of the increase were their cronies and friends in the business community and those who received kickbacks. It was also noted that the Dollar for Dollar programme that was delivered was different from what had been promised, and that only first year students attending The University of the West Indies and certain other institutions in Trinidad and Tobago had benefitted, and not to the extent that parents had been led to believe. Only tuition costs were met. It was also observed that nothing was done to increase space and other facilities needed to increase registrations in tertiary institutions as had been promised and that a UNDP Report had revealed that 34,623 children between 5 and 11 were not enrolled in schools despite UNC boasts that it had left no one behind (*Express*, December 5, 2001). The general criticism was that the UNC had focussed on improving numbers and constructing buildings as an election gambit and had done little that was meaningful to increase the quality of what was offered. It was noted that while the Common Entrance Examination had been abolished, it was replaced by an equally difficult competitive alternative, the Secondary Entrance Assessment examination (SEA).

The Battle for Political Survival

As election day drew near, the three political parties and their leaders were locked in near mortal political combat. The UNC felt that if it were to lose, it would not only mean the effective end of Mr. Panday's political career, but would in all probability also involve political humiliation for him and some of his ministerial colleagues and their respective cronies. Mr. Panday simply could not afford to lose. Too much was at stake. He thus had to use every arrow in his quiver to defeat his challengers. Money wrapped in T-shirts, the promise of an enhanced package of goodies, and much more that was unconventional was used to ensnare voters. Mr. Panday summoned all the ancient ghosts of the plantations to do battle on his behalf. He played the race, religious, and secular nationalist card with the dexterity of a 3 card con artist.

The PNM and its political leader also could not afford to lose since defeat would have meant retirement for Manning. The latter saw himself in a "scavenging" or salvationist role. In his view, Trinidad and Tobago faced a deep social and political crisis, and had to be saved from those who were pauperising it materially and spiritually. The country had to be spiritually cleansed. Political evil had to be exorcised. As Manning put it dramatically in his campaign launch, paraphrasing Churchill's speech during the second world war in 1940, "the battle for the survival of Trinidad and Tobago is about to begin. Upon this battle depends the survival of our civilisation. Let us therefore brace ourselves to our duties, and so bear ourselves that if Trinidad and Tobago should last for a thousand years, people will say of us and of this time, 'this was the finest hour.'"

Manning took the high ground on the issue of good governance and probity in public affairs, and invoked Judeo-Christian iconic figures such as Isaiah and St. Paul to give witness to his calling. To those who doubted his ability to lead, he advised that he had gone deep within himself, had done the necessary introspection, and was now better equipped to lead the crusade to save Trinidad and Tobago and take it to the "Promised Land." He also advised those who either hated or feared the PNM, that the party had done the necessary rethink, and had returned to its 1956 roots. If it did in fact lose its way, it had found it once more. This was a new PNM. Those who had left the church or who had never joined it, were urged to come to the fold where they were certain to "find political rest."

While Manning pitched his tent on the moral high ground, he had clearly learnt that political man does not live by spirit alone, and that material inducements were necessary to attract voters to the political Jerusalem. The political marketplace was thus segmented and goodies brandished to attract senior citizens, youth, public servants, the young, the overtaxed, and the business community. In 2000, the UNC outbid the PNM. It promised the moon and the man on it! In 2001, the PNM sought to ensure that this did not happen. They had to reclaim the moon and also promise the stars, "dollar for dollar." The party also paid more attention to the voters list and its election day machinery which it recognised had not performed as well as it should have in the 2000 elections, particularly in the critical marginal seats of Tunapuna and San Fernando West. A great deal of energy was expended to target the middle class vote which was seen as crucial "swing" votes.

The leaders of Team Unity were also locked in a battle for survival. Team Unity saw itself as making a strategic intervention which could be decisive. Maharaj in fact boasted that Team Unity would be the instrument through which the country would be saved. Sudama likewise boasted that Team Unity would "lay down the conditions for the next government." The break away party claimed that its support was silent out of fear of victimisation. It also hoped to pick up votes from persons who would normally have voted PNM but whom they expected to switch for strategic reasons. It also hoped to win votes that would otherwise have gone to the UNC or which might have stayed at home in protest. Team Unity answered the charge that they had committed a social sin by consorting with the enemy that it was Panday who had sold out the UNC and the sugar workers to erstwhile PNM elements who had captured the UNC. Maharaj *et. al.* believed that their task was greater than that which faced Manning. They had to save both the UNC and the country at large.

The General Public and the Campaign

Corruption was the touchstone or defining issue in the 2001 election. In a survey carried out in October 2001 by SARA, 58 percent of the population said they considered the problem to be "very serious." Another 17 percent considered the problem to be "serious", an aggregate of 75 percent! More Afros (79 percent) deemed the problem "very serious" or "serious" (15 percent) than did Indians, 37 and 19 percent of whom so described it. The aggregates were 94 and 56 percent respectively. Hindus (34 percent) were less inclined to define the problem as "very serious" than were Catholics (71 percent), Anglicans (66 percent) or Muslims (46 percent) (Table 9).

Table 9
How Serious is the Problem of Corruption in Trinidad and Tobago?
(%)

Response	National	Indo	Afro	Hindu	Islam	Anglican	Catholic
Very serious	58	37	79	34	46	66	71
Serious	17	19	15	23	16	17	15
Not very serious	12	23	3	26	22	7	4
Uncertain	9	16	3	15	8	5	7
Refuse to say	4	6	0	2	7	6	3

The public was virtually unequivocal in its view that Mr. Panday had not dealt with the problem of kleptocracy within his regime. Eighty-two percent of the sample agreed (53 percent strongly) that he had not dealt seriously with the problem. Eighty-nine percent of the Afros were of this view compared to 71 percent of the Indos. Hindus were again less likely to "agree strongly" than members of other confessional groups. A quarter of them did, compared to close to half of the Catholics (48%) and Anglicans (44%) and 39 percent of the Muslims (Table 10).

There was much speculation and contestation as to whether Mr. Panday was chairman of the board of the felonious state or whether he was above the board but unable to act because of the nature of his majority. When asked for their opinion as to whether Panday himself was guilty or innocent of the accusations about his involvement in corruption, close to half of those interrogated (49 percent) believed that he was guilty. Nineteen percent felt he was not. Afros (69 percent) more readily agreed that he was guilty than were Indos. Twenty-nine percent of the latter deemed him guilty while 35 percent absolved him from the charge. About a quarter of each groups said they did not know what was true or what was fabrication (Table 11).

Turning to religion, Hindus were again more inclined than other groups to deem their "hero" innocent of the charges of financial turpitude. Forty percent held him to be innocent compared to 33 percent of the Muslims and only 6 and 10 percent of the Anglicans and Catholics respectively (Table 11).

When asked whether their voting preferences would be influenced by their perceptions of corruption in the Panday regime, a third of the sample said it would be. Half the Afros (48 percent) reported thusly, compared to one fifth (20 percent) of the Indos (Table 12). Hindus were less inclined to allow the allegations to influence their voting behaviour than were other denominational groups. Many seemed to be saying that he might be a rascal, but he was their rascal. Many were

Table 10
Panday has not Dealt seriously with Corruption
(%)

Response	National	Indo	Afro	Hindu	Islam	Anglican	Catholic
Agree strongly	53	49	56	25	39	44	48
Agree	29	22	33	14	12	28	25
Disagree strongly	5	9	3	8	5	1	4
Disagree	8	14	5	10	6	7	6
Uncertain	4	6	3	4	4	1	4
Refuse to say	1	0	0	0	1	0	1

Table 11
Panday Guilty or Innocent of Accusations of Corruption
(%)

Response	National	Indo	Afro	Hindu	Islam	Anglican	Catholic
Guilty	49	29	69	28	37	58	61
Innocent	19	35	3	40	33	6	10
Do not know	25	27	22	28	23	26	23
Refuse to say	7	9	6	5	7	10	6

also in denial or were inclined to saying that everybody does it. Only 15 percent of them said it would affect their psychological behaviour compared to 26 percent of the Muslims, 31 percent of the Anglicans, 22 percent of the Presbyterians, 46 percent of the Catholics and, 51 percent of the Pentecostalists.

Was unseemly political ambition and greed for political power the principal cause of the fragmentation of the UNC? Did rampant corruption trigger the collapse, or was it concern that Carlos John and C L Financial had established a hammer lock on Mr. Panday and the state machine? When asked their view as to what was the principal cause for the split, 29 percent of the sample felt that Panday's failure to deal with the problem of corruption was the cause, 30 percent blamed Maharaj's power urge, while 16 percent felt that a grasp for economic and political power by Carlos John and C L Financial was the precipitating factor. Indians were more inclined to blame the crisis on Maharaj's ambition than were Afros. Forty-three percent of them held this view compared to 17 percent of the Afros who did (Table 13).

Table 12
Will Feelings about Panday's Involvement Influence the
Way you Vote?
(%)

Response	National	Indo	Afro
Yes	34	20	48
No	16	8	25
Uncertain	2	1	2
Refuse to say	48	71	25

Table 13
Single Most Important Cause for UNC Split
(%)

Response	National	Indo	Afro
Panday's refusal to deal with corruption	29	29	29
Maharaj's leadership ambitions	30	43	17
Opposition to Carlos John as successor to Panday	8	5	11
Opposition to CL Financial	8	4	13
Other	10	4	16
Do not know	11	10	11
Refuse to say	4	6	3

Notwithstanding the widespread view, even among a sizeable number of Indians, that the UNC regime was very corrupt, the survey revealed that Panday was preferred by a majority (54 percent) of Indians for the post of Prime Minister. Manning was the preferred choice of a plurality (46 percent) of Afro-Trinidadians, 18 percent of whom chose Keith Rowley, who had almost successfully challenged him for the PNM leadership in 1995 (Table 14).

Table 14
Preferred Person as Prime Minister
(%)

Response	National	Indo	Afro
Panday	29	54	6
Manning	26	7	46
Rowley	9	1	18
Maharaj	4	8	4
Persad-Bissessar	3	4	2
Mottley	2	1	2
Other	8	7	3
Uncertain	10	10	8
Refuse to say	9	7	11

When asked which party or combination of parties they would prefer to see in office following the election, 36 percent of our sampled electorate said they would prefer the PNM, 31 percent plumbed for the incumbent UNC loyalists, while 2 percent chose the dissident Team Unity. When broken down in terms of ethnicity, 57 percent of the Indos preferred the UNC "orthodoxos," 4 percent the dissidents, while another 7 percent supported the PNM (Table 15).

Table 15
Party or Coalition Prefer to See in Power After Election
(%)

Party/Coalition	National	Indo	Afro
PNM	36	7	65
UNC	31	57	5
Team Unity	2	4	1
PNM-Team Unity-NAR	5	6	4
NAR/Citizens Alliance	1	0	2
NAR	1	1	1
Other	3	0	3
Uncertain	11	17	7
Refuse to say	10	8	11

The PNM was the choice of 65 percent of the Afros. Five percent of them supported the Pandayites, while 1 percent endorsed Team Unity. Four percent said they would endorse a coalition consisting of the parties to the Alliance and the NAR, while 2 percent indicated they would have endorsed an alliance between the NAR and the Citizens Alliance if it had entered the fray.

When one looks more closely at the data, we note that the percentage of Afros and Indos who said say would cross the ethnic aisle was about the same. We also note that as many as 13 percent of the Indos said they would resolve their cross pressure by not voting. They were unable to vote for either the UNC or the PNM. Only 3 percent of the Afros said they would abstain (Table 16).

Table 16
Party Voting for on December 10
(%)

Party	National	Indo	Afro
PNM	37	7	68
UNC	31	57	6
Team Unity	4	7	2
NAR	1	0	2
Other	2	1	1
Will not vote	8	13	3
Refuse to say	17	15	18

There were indications that some Afros who voted for the UNC in 2000 were planning to return to the PNM. Thirteen percent of our Afro respondents said they voted for the UNC in 2000. Only six percent of them reported that they would vote for the UNC and 2 percent for Team Unity. Seven percent of the Indos said they voted for the PNM, the same percentage which expressed an intention to do so in the forthcoming election. What the data suggested was that Indos who were planning to abandon the UNC were abstaining rather than switching to the PNM (Table 17).

Table 17
Party Voted for in 2000 Election
(%)

Response	National	Indo	Afro
UNC	46	80	13
PNM	33	7	59
Other	3	2	4
Refuse to say	18	12	24

When an electorate votes, some do so because they identify with the leader; some do so because they agree with or value the benefits which they get from the policies of the party even though they may not like the party's priest, pundit or Imam. Some also consider themselves supporters of the party which they view as an institution which is part of their traditional stock of social capital. Voting is "mindless" and virtually automatic. The manner in which these orientations interact varies from culture to culture, from conjuncture to conjuncture and among various social structures. Our data suggest that in the 2001 election, ethnicity and party counted for more than the quality or character of the leaders of the two major battalions about whom much controversy swirled. Only 13 percent of the Indos said that the leadership of the party would be the factor that would be uppermost in their minds when they voted on December 10, 2001. Sixty-seven percent said they would be influenced more by the Party and its policies. Looking at the PNM, only 11 percent of the Afro-Trinidadians say that their vote would be primarily a vote for Mr. Manning. Seventy-four percent of them said they would give more weight to the party and its policies than to who the leader was. In sum, neither leader seems to have had "heroic" dimensions in the eyes of their supporters (Table 18).

Table 18
Most Important Factor which will Determine Vote on
December 10, 2001
(%)

Response	National	Indo	Afro
Party Policies	40	43	37
Party Leader	12	13	11
Party as a Whole	30	24	37
Other	5	4	6
Will not Vote	6	10	2
Do not Know	2	1	2
Refuse to Say	5	5	5

Deadlock

The 2001 elections resulted in a historic 18-18 tie. This "political accident" precipitated a major political and constitutional crisis. The UNC called the elections in an attempt to get a vote of confidence from the electorate, and spent some TT$20m dollars on a sophisticated advertising campaign to seduce the electorate with claims about how well it had performed. The party won four of the five marginal seats but lost the pivotal Tunapuna constituency by a margin of some 276 votes, and also recorded an overall decline of popular support (see Tables 19 to 23 below). Whereas it had received 307,546 votes in the 2000 elections, it was only able to muster 278,781 votes, 26,765 less than in the previous election. The margin separating the two parties was 19,341 votes compared to 31,000 which obtained in December 2000. Mr. Panday deemed the tie a "miracle" given the role of the media in the campaign. TV6 was described by Panday as "the devil," and the *Express* as the "son of the devil." The TV channel was also said to be "the most biased, prejudicial, diabolical, satanic element of the media" (*Express,* November 22, 2001). Mr. Panday neglected to comment on the role of the state owned station, Trinidad and Tobago Television (TTT) and the numerous Indian owned radio stations.

The PNM for its part won two additional seats, Tunapuna and another in Tobago which it now fully controlled. In Tobago East, the PNM won 4,866 votes, the NAR 2,384, and the UNC 1,066. The PNM did not secure as many crossover votes from the UNC as it had hoped, much of which seemed to have gone to Team Unity. In fact, the PNM's vote also declined. The party secured 259,450 votes compared to the 276,288 which it won in December 2000, 16,838 fewer than in the previous election. Team Unity, which had hoped to make a critical difference by winning one or two seats, secured a mere 14,165 votes and no seats whatsoever. All of its candidates, Mr. Maharaj excepted, lost their deposits. The National Alliance for Reconstruction secured 5,925 votes, but lost the two seats in Tobago where it was once dominant.

In what had promised to be an exciting and closely fought election with a high turnout, only 560,726 voters or 66 percent of the electorate of 849,874 exercised their franchise. The turnout in the 2000 election was 63 percent. Had the list not been revised and 97,815 names removed, the turnout would have fallen to 59 percent. The result clearly indicated that significant sections of the electorate were either weary of the process and the parties or were disenchanted by allegations and counter allegations about corruption. Both factors seemed to have been operative. It is worth noting that the UNC won a plurality and not a majority. The combined votes of the PNM, Team Unity, and the National Alliance For Reconstruction exceeded its total by 759 votes. The relevant percentages were UNC 49.72 percent, PNM 46.28 percent, Team Unity 2.53 percent and NAR 1.06 percent. In the 2000 election, the UNC got 51.42 percent of the votes.

The election outcome surprised many who did not believe those (like the author) who had anticipated a hung election. Among the most disappointed were the members of Team Unity, the political leader of which nevertheless claimed that he had not really "lost," but had in fact won a moral victory by helping to legitimate the PNM's allegations about corruption among Indian voters who were minded to doubt that the charges had any substance. As he put it, "I won by exposing corruption." In this, he was quite correct. Maharaj argued that Mr. Panday had led the UNC into opposition because he had refused to deal with corruption in Government and democracy in the country (*Newsday,* December 25, 2001). Maharaj boasted, albeit hopefully, that Team Unity had changed the politics of Trinidad and Tobago. "We can now expect that no government in the foreseeable future will allow corruption to flourish" (*Newsday,* December 11, 2001). Maharaj also believed, prophetically, that Panday had ceased to be an important political factor in the politics of Trinidad and Tobago (*Newsday,* January 21, 2001).

Also expressing acute disappointment was UNC foundation member, Trevor Sudama, who, to the surprise of many, lost his deposit in a constituency that he had loyally served for many years. Sudama, who received a mere 1,781 votes to the UNC newcomer's 13,344, complained that "we were portrayed as anti-Indian for having betrayed the Indian Government. The general elections have shown clearly that ethnic loyalty to tribe remains overwhelming. I had, in Panday's own words, taken the 150 years struggle and sold out to the Nigger Party. I would have to pay for such treachery" (*Mirror,* December 16, January 6, 2002). Sudama complained that racial loyalty was too strong to allow people to see the issues. "We tried to shift politics to the issues, especially corruption, but they (the people) like it so. We tried between two ethnicities and failed. If people want corruption, what can we do? (*Newsday,* December 12, 2001). It was the same comment that the Organisation For National Reconstruction (ONR) had made following its defeat by the PNM 20 years earlier (Ryan 1989). Mr. Sudama also noted that he had not received any support from the Afro-Trinidadian elements in his constituency who had promised to vote for him. He considered himself a victim of dual tribalism.

Following the election, UNC spokesmen admitted that the corruption issue had hurt the party, and expressed regret that they had taken the advice of their PR consultants that they should ignore the corruption issue and focus on "performance" (*Express*, March 4, 2002). The Minister of Finance felt that Mr. Panday had erred in his judgement in his handling of the allegations about corruption in the construction of the new Airport (*Guardian*, March 28, 2002). The Attorney General agreed. She also claimed, somewhat disingenuously, that the UNC wanted Trinidad and Tobago to become as "clean" as Hong Kong, Singapore and Botswana and that the Government had a Corruption (Amendment) Bill on the Order Paper when Parliament was dissolved in October 2001. The Bill made "illicit enrichment" an offense, and the proposed Anti-Corruption Commission was to be empowered to investigate allegations that people holding public office had abused their positions to enrich themselves. There was also to be protection for whistle blowers. The purpose of that provision was to encourage people to come forward and give information about criminal activity. "This is very important, especially in corruption crimes which are so difficult to detect" (*Newsday*, April 16, 2002).

Table 19
Election Results - Barataria/San Juan, 1991-2001

Year	Electorate	Party	Votes	Margin
1991	21,982	PNM	6,052	1,363
		NAR	2,652	
		NJAC	188	
		UNC	4,689	
1995	22,603	PNM	6,666	
		UNC	7,611	945
2000	25,021	PNM	7,121	
		UNC	9,098	1,977
2001	20,905	PNM	6,343	
		TU	163	
		UNC	8,007	1,664

Table 20
Election Results - Ortoire/Mayaro, 1991-2001

Year	Electorate	Party	Votes	Margin
1991	22,214	PNM	7,578	1,565
		NAR	2,593	
		UNC	6,013	
1995	22,948	PNM	8,201	
		UNC	8,944	7,43
2000	25,640	PNM	9,303	
		UNC	10,923	1,620
2001	22,289	PNM	9,433	
		TU	174	
		UNC	10,252	819

Table 21
Election Results - San Fernando West, 1991-2001

Year	Electorate	Party	Votes	Margin
1991	21,506	PNM	6,934	1,847
		NAR	5,087	
		NJAC	88	
		UNC	2,073	
1995	22,253	PNM	7,748	1,288
		NAR	616	
		UNC	6,460	
2000	25,828	PNM	8,233	
		UNC	9,176	943
2001	22,059	PNM	7,810	
		TU	174	
		UNC	8,244	434

Table 22
Election Results - St. Joseph, 1991-2001

Year	Electorate	Party	Votes	Margin
1991	22,214	PNM	5,527	712
		NAR	3,497	
		NJAC	185	
		UNC	4,815	
1995	22,948	PNM	6,960	
		MUP	327	
		NLP	69	
		UNC	7,564	604
2000	25,640	PNM	7,387	
		UNC	9,753	2,366
2001	22,289	PNM	6,793	
		TU	242	
		UNC	8,824	2,031

Table 23
Election Results - Tunapuna

Year	Electorate	Party	Votes	Margin
1991	22,214	PNM	6,872	2,699
		NAR	3,266	
		NJAC	257	
		UNC	4,173	
1995	22,948	PNM	7,467	244
		NAR	368	
		NLP	43	
		TPV	16	
		UNC	7,223	
2000	25,640	PNM	8,726	
		UNC	9,062	1,503
2001	22,289	PNM	8,819	276
		TU	184	
		UNC	8,543	

Chapter 6

THE HUNG PARLIAMENT

*T*he outcome of the election presented a major challenge for the country generally, and for the President who had to decide which of the two leaders he would call upon to assume the role of Prime Minister and Leader of the Opposition respectively. The Constitution was not entirely silent on what the President could do. Section 76 provided as follows:

> 76. (1) Where there is occasion for the appointment of a Prime Minister, the President shall appoint as Prime Minister:
>
> (a) a member of the House of Representatives who is the Leader in that House of the party which commands the support of the majority of members of that House; or
>
> (b) where it appears to him that that party does not have an undisputed leader in that House or that no party commands the support of such a majority, the member of the House of Representatives who, in his judgement, is most likely to command the support of the majority of members of that house; and who is willing to accept the office of Prime Minister.

Clearly, The President could not act on the basis of 76a. He could however act on the basis of 76b which anticipated a hung parliament or one in which no party enjoyed majority status. Wisely, however, the President chose not to impose a solution, and instead summoned both leaders whom he urged to try and resolve the impasse themselves, in the process making reference to the entente which had been negotiated between Dr. Williams and Dr. Capildeo at the pre-Independence Conference in Marlborough House in 1961 (Ryan 1972). Robinson told the two leaders that the country was faced with a critical moment which however offered opportunities for progress. The leaders were told that they were required to act decisively and creatively in the national interest (*Guardian*, December 12, 2001).

Both leaders staked out claims to the Prime Ministership. Mr. Manning declared that he was ready and able to form a government and that he had campaigned on the themes of corruption and the need for good governance. The PNM also noted that it had won two seats, including an additional one in Tobago. Mr. Panday based his claim on the fact that he was the incumbent who had not been defeated at the polls. He argued that as in boxing, the incumbent should be given the benefit of the doubt since he did not lose.[1] He also noted that the UNC secured more votes than the PNM. Panday also sought to preempt the President by offering to share power with the PNM leader. As he declared publicly:

> I consider it mandatory that both political parties should respect the expressed and collective will of the electorate. I shall therefore propose to the PNM leader that we make partisan agendas secondary to the national interest and that we work out an appropriate arrangement for sharing power in a Government of national unity. With the seats in parliament evenly divided, neither the PNM nor the UNC can effectively govern T&T for any significant period of time. Discussions for such an arrangement should place high priority on several pertinent issues, including:
>
> • Immediate rationalisation of the EBC's operations and matters related thereto, subject to approval of the President.
>
> • The swift establishment of mechanisms to examine and recommend constitutional reform.

- The appointment of an omnibus Commission of Enquiry to investigate persistent allegations of corruption in Government transactions.

I trust that the PNM leader will be willing to consider my proposal for sharing power in a Government of national unity. To do otherwise would leave the country in gridlock, the society polarised, and the economic advantages and strength that Trinidad enjoys under serious and continuing threat. (*Guardian*, December 12, 2001)

Mr. Panday was at pains to add that while he was prepared to share power, he was not "for one moment surrendering power" (*Express*, December 13, 2001). He nevertheless allowed that he was willing to alternate leadership of the government. This he opined was a better option than returning to the polls. "I do not wish to return to the polls. It is too tiring and costs too much money." He would only do so if necessary. He nevertheless felt that the results showed that the country wanted unity. Thus his offer of power sharing in a government of national unity.

Some analysts argued that the 18-18 tie indicated that the electorate consciously voted for some sort of government of national unity. According to the Director of the NACTA polls, Vishnu Bisram, "the electorate has spoken unambiguously that it wants a joint or collaborative government." That statement was however untrue. A NACTA conducted poll infact indicated that only a quarter of the population (24 percent) believed that the parties should share power. Fifty-five (55) percent were opposed. The remainder, 21 percent, were unsure or refused to say. According to the survey, 53 percent of the Afros in the survey and 59 percent of the Indos opposed power sharing. Only twenty-three percent of the latter and 27 percent of the former said "yes" to power sharing. Whites and other minorities were 21 and 51 percent respectively (*Sunday Express*, January 6, 2002). The fact that the outcome was a tie could not be adduced as evidence that a government of national unity involving executive power sharing was what the electorate intended or wanted. The fact of the matter is that in 2001, Trinidad had a dual electorate, which mechanically produced a "dual mandate." The electorate was given a choice from among two dominant organisations which displayed governance styles and cultures which seemed to be dramatically opposed. A tie was an accident, no more, no less.

Lloyd Best however saw the result as being the by product of the genius of history and a time of opportunity. As he opined:

> Faced with not only a hung country and a hung electorate, the only conceivable shot the country could play was to bring the country to stalemate by ensuring that the parliament too was hung. This is precisely what we've contrived, but as no sudden impulse. Three time times over, we've discovered the genius. In 1995, it was 17-17; in 2000, 19-17. And now it is 18-18. If this is accident, it merely confirms that history works mostly through the unanticipated and unplanned. The reason this is no guesswork, is that we were all near certain that this result was securely on the cards. If this tie is the beginning of wisdom, no less is it a responsible beginning.

Some argued that even if the electorate had not consciously and unambiguously opted for an abandonment of the Westminster "winner take all" political paradigm and for its replacement by a collaborative "all take win" power sharing alternative, power sharing was the only fair option, and that the President should have used his constitutional prerogative and his skill as a political alchemist to engineer such an arrangement. Yet others argued that power sharing was not only a political necessity but an ideologically desirable option. They saw cohabitation as a formula for bringing to an end the ethnic polarisation that was threatening to consume the country. In their view, the election result presented the country with a magnificent and perhaps a once in a lifetime opportunity to experiment with a political formula that had creative possibilities for rekindling the spirit of 1986. Idealists felt that the need to live in the same political mansion and lie in a national as opposed to a UNC or PNM bed would encourage the political class to develop conventions of political behaviour and manners which would help to make the marriage work. The need for such conventions was said to have become necessary in a (hopefully) "post racial" world. Lloyd Best, for example, saw Panday's offer as an "excellent initiative." Best felt that the option provided the country with an opportunity to break the deadlock and to practice constitution reform and do some things we have never done before. He felt that the Prime Ministership should be alternated, and that voting in the Parliament should be free of party whips (*Express,* December 12, 2001).

Former Member of Parliament, John Humphrey, argued similarly. As he advised the President by letter dated December 20, 2001:

A golden opportunity seems to present itself to you with the 18-18 split in the House.

- Before you appoint a Prime Minister, could you not propose to the two party leaders that they work with you in appointing the Senate [sic] to be representative of the varied interests of the national community?

- Having done so, could you not then request that the two leaders work together in assembling a government of national unity that would transcend party divisions?

- The Prime Minister could then be appointed on the basis of his commitment to this task with the other leader to be appointed as Deputy Prime Minister.

- This could rotate annually by agreement until the country returns to election.

- Having achieved the above, could the Senate and the House be persuaded to meet concurrently to debate Constitution Reform on a motion that encapsulates the recommendations of the Wooding Constitution Commission with appropriate amendments, until resolution is reached?

- Then could the country not face new elections on the basis of the new Constitution?

- Could this not give us a formula for lasting national unity?

- The first tasks of the new Parliament would be to amend the Constitution to validate the above and to extend your tenure in accordance with Section 33, sub-section (2).

Realists however argued that politics is a functional equivalent to war, and that the attempt to change the arena or the terms of engagement does not alter that brute fact. At most, it may disguise it until the parties involved calculate that political divorce is a more profitable option than an unhappy condominium arrangement. As soon as crises strike or elections loom, the separatist itch begins to manifest itself, and the alchemy becomes tarnished.

The PNM made it clear that it was only interested in power sharing at the parliamentary and not at the executive level. The party in fact refused to entertain the sharing or rotation of the Prime Ministership. The General Council also categorically rejected the suggestion that one or two cabinet posts be offered to UNC's MPs whom the PNM could "stomach." This rejection was perhaps unwise since such a gesture would have shown that the PNM was flexible, and recognised that it had not won the election. A majority on the Council and the elected MPs however insisted that they could not possibly share cabinet space with any former UNC minister, even assuming that any dared to accept the offer. Typical of this view was Keith Rowley who made it clear that he would prefer to give up office rather than work with certain UNC MPs. As he put it:

> People are talking about PNM trying to entice somebody to cross the floor. I made it quite clear: It does not necessarily mean the balance would change; because there are some people who served within the last UNC cabinet whom I'm not prepared to serve with in a Cabinet. You either stand for something or you don't. I can't spend six

years telling the country you're "tiefing" the country dry
and you want to save your own skin and run to me now
and say, "I will join you so we can stay in power." We refused
that before, you know. The behaviour of the UNC in the
last six years [was disgraceful]. I'm talking about the UNC
leadership attacking every institution, denigrating officials,
cussing Archbishop. There was nothing unscathed in the
last six years. The people will determine if it's going to be
18-18 or 25-11. 18-18 meant the electorate did not make a
clear distinction between right and wrong. Mr. Panday's
conduct has been reprehensible and it has damaged this
country!

The fact that a government of national unity meant that there
would be no formal opposition was also one that PNM Political Leader
Patrick Manning, who is a Westminster fundamentalist, was not prepared
to contemplate. His view was that this was not only unconstitutional,
but a formula for bad governance. In this view, Mr. Panday was not a
person with whom he could deal. As he later put it, "Panday and I are
two different people. We come from two different perspectives. We
come from a perspective that stems from integrity. We understand the
administration of the public trust" (*Guardian*, April 5, 2002).

At a historic "summit" meeting which took place on December
13th and 14th, the two leaders however managed to agree on 10 items
but disagreed on several others. The Crowne Plaza Agreement, as the
entente came to be known, provided as follows:

Matters Agreed Upon

- Prime Minister to be appointed by the President in accordance
  with the provisions of the Constitution of the Republic of Trinidad
  and Tobago

- The Parties to agree on a Speaker of the House of Representatives
  who is to be identified before the appointment of the Prime
  Minister

- Electoral reform including the removal of systemic and personnel constraints

- Constitution reform relevant to a plural society so as to foster *inter alia* a cohesive national community

- The appointment of Commissions of Enquiry into the following:

  - Piarco Airport Terminal construction and associated projects

  - Project Pride

  - La Brea Industrial Complex

  - South West Soldado project

  - InnCogen

  - Desalination Plant

  - Sale of Trinidad and Tobago Electricity Commission power generation facilities

  - Sale of shares of Trinidad and Tobago Methanol to Ferrostal

  - Severn Trent contract

  - Regional Health Authorities

  - Award of Telecommunications licences

  - State-owned financial institutions' write-off of customer's debts.

- Consensus building at the parliamentary level but not at the executive level, i.e., to establish mechanisms to achieve collaboration and cooperation on legislative matters and other parliamentary business

- Give effect to "Crossing of the Floor" Act and associated regulations

- Fresh elections, but no agreement on time

- Establishment of Standing Parliamentary Committees on Energy Policy and Foreign Affairs

- Referral of the Prevention of Corruption Bill to joint select Committee of Parliament without prejudice to the PNM's proposal for the appointment of a special prosecutor.

Matters Not Agreed Upon

- Coalition government with executive collaboration

- Timing of Elections

- Commission of Enquiry into the Elections and Boundaries Commission

- Special prosecutor

Positions on Matters not Agreed Upon

• POWER SHARING

UNC proposes power sharing at the executive level, i.e. cabinet and the appointment of senators

PNM rejects UNC proposals for executive collaboration

• TIMING OF ELECTIONS

UNC proposes elections to be held after electoral and constitutional reform

PNM proposes fresh elections not before the availability of a new voter's list generated from a national re-registration

• COMMISSION OF ENQUIRY INTO THE EBC

UNC rejects the PNM's proposal for a Commission of Enquiry into the EBC and instead proposes reform of the electoral system

PNM proposes a Commission of Enquiry into the EBC as a prerequisite to electoral reform

• SPECIAL PROSECUTOR

UNC rejects PNM's proposal for a Special Prosecutor and proposes Prevention of Corruption Bill which provides for a permanent anti-Corruption Commission with full investigative powers.
PNM proposes the appointment of a Special Prosecutor to deal with allegations of corruption (*Guardian,* December 16, 2001).

The document was signed by both leaders who declared themselves well pleased with it. Mr. Manning was of the view that it was much more than a political arrangement between two parties:

> It is a major step in the process of consultation and the evolution of the political process in Trinidad and Tobago. I will take it a step further.... If that process works, it has implications for reform of the country's Constitution and proper social integration for Trinidad and Tobago. May I say that it is a power sharing arrangement at the parliamentary level. (*Express,* December 28, 2001)

Mr. Panday was equally enthusiastic and felt that anyone who walked away from it would pay a heavy price:

> The enforcement of this agreement depends on good will. There is nothing legally binding. We expect that people are going to abide by their undertaking. The electorate as you know is always the final arbiter in these matters, and anyone who walks away from it will pay for it politically and pay dearly. There is nothing to prevent anyone from walking away, and as I said before, if anyone walks away from this agreement, then the Government collapses. And if the Government collapses, then we are back to square one. (*Guardian,* December 16, 2001)

Messrs. Panday and Manning were subsequently asked by the President to assure him that they commanded the support of all the Members of Parliament who were elected on their slates. Both did. One assumes that the President wished to be assured that no one was planning to cross the floor, tipping the balance between the parties in the process. Having thus been assured, the President, on December 24, 2001, (Christmas Eve) advised the country in a nation wide address that he had decided to appoint Mr. Manning as the new Prime Minister. The President indicated that he would have preferred not to have had to make the decision, but the leaders had left the burden for him to bear. He had no choice but to break the tie, a role which he was constitutionally empowered to undertake under 76b. Robinson's problem, however, was to find a constitutional peg on which to hang his choice. To do so, he chose to turn for help to the Almighty, the Preamble to the Constitution, his oath of office, and those of Members of Parliament. As he declared:

> Having considered the oaths of office, I considered our Constitution which begins 'Whereas the people of Trinidad and Tobago have affirmed the supremacy of God, faith in fundamental human rights and freedoms in the society, and the free institutions.' And that preamble of the Constitution went on to say to the people of Trinidad and Tobago, it may not be the exact words - that when a society remains free,

when freedom is founded on moral and spiritual values and the rule of law. I emphasise - the moral and spiritual values and the rule of law - and it is against that background, taking into account the oaths of office of a member of parliament, a minister, and my duty as President, I … came to a final decision.

It is a decision that I would not normally want to have to take. Where two people are concerned in such a position, there is bound to be disappointment of one side, and that disappointment may extend way beyond the particular person, and would include followers or supporters of that particular person. But when a decision has to be made in the national interest, it has to be made; and when the responsibility falls upon my shoulders, I cannot shirk that responsibility, however burdensome it may appear to be. I cannot shirk that responsibility. I have not done so in the past, and I have not done so even at the risk of my own life, and I don't think I should do so now. However burdensome that responsibility may have been, I had to discharge that responsibility. My decision is that the mantle of Prime Ministership should now be handed over to Mr. Patrick Manning, and I have appointed him as the Prime Minister of Trinidad and Tobago. (*Newsday*, December 25, 2002)

PNM supporters and the Christian creole community were ecstatic. For them it was a beautiful Xmas present. The UNC cohorts were shocked and went into deep mourning. For them, there were no Christmas celebrations. Panday was enraged that Mr. Robinson had chosen Mr. Manning to serve as Prime Minister in what he deemed "a most cavalier fashion." Claiming that he was "misled" into believing that he would be chosen, having regard to the fact that he was the incumbent, Panday accused Robinson of acting unconstitutionally and illegally and out of spite and bitterness. According to Panday, "I did not think he would carry his spite, bitterness, whatever it is he had in the past, to this point" (*Guardian*, March 3, 2002). Declared a politically bereaved Panday:

The President's perverse decision to install an unelected Government has created a political crisis of ominous dimensions and a political precedent that can profoundly alter the common framework of democracy in which the countries of the English-speaking Caribbean operate.

He also affected to be shocked and outraged by the reasons which Robinson adduced to justify his choice, which he deemed "disrespectful." Fumed Panday:

President Robinson has struck a severe blow to our nation's struggle for inclusion and national unity.... Implicit in the President's explanation was an irrelevant, gratuitous, injudicious, divisive, highly offensive dismissal of the moral and spiritual values of members of the Government who have been elected free and fair by the legitimate, popular will of the people (*Newsday*, December 30, 2001).

Panday and his Attorney General believed that the President would have taken the advice of Professor Vernon Bogdanor of Oxford University whose advice they had sought, reportedly on the suggestion of the President. They claimed that they were misled into believing that he would have taken the Professor's advice. Professor Bogdanor, author of the erudite and highly acclaimed book, *The Monarchy and the Constitution (1995),* noted (in the two opinions which he gave to the Attorney General by way of letters dated 13th and 15th December, 2001) that under the 1976 Republican Constitution, the President inherited "any rights, powers and privileges, duties or functions which are vested in or imposed on the Governor General." Among those rights was the power to appoint either the existing Prime Minister or someone else to replace him.

On the question of what factors should guide the President in coming to his decision as to whom to appoint, Bogdanor argued that the question of which party won more votes "was not a relevant consideration since the Constitution does not provide for any account to be taken of the number of votes, only of the number of seats."

Trinidad and Tobago was a parliamentary and not a plebiscitary democracy. Having regard to the Crown Plaza *entente*, Bogdanor dismissed the claim that the incumbent had a superior claim to being appointed. As he put it, "the fact that Prime Minister Panday is the incumbent Prime Minister cannot be a dominant consideration." Another question concerned the PNM's allegations about UNC corruption. Bogdanor's opinion was that that was a matter for the "courts to investigate through the proper legal process. It is not an allegation upon which the President can adjudicate. The President cannot as it were, look behind the number of seats which each party has gained unless and until the courts have pronounced on the issue." It is however questionable whether the President could have gone behind the number of seats even if the courts had deemed the Prime Minister or any other UNC Minister corrupt, since the electorate could have endorsed and absolved the regime by giving it a majority even if the courts had found the Prime Minister or some other minister or ministers guilty of corruption. As the saga of President Bill Clinton demonstrated, charisma and the "gift of gab" seem to beat moral rectitude almost every time.

In Bogdanor's view, the key consideration that should have guided the President was that the UNC did not lose the election. If the President were to appoint the former leader of the Opposition, he would be "open to the criticism that he was acting on the basis of enmity towards Mr. Panday…. *The least dangerous course would [thus] be for the President to reappoint Mr. Panday. The grounds for reappointing Mr. Panday are narrow ones, but in the absence of other considerations, they remain, I think, decisive."* Professor Bogdanor did not however say unequivocally what were the considerations, albeit narrow, which the President should have taken into consideration once he had conceded that incumbency could not be a dominant consideration. He also never indicated why appointing Mr. Panday was the "least dangerous course."

Bogdanor's suggestion that the President should not have sought to resolve the deadlock himself, and that he ought to have tried to persuade the political leaders to resolve the issue themselves, had already been tried. His other suggestion, *viz.,* that failing agreement by the chief actors, the President was better advised to ask the electors to resolve the issues, was academic and impractical in the short run since the electorate had already had two bites at the cherry, so to speak, and had spoken with an uncertain voice. The electorate was hung and the likelihood was that it would again have difficulty producing a result that was clear, legitimate and universally acceptable, given that arrangements for ensuring fair elections were not in place. No PNM leader could have agreed to contest fresh elections unless his followers and the society at large were satisfied that the systemic problems of the Election and Boundaries Commission had been dealt with. Any attempt by the UNC to force new elections before the EBC was demonstrably ready would have provoked the unrest that no one wanted. And what if one hung parliament were to be succeeded by another, as then seemed likely? Who would be favoured by the President?

Bogdanor seemed to have sensed that his advice was impractical when he conceded that in certain circumstances a President might have to break the deadlock himself. As he wrote, "only in the case of repeated deadlock which cannot be resolved either by politicians or by the people, and when this has become generally recognised, should the President seek to take an active role." Clearly, the President had to break the deadlock. Moreover, the Westminster conventions were not of much use. Bogdanor had in fact noted that if one hung parliament was succeeded by another as almost occurred in England in 1974, "the current conventions might well have come under strain." The Professor correctly suggested that the President ought to be neutral; but since the text of the Constitution and the reigning conventions offered no guidance as to what ought to be done in the given circumstances, President Robinson had to exercise his own deliberate judgement as to what was in the public interest.

Clearly, however, whatever choice the President made would have provoked a firestorm of protest. Partiality is in fact an inevitable by-product of the exercise of the prerogative. As Bogdanor (1995: 153-154) himself noted in respect of the United Kingdom:

> The truth is that the existing conventions are not - and perhaps cannot be politically neutral…. The ambiguities in the basic principle of parliamentary government could easily embroil a sovereign in political controversy. The problem is not so much that the sovereign would use his or her powers in the formation of a government in a deliberately biased manner, but rather that, even if the sovereign were to act in a way which he or she genuinely believed to be in accordance with the constitutional proprieties, the supporters of one (or more) of the parties might come to feel that their party had been unfairly treated.

Part of Professor Bogdanor's problem was that the UNC had only provided him with part of the reality with which he had to be familiar in order to come to a sensible judgement. Had he had an opportunity to immerse himself more deeply in the political discourse taking place in the country, he might have come to an entirely different conclusion as to what the conjunctural imperative required the President to do to break the deadlock. The problem was not only a constitutional one, it was a political one as well.

Bogdanor's classic study contained other observations about hung parliaments which had some relevance for the Trinidad case, especially since many Trinidadians insist on regarding British precedents as guides whether they are appropriate or not. After reviewing a number of cases in which the British Parliament was hung, Bogdanor observed that the neutrality of the Monarch in such situations was difficult to achieve. He also noted that there was no obligation on the part of the sovereign to ensure that the Prime Minister commanded the support of a majority in the House. As he writes, "it is clear, that there is normally no requirement for a Prime Minister to seek majority support in a hung parliament. This has profound effects on the fortunes of the political parties, and perhaps also on the future of the party system. Were he or she to act on the basis of precedent, therefore, the sovereign would not require a government in a hung parliament to command majority support. Were he or she to depart from precedent, the sovereign would be open to criticism from the major parties of acting partially...since he or she would not be allowing a prime minister to form a minority government without negotiating its terms" (*ibid.*: 163).

Bogdanor further observed that the principle that a government must enjoy the confidence of a majority in the Commons - a basic principle of parliamentary government - was "unfortunately, not free from ambiguity [since] it can either mean that a government commands the *positive* support of a majority in the Commons, or that there is no majority in the Commons *against.* In a hung parliament, the first interpretation of the principle that a government must enjoy the confidence of the Commons entails a majority coalition or a minority government with outside support and operating on an agreed programme; the second would allow for a single-party minority government, perhaps living from day to day" (*ibid.*: 152). Clearly, while the PNM may not be supported by a majority in Parliament when it meets, neither was there a majority *against* it.

Bogdanor also sagely observed that "constitutional conventions do not exist in a vacuum. Rather, they reflect the facts of political power... No alteration in conventions was likely until the existing ones had been shown to be no longer applicable, and therefore exhausted. This would require a succession of hung parliaments and/or the introduction of proportional representation, forcing the political parties to accept that single-party majority government would rarely recur. What can probably be expected is an extremely messy intervening period in which different conceptions would reflect a conflict between a party system that is dying and one that is struggling to be born" (*ibid.*: 163). Much of this was relevant to Trinidad's political predicament which was certainly "one for the books."

A peeved Mr. Panday subsequently advised the President and the new Prime Minister that he would not accept the PNM's choice for the Speakership whose candidacy he had previously endorsed, on the ground that the PNM had concealed the "fact" that their nominee was a party supporter who had spoken on their platform in 1995, an allegation which was never substantiated and which was patently false and deliberately manufactured to provide the fig leaf needed to break the Agreement. He also indicated that he would not assume the position of Leader of the Opposition since he had not lost the election and had not been consulted by the President prior to the offer being made as the Constitution prescribes. Mr. Panday identified the problem he now faced when he observed that the Westminster system was cruel to the opposition:

> It is a system (Westminster) in which winner takes all and the Opposition is really powerless. It can be extremely frustrating to be powerless. And that is why people behave the way they behave in Parliament. But I am not condemning anybody because I didn't behave too well myself when I was in Parliament because the system requires you to behave that way. It is an expression of the frustration of the system. (*Guardian*, December 16, 2001)

In response to the charge that he had broken his commitment to accept the President's decision, Panday made the ridiculous claim that it was the President and not the UNC which had broken the Agreement. By way of an apology to MPs and other supporters who clearly felt that he had struck a poor bargain which caused them to lose control of the government, Panday vowed that he would be more careful the next time round. "I am a human being, not God, and I had trusted people. I don't blame myself and neither have I committed a sin by trusting people. I would be a fool to make the same mistake if such a situation arose again" (*Express*, January 26, 2002). Interestingly, UNC MP Carlos John openly expressed the view that the UNC would accept the President's decision, a view that was however not shared by his other UNC colleagues who successfully urged Mr. Panday to break the Agreement. As John opined:

> We respect and abide by the President's decision. This was part of the recent accord between the two leaders. As a party, we do that. Our word continues to be our bond. We left it in the hands of the President in accordance with the Constitution and in God's hands. When you're in politics,

you have those who win and those who lose. There's no draw. (*Trinidad Guardian*, December 25, 2001)

It would appear that Mr. Panday was at first minded to abide by the Agreement but was pressured into breaking it by colleagues who offered him the excuse that by failing to appoint the person who had offered power sharing and who thus had the best chance of commanding a majority, it was the President who had broken the Agreement.

Trevor Sudama was however correct in his view that Panday made a fatal *faux pas* in the manner in which he handled the 18-18 crisis. Sudama believes that as the incumbent, Panday could have forced the President to give him the first opportunity to attempt to form a government. As he argued:

> Logically, he was not obliged to vacate office except he was unable to convene a sitting of the House and elect a Speaker, or, if the House was convened, he was not able to command a majority there. Panday was on solid ground to insist that, as the incumbent, he be given the opportunity to prove that he can command a majority in the House. If President Robinson chose to do otherwise in the light of the facts stated above, then the onus was on him to justify his action in removing an incumbent who had not lost the elections and whose party had gained more votes nationally than the major opposition party. Protest against such action ·by the President would have been justified.

> But the case had to be publicly made by Panday immediately after the results were announced and not after the Crowne Plaza fiasco. Instead, Panday was hoisted on his own petard and in the world of real politik proved to be anything but a silver fox. Amazingly, he went to the Crowne Plaza Hotel to meet with Manning and his team to negotiate to establish a Government of national unity. Panday should have known beforehand that the probability of agreement on a national unity Government with the PNM was the same as wishing

to preserve a snowball in hell. Any layman could have told
him as much. (*Newsday*, January 5, 2003)

An appraisal of the post-election events brings a few questions to
mind. Did the President send any coded messages to either Mr. Manning
or Mr. Panday causing them to believe that they would be the anointed
one? Was the message unambiguous allowing either to read into it
whatever he wished to hear? Did the President deliberately "wrong
foot" Mr. Panday as some believe and as seems to have been the case?[2]
How else could Mr. Panday ever have concluded that given all that had
happened between them after the 1986 and 1996 elections, and all that
President Robinson had said in his national addresses about the
democratic system being destroyed by Mr. Panday, and that he could
not be expected to "fiddle like Nero while the country burns," think
that Mr. Robinson would agree that appointing him was the "least
dangerous course"?

The more important question, however, was whether Mr. Panday
initialled the terms of the Agreement only because he assumed that he
would be the "selected one." This is the only conclusion that one
could come to. It also seemed that he agreed to the PNM's nominee
for the office of Speaker as a concession to the PNM, believing that he
would be the Prime Minister. If this is correct, as seems to be the case,
it would also follow that much of what Mr. Panday had to say about
the responsibility on the part of leaders to sell unpleasant policies to
their followers, and about the high price that any leader would pay who
broke the Agreement was meant for Mr. Manning and not for him. It
would also explain why Mr. Panday wanted fresh elections to follow
constitutional as well as electoral reform which would have meant a
possible 3-year hiatus. It also seems clear that the argument about the
President acting illegally and unconstitutionality only applied because
Mr. Manning was chosen. What would have made the choice of Mr.
Panday constitutional and legitimate that was not applicable in the
President's choice of Mr. Manning? Clearly, any choice which the
President made would have met with critical comment. Taking
everything into account, it would seem that the President made the

right choice since to do otherwise would have been to go against the *Zeitgeist*, the intellectual and moral spirit of the times, which was clearly unfavourable to the Panday administration which was seen to be ethically challenged, even in the eyes of many of its supporters, their vote for it or against the PNM notwithstanding.

In emphasizing the importance of moral and spiritual values, the President was however not indicting 269,000 Indo-Trinidadians or the religions to which a majority of them subscribe. A careful reading of what the President said indicates that he did not in fact base his decision on these principles, though he alluded to them in his preamble. This argument was used by UNC spin doctors to delegitimise the President's choice. The President was criticising the Panday administration which, over the preceding six and a half years had done more to scandalise Trinidad and Tobago than had any previous regime, boasts about performance notwithstanding. All the signals warning about civic decay and eventual collapse were flashing red. Mr. Robinson pointedly underlined this when he subsequently opined that: "white collar crime brings down regimes and destroys society and was much more destructive than street crime. What is happening in society was a deterioration of civic responsibility. If we are to address our civic responsibility, then that must not stop at the lowest level. It must go to the highest level; it must go to the level of persons who are our leaders in society and see that they discharge their responsibility and they adopt and act in accordance with standards which are acceptable in a society that has civic responsibility."

Once Mr. Panday's expectations were not fulfilled, it was no longer in his interest and that of his UNC colleagues to honour the Agreement. Thus his demand for fresh elections sooner rather than later. His preferred date for the election was July 8, 2002. In his view, if a Speaker or deputy Speaker could not be elected at the first sitting of the Parliament, Parliament could not be prorogued by the President with the aim of seeking to convene a new session for any purpose whatsoever. "The categorical reality is no Speaker, no Parliament; no deputy Speaker, no Parliament." In Panday's view, it was not open to the PNM to try and govern by executive fiat under the guise of the Doctrine of Necessity. "To go that route would be stretching the tolerance of those members of the population, spanning all demographic groups, who consider themselves victimised, disenfranchised and marginalised by the PNM's patent agenda for group domination" (*Express,* January 10, 2002).

To underline his refusal to accept the President's decision, Mr. Panday declared that he would establish an alternative government with its own "cabinet" to determine government policy. The "cabinet" meetings were to be held at the same time when the official Cabinet met at Whitehall, a decision that the PNM called "sheer madness and a recipe for instability" (*Express,* June 3, 2002). He likewise warned that he would bring his supporters out on the streets in a campaign of civil disobedience to dislodge the PNM whom he said would try to keep power legally or illegally, lawfully or unlawfully. Panday's statement, which was quite irresponsible and widely criticised, was as follows:

> If we give Manning a Speaker who will bend to his will, Manning will have 18 seats and 19 votes in Parliament. We will have 18 votes and he will have 19 votes in Parliament. And with 19 votes, he could run this country for five long years. We cannot do that to our country. We cannot inflict PNM upon this country for five more years…. The PNM, over the past three weeks, has unleashed a terrifying reign of religious intimidation, group domination, political victimisation and disenfranchisement of political opponents, entirely without precedent in this country…. The [PNM] will stop at nothing and you can expect them to do anything. So it is going to be a long and bitter struggle. But we are no strangers to struggle. We were born in struggle. The weapons of that struggle will be the weapons used by Mahatma Gandhi and Martin Luther King Jr. These weapons will be marches and demonstrations, boycotts and civil disobedience. (*Express,* February 23, 2002; *Guardian,* January 1, 2002)

Panday, who in 1996 had accused Mr. Manning and the PNM of trying to overthrow his government, told his supporters to get ready for "a long hot summer" as the UNC mobilises to dislodge the "born again demons" in the PNM. He also warned Manning, whom he said was "waiting for something to happen," not to attempt to induce anyone to cross the floor, a reference to reports that such a possibility was real. It was widely believed that one or two UNC MPs might seek to avoid criminal charges by doing a deal to avoid being arrested. He also warned the PNM against trying to change the balance in Parliament by arresting any UNC MP. Shouted Panday: "arrest falsely one of our men, and you touch all. You will see a reaction such as you have never seen in your life." Panday warned Manning that there were no other options available to power sharing. If this was refused, he should summon Parliament to show the country, and above all "King Arthur," that "capital 18 is more than common 18" or that he could command a majority through "moral and spiritual values" (*ibid.*). Panday was clearly shooting an arrow over Manning's bough in the hope of forcing early elections.

Panday also sought to mobilise regional and international opinion. He claimed that the President and the PNM had violated the doctrine, arrived at the Quebec Summit of the Americas, which was held in 2001, that any unconstitutional alteration or interruption of the democratic order in a state in the Hemisphere constituted an insurmountable obstacle to that state's participation in the Summit of the Americas process. "Steps thus had to be taken to reverse this desecration of the Constitution which had taken place by returning to the polls in six months" (*Newsday,* January 13, 2002). CARICOM was also invited to mediate the crisis which it agreed to do as had been the case in the Guyana and St. Vincent crises (see Ryan 1999).

Some CARICOM Heads were known to have expressed concern about what they feared the President might do if the Leader of the People's National Movement (PNM) and the three dissidents who had been expelled from the governing United National Congress (UNC) earlier that year, and who had joined forces with the PNM in a "strategic alliance," had advised him that Mr. Manning now commanded the support of a majority of the members of Parliament and not Mr. Panday who now only spoke for 16 MPs. The then Attorney General, Mrs. Kamla Persad-Bissessar explained the concern of CARICOM Heads as follows:

> Caricom states are voicing concern at the proposition being put forward that consequent upon a deal struck by the renegade UNC MPs and the PNM leadership, President Arthur Robinson is about to revoke the appointment of the constitutionally-appointed Prime Minister to replace him with the PNM leader. Although there is no evidence whatsoever that President Robinson is even contemplating such an action, reports of this possibility have generated widespread alarm among Caricom governments, which essentially operate within a common constitutional framework with Trinidad and Tobago. (*Sunday Express*, October 6, 2001)

Whether the President ever seriously contemplated appointing Mr. Manning to replace Mr. Panday is not known. The available evidence seems to suggest that he was approached informally, and took the view that the Constitution required him to act on the advice of the Prime Minister to dissolve the Parliament and set in train the process of conducting new elections.

Meeting in the Turks and Caicos Islands in January 2002, the Bureau of the Caricom Conference of Heads expressed concern about the situation in Trinidad and Tobago, and declared themselves anxious that a state of normalcy should return soon. They felt that the "community owes it to the people of Trinidad and Tobago and the wider Caribbean community as well to do whatever lies within its capacity to bring about normalcy" (*Express*, January 13, 2001). The Bureau arranged for Messrs. Ingraham of The Bahamas, Ralph Gonsalves of St. Vincent and the Grenadines, and the Secretary General of Caricom to meet with the President, Mr. Panday, and Mr. Manning, all of whom agreed to meet with the delegation, though the President was clearly not keen to do more than be courteous to the delegation. It would seem that the delegation left thinking that they had brokered an agreement between Messrs. Panday and Manning which would involve Mr. Panday accepting the President's formula which gave Mr. Manning the Prime Ministership and Mr. Panday the leadership of the Opposition, but in retrospect, it appears that the mission went through the motions ritualistically knowing that it had not succeeded in bridging the gaps that divided the two leaders. In sum, the mission failed.

From Crowne Plaza to the Hilton

Panday's refusal to honour the Crowne Plaza Agreement was met with consternation by PNM supporters. Panday was sharply criticised for going back on his word. Supporters of Team Unity were also critical of Mr. Panday and their former UNC colleagues whom they deemed "obstructionist." Others however argued that the Agreement was flawed and should have been reprobated. Arguing this was former Senator Martin Daly, SC. Daly opined that the Agreement gave an

> ...unqualified extra-constitutional licence to the President to choose a Prime Minister. Given this, it was difficult to see how a complaint could be made against the choice of a Prime Minister by the President. The want of authority in the President must have been known to those who negotiated the Agreement and they chose to invite him to make a choice nevertheless.... The country and Mr. Panday is now stuck with the President's decision which was made on the basis of an incomplete and deficient agreement.

Daly argued that the leaders ought to have set a firm date for fresh elections. He also advised the Prime Minister that while his Government had legal status, it lacked political legitimacy since its actions were not legitimated by Parliament. He urged the two leaders to conduct further negotiations to cure the deficiencies of the Crowne Plaza Agreement for the good of the country (*Guardian*, January 16, 2002).

In response to intense public pressure by high profile individuals and civil society groups, including those in the business sector, the PNM and the UNC met to consider ways of resolving the crisis. The UNC reiterated its position that there must be equal power sharing or nothing. The UNC's position and proposals, which we reproduce in full, were as follows:

- The 18-18 results of the last elections demonstrate clearly that the electorate is divided in its support for both parties. The will of the people demands that the country return to the polls and that an interim formula be found for governance which reflects the reality that no party was given a clear mandate to govern.

- The UNC firmly believes that power sharing provides us with an historic opportunity to reduce the adversarial style of our inherited Westminster system of governance which has not always operated in the interest of all the people of our country.

- Power sharing also provides the country with a unique opportunity to promote nation building through consensus rather than conflict, and inclusion rather than exclusion.

- Interim power sharing arrangements will provide the country with an alternative model of governance. The very useful lessons that can be learnt from this temporary arrangement will assist us as we undertake the necessary task of reviewing our constitutional arrangements.

Interim Arrangements in Respect of the Cabinet

- We propose that the existing Cabinet be reconfigured, as it was on December 10, 2001 (Cabinet size - 18). This will facilitate efficient financial management and eliminate the budgetary nightmare where funds allocated to previous Ministries have to be redistributed to those created in January 2002. The reconfiguration of the Cabinet in this way will keep the cost of government down.

- The cabinet should consist of equal numbers of UNC and PNM Ministers.

- Ministerial appointments at the level of Cabinet will be done by agreement between both leaders. Failing that, a system of alternative selection can be used.

- Non-Cabinet ministerial allocations will be equally shared and selected on the same basis as Cabinet appointments.

Cabinet's Modus Operandi

- For the purpose of establishing an interim government until the next General Election, the UNC is prepared to acknowledge the current selected Prime Minister as the interim Prime Minister of the country *pending fresh elections.*

- It is expected that the interim Prime Minister, as Chairman of the Cabinet, will seek always to obtain a consensus on matters before the Cabinet, and where there is no consensus the question at hand shall be resolved by a vote of the majority. The Chairman shall not have a casting vote. Those matters for which no agreement can be obtained will not go forward.

Parliament's Modus Operandi

- It is proposed that the leader of Government business in Parliament will be a PNM appointee, while his Deputy shall be a UNC appointee.

- The role of elected members of Parliament not in Cabinet will be similar to that of members of the US Congress and Senate. They will be allowed to vote by conscience. Under this system, there will be free and open debate on the issues at hand rather than on strict adherence to party line.

- The Senate will consist of 11 Senators appointed by the PNM, 11 by the UNC and 9 Independent Senators.

- The requirements of the Constitution will be maintained by the interim Prime Minister who will include in his 16 nominees, five persons nominated by the UNC.

Interim Budgetary Arrangements

- The UNC notes that there is already in existence a budget for the year 2001/2002 approved by parliament.

- Variations to the approved budget must be agreed to by Cabinet and approved by Parliament. Agreement must also be arrived at if government intends to engage in deficit spending.

Boards of State Enterprises and Statutory Bodies

- Where the bye-laws do not prevent it, there must exist an even number of Board members, and both parties must nominate equal numbers.

- Where the law requires an uneven number of Board members, the additional person will be selected by agreement by both parties.

- In all circumstances however, chairpersons will be selected either by cabinet or by the leaders of the two parties.

"The UNC is of the view that with goodwill and mutual understanding, the foregoing can provide a mechanism for resolving the problems of governance arising out of the 18-18 results of the last general election. We stress that these are merely interim arrangements pending fresh elections, and can provide useful insights that will help us as we commence the necessary task of constitutional reform. Timely fresh elections and fundamental constitutional reform will provide the final resolution for the electoral draw of 18-18. In the interim, however, government, its Executive and its parliament must reflect the equal will of the electorate, respecting the rights of all citizens of our beloved country, Trinidad and Tobago" (*Guardian,* February 14, 2002).

The PNM's counter proposal was a repeat of what had been offered earlier, *viz.,* the creation of joint select committees with an equal number of members from the government and the opposition. The government would implement all majority decisions of the committees. Special mention was also made of the need for parliamentary consensus on policies in respect of Energy, Agriculture and Foreign Affairs.

Predictably, the PNM's General Council rejected the UNC proposals as being utterly unacceptable, arguing that they were unconstitutional, unworkable, and "downright dangerous." It was recalled that Mr. Panday had campaigned on the theme that any relationship with the PNM was "bad, bad, bad." The prevailing view was that Mr. Panday simply could not be trusted as a coalition partner. As one PNM MP put it, "we do not respect Mr. Panday's version of national unity. He is talking peace and waging war. He talks of national unity and he is Mr. Divider himself. As such, we will never want to be part of any national unity government with Mr. Panday, especially seeing how his national unity worked with NAR in 1986 to 1988 and in 1995 and 1996" (*Guardian,* December 14, 2001). Another PNM MP noted that Cabinet was a difficult place even when controlled by one party. How much more difficult would it be when managed by two evenly matched parties. In the PNM's view, an opposition was an essential part of government. That is why, when the PNM was invited to form a government of national unity following the elections of 1995, it rejected it, and went into Opposition. In a further comment on the UNC's power sharing proposals which he said had no precedent in the Commonwealth, Manning warned that Trinidad and Tobago must avoid

being characterised as a "forced ripe banana republic," a development
that he felt would follow "if the country entered makeshift political
agreements that objective reality forced it to change every third day"
(*Express*, March 5, 2002).

Questions were also raised by the PNM, perhaps rhetorically, as
to whether the proposal meant that the UNC would effectively govern
half the country and the PNM the other half, and whether this would
eventually lead to partition as some Indian militants had called for in
1962. As Mr. Manning himself averred, "the 18-18 power sharing
arrangement was just a forerunner to a proposal that the PNM govern
18 constituencies and the UNC govern 18…. The General Council felt
that the power sharing proposal could lead to a renewed call for the
partitioning of the country (*Express*, February 18, 2002). The assertion
was absurd, but indicated that the elites responsible for "spinning"
were doing their work. The UNC's predictable response was that under
its proposal, each ministry would deal with the whole country. This of
course did not answer the question as to whether given what was "in
the river," the formula was workable.

Team Unity likewise raised questions about Mr. Panday's offer.
The former Attorney General, Mr. Ramesh Maharaj, noted that while
"national unity was always a good thing," it should not be a "convenience
machinery." Maharaj noted that "national unity does not come from
taking a Syrian, a Chinese and an Afro-Trinidadian from the business
sector and appointing them to the Cabinet" (*Express*, December 3,
2001). "Power-sharing is good for the country, but it must be based
on genuine concern for a cohesive society and a genuine willingness to
have it. This cannot be achieved successfully when you have to act
under compulsion. I don't think in the present circumstances it will be
able to work. The PNM [had] accused the UNC of stealing the country
and the UNC accused the PNM of not performing and also of stealing
the country. The voting showed that the public was not going to forget
corruption. It is not in the public interest for the UNC to investigate
itself. Panday himself is under investigation for corruption. He in fact

called the election to cover up corruption" (*Guardian,* December 14, 2001).

Both parties were clearly playing games with the negotiations which had in effect become part of the "long campaign" for the elections, whenever they were held. The UNC's proposals seemed very reasonable. Mr. Panday however wanted power sharing because he was acutely concerned about the investigations that were taking place in all the pivotal state enterprises and statutory bodies which were not only revealing massive and unconscionable corruption and civic malfeasance, but which threatened to bring into question the claim that it had "performed." He was also concerned that these investigations could lead to criminal prosecutions involving ministers, including the Prime Minister, who many believed did not have what the Italians call *mani puliti,* (clean hands), protestations to the contrary not withstanding.

The PNM, for its part, believed that possession was nine tenths of the law, and wanted to remain in office for an extended period, if possible, but in any event for a period that was long enough to allow investigative teams to marshall the evidence that would compromise UNC MPs and Mr. Panday himself in the hope that in doing so, they would be rendered inelectable. All of this however assumed that sufficient UNC supporters would "churn" if hard evidence was available to convict UNC frontliners. The 2001 election results however suggested that many UNC supporters would find ways to shrug off the revelations and continue to support their tribal leaders even if they were seen to be culpable. The PNM however assumed that less ethnically anchored voters would abstain or vote against the UNC, and that these votes would make a difference in the swing constituencies.

The two leaders and their advisers met on three occasions to try and resolve their differences, but failed to do so. Following the last meeting on March 6, 2002, Mr. Panday expressed the view that the PNM was not approaching the discussions seriously and that they were a waste of time. The PNM was said to be shifting their positions on key issues. The talks were declared to have broken down. In Mr.

Panday's view, this was deliberately done. Mr. Manning, perhaps ritualistically, insisted that the talks should continue. His position was that the Crowne Plaza Agreement was legally enforceable, and should therefore form the basis of any forward movement. He further argued that he had been advised that the country had a legally constituted government, and that contrary to what was being asserted, there was neither gridlock nor political crisis, a statement that was palpably false. He likewise took issue with the assertion by the Elections and Boundaries Commission that they would be ready for elections if they were to be called in July 8, 2002 and thus refused to meet with the Commission. He however gave the assurance that Parliament would be convened prior to April 9, 2002 when it was legally and constitutionally due. Mr. Manning's various assertions led Mr. Panday to declare that the time for civil disobedience was "getting close" (*Express,* March 7, 2001).

Power Sharing Revisited

Power sharing as an option for Trinidad and Tobago died in March 2002. Its ghost however continues to haunt the community. Ironically, the initiative failed even though almost all the major stake holders and civic elites openly agreed that the Westminster architecture had to be modified and replaced by an "all take win" formula that they believed was better suited to the country's complex demographic and political reality. Some placed the blame for failure at the feet of the President whom they say failed to grasp the historical opportunity presented by the tie to force the two leaders to work out a condominium arrangement that could well have provided a platform for a more durable political unity. This school of thought was of the view that given this standoff, the President should have used his diplomatic skills to advise, warn, delay and broker a power sharing formula, and also to fix a firm date for election.

Lloyd Best was among several who believed that Robinson had what was required to negotiate a power sharing revolution. To quote him; "his best option was always to preside over a joint Administration, led by a toss of the coin, comprised of a handful of ministers only, one charged to carry out limited measures and to undertake restricted spending within a fixed time horizon given by an agreed election date, determined by reasonable EBC readiness." Best argued that Robinson's choice of Manning was the "wrong error." "Though the Manning appointment is legal, on both political and constitutional grounds, it is clearly illegitimate" (*Express*, April 9, 2002). Best insisted that Robinson ought to have called on Manning to form a government with Maharaj *et al* in October, 2001 instead of agreeing to have Parliament dissolved. That, he said would have been the "right mistake." Much of this was unrealistic, even if well meaning. Mr. Robinson had no choice but to accept Mr. Panday's advice to dissolve and it was totally unrealistic for him to seek to impose Best's proposed solution in December 2001 when both sides were negotiating and confidently expecting to win and hoard everything, offers to power share notwithstanding

Best has argued that Panday's decision to resile on his commitment to abide by the Crowne Plaza accord could be justified by the nature of politics. To quote Best:

> By the very nature of politics, of which the main prize is control of the State, any suggestion by a practitioner that he or she would give up his/her right can only be a tactic, whatever the context. Even Robinson cannot seriously query Panday's right to change his mind at any moment and to repudiate whatever commitment he had given especially when he had made it clear that the Constitution, if not the Constitution as law and as text, required the incumbent Prime Minister to be retained, so long as there was no compelling electoral basis for changing the government. (*Express*, July 13, 2002)

Best also dismissed as "humbug" Robinson's talk about "moral and spiritual values." He argued that such judgements should be the prerogative of the "electorate alone." It should not be usurped by any official, least of all an unelected official who might have all kinds of biases and hang-ups of recent vintage. Best also noted that over the past two years, Robinson had in some respect emerged as the leader of the anti-Panday forces in the country, even though not quite as the leader of the post-Williams PNM. "As such, he ought to have exercised more care in what he said or did (*Express,* July 13, 2002). One however senses that Best's judgement was clouded by his patent and barely disguised antipathy to Mr. Manning and the PNM. His conscious or unconscious biases were showing as clearly as were Robinson's.

While it may be arguable that some blame should attach to Mr. Robinson for not insisting on a more precise agreement, it is also arguable that the President had no way of knowing in advance that Mr. Panday would renege on the Crowne Plaza Agreement which he had faithfully promised to sell to his supporters. Did Mr. Panday not say that it was the responsibility of leaders to sell unpopular things to their followers if it was in the public interest, and that no one would take the risk of allowing the Government to collapse? Did he also not say that while the Agreement was not legally binding, anyone who walked away from it would pay for it, and pay dearly? From this latter perspective, blame for the collapse of the power sharing initiative must be placed squarely on the shoulders of Mr. Panday and his UNC colleagues who put their political fears, ambitions, and agendas above the public weal. Mr. Manning and the PNM leadership would never have broken their word as cavalierly and cynically as Mr. Panday did. The PNM and its support base would certainly have puffed and grumbled, but in the final analysis, the party would have taken the view that "a deal is a deal" and that gentlemen must honour their word.

Clearly, followers of Mr. Panday and Mr. Manning were not using the same civic yard stick to judge them. Mr. Panday's flock seemed to allow him greater latitude than did Mr. Manning's. According to a NACTA poll conducted in January, 2002, only 13 percent of the Indians interviewed felt that the UNC should honour the Accord; seventy-nine percent felt it should not be honoured. The community may well have been echoing the voices of its leader, but few openly criticised his posture. It may well be that they were so chagrined and humiliated, felt so emotionally and materially insecure as a result of their loss of political power, that they were prepared to condone any behaviour that would have led to its retention in part or wholly.

By walking away from the Crowne Plaza Agreement, as casually as he did, Mr. Panday reminded the country that he could not be trusted as a political partner. Mr. Panday's legendary reputation for being cunning and of being too clever by half, made it easy for the PNM to write him off as an unreliable and an untrustworthy political ally. The message about the potential benefits of power sharing was contaminated by the medium. Panday himself had the following to say about the dynamics of politics. "There is one thing that you do not escape in politics and that is the consequences of your actions. Whatever action people take, they are going to pay the consequences for them" (*Guardian*, September 6, 2001). Clearly, Mr. Panday was paying for his previous indiscretions. Several trade unionists and supporters of the United Labour Front and the National Alliance for Reconstruction also recalled Panday's many betrayals. The *Trinidad Express* likewise warned editorially that Panday would treat power sharing as a short-term means to secure the long-term gain of overall dominance (*Express*, December 13, 2001).

Panday must also be blamed for the collapse of the Hilton Summit since the proposals which he put on the table must surely have been among the most extreme ever to have been presented by one party to another following an election. It was utterly unacceptable to the PNM and at least half of the country, and it was therefore easy for Mr. Manning to dismiss it as unworkable and "downright dangerous." While it seemed reasonable on the surface, it could in fact have led to so much unseemly conflict that the concept of power sharing would have been tarnished for many moons to come. One in fact agrees with a statement made by Manning in May 2001 that conjunctural factors would have rendered power sharing at the executive level unworkable. As he said then:

> If a government of national unity had happened after the
> elections of 1995 or 2001, the country could have easily
> been destroyed ... But it would not have lasted anyway. The

> partnership would have been broken as soon as things like
> the airport scandal and others came up. The opposition was
> there to show the other side of an issue and, without that,
> there would be room for civil unrest and even military
> intervention. It is not in the national interest to have anything
> like a national unity government without an opposition.
> (*Express*, May 23, 2001)

One might argue that the proposals were merely meant to be a basis for negotiation, but Mr. Panday made the mistake of presenting it in a confrontational manner, complete with the threat of civil disobedience if things did not go his way. Mr. Panday in fact boasted that in his talks with Manning, "we asked for power sharing, and not any "mambie pambie" Mickey Mouse type of power sharing. Based on the results of the election, 18-18, 50-50 in everything; 50-50 not only in the Parliament; 50-50 in the Government …. No power, no sharing of responsibility" (*Sunday Guardian*, February 24, 2002).

The UNC of course blamed Manning and the PNM for the collapse of the talks. The PNM was accused of not taking the discussions seriously, of not making serious counter proposals, and of playing for time. All these accusations were correct. The PNM stood pat on the viability of the Crowne Plaza Accord, insisting that informal power sharing at the parliamentary level and other veto points in the system had to be the basis of any forward movement instead of a formal sharing of juridical power. In Manning's institutionally conservative view, one simply could not negotiate away the notion of a parliamentary opposition which he saw as a fundamental ingredient of parliamentary democracy as he understood it. Manning had on more than one occasion insisted that he does not like coalitions. "They sometime call on one to make compromises that are not acceptable and which might amount to too high a price." He was however prepared to forge an "accommodation" if the circumstance now dictated that this was necessary to achieve an important goal such as combatting corruption (*Guardian*, October 12, 2001). If an opposition did not exist, one would have to create it as Dr. Williams felt compelled to do in 1971 when the PNM won all thirty six seats in the elections which were held in that year (Ryan 1989a). The suggestion that the function of opposition could be achieved by allowing MPs to vote freely in accordance with their consciences was not an adequate safeguard, since party players would want to avoid scoring "own goals."

Mr. Manning clearly wanted the Hilton talks to fail, and Mr. Panday obliged him by putting forward proposals that no leader who had tasted restored power could countenance. Mr. Panday should have understood that once Robinson had pulled the rug from under his legs, he had to find another way to negotiate with Mr. Manning other than by saying that the game had to be played his way, and on his playing field, or not at all. Mr. Manning in fact had no incentive to share juridical power with Mr. Panday once there was mutual agreement that fresh elections had to be called soon. Why share power when there was nothing to gain other than a few extra months in office, and everything to lose by having to deal with Mr. Panday in a Cabinet in which he had the power to block or frustrate everything? Mr. Panday wanted power sharing primarily to abort the various inquiries that were taking place or which were being planned. The PNM hoped the inquiries would allow the country to determine who was responsible for what, and who should be targeted for legal punishment. One notes that a NACTA survey conducted in January 2002 indicated that 85 and 84 percent of the Indians and Africans in the sample respectively felt that corruption should be investigated.

The collapse of the power sharing talks led to feverish attempts on the part of the Prime Minister to find a formula to avoid returning to the polls immediately. Mr. Manning assured the country that a Speaker would be elected, and it may be that he had been given reason to believe that someone from the UNC would cross the floor in return for a promise of office and/or some other consideration as two PNM MPs had done in 1995. One UNC MP had in fact publicly declared that he would vote as his conscience dictated, and it was believed that one or two others might also have been willing to cross. No one crossed, however, and it would appear that the Prime Minister was misled into believing that such a betrayal was likely.

Another possibility was that someone had a change of heart or was dissuaded from executing the planned cross. But given the siege mentality that obtained within the Indo-Trinidad community, one would have been surprised if anyone had seriously considered defecting since to do so was to invite the imprecation that one was a *neemakharam*, a betrayer of the most heinous sort. Such a person would also be courting physical elimination unless he chose to "live in the sky," to use Panday's phrase. One was also surprised that Mr. Panday felt he had to billet every UNC MP in the Crowne Plaza Hotel and to ferry them in a chartered bus to the opening of Parliament, ostensibly because of concern that one of them might have been arrested, kidnapped, assassinated, seduced or suborned prior to the start of the sitting. It is however likely that the initiative was intended to boost morale and feelings of group solidarity for what was intended to be a long drawn out parliamentary session in which games would be played by both sides to ensure that a Speaker was elected (or not elected).[3]

Predictably, no Speaker was elected when Parliament met. Mr. Manning's response was to advise the President to prorogue Parliament. His decision to do so clearly caught Mr. Panday by surprise. The latter argued that the President should have dissolved Parliament and called new elections since it had now become palpably clear that the PNM could not secure the majority necessary to elect a Speaker without whom Parliament could not be properly constituted. This meant that no legislation could be enacted. It also meant that there could be no amendments or variations to the Budget which the UNC had put in place in October 2001. Mr. Panday felt certain that Mr. Manning and Mr. Robinson had conspired to subvert the Constitution and to establish an "executive dictatorship." Mr. Panday repeated the charge that Robinson's actions were motivated by racial considerations. As he declared, "I believe he did not want the UNC in office for reasons which probably had racial overtones, but which certainly had historical antagonisms between ourselves as political persons. The President has been carrying out a political campaign against the UNC since he entered office. That is as blunt as I possibly can put it." Mr. Robinson initiated legal proceedings against Mr. Panday for the above remark which he deemed libellous and which is still pending (*Sunday Express,* May 19, 2002). Mr. Manning conceded that he had raised the matter of prorogation with the President during their weekly meetings, and one assumes that he was assured by the President that he would accept his advice to do so rather than force a dissolution. Having helped Mr. Panday to come to power in 1995, Mr. Robinson may have felt that he had erred in doing so and that he had to correct that historical error.[4]

While power sharing was theoretically and ideologically attractive, it was unworkable in the concrete circumstances and would merely have transferred gridlock from the country and Parliament into the Cabinet.[5] For horizontal power sharing to work, the political "planets" either have to be lined up in favour of it, or the concrete reality such as to make it clear that it was the only alternative to civil unrest or state collapse. No party voluntarily gives up power once it has it and thinks that it can maintain its hold on it. My own judgement is that while power sharing is desirable and would be necessary sometime in the future, the country was not yet ripe for the paradigm shift that shared governance involves. Its indispensability would however have become evident to all if the country had gone back to the polls and had again elected a hung Parliament. This would have meant that no Appropriation Bill could have been passed unless Parliament was properly constituted and both parties agreed to put a budget in place to provide the country with the funds needed to meet salaries and services. Then and only then would the President have gotten the cross ethnic support which he would have needed to do what it was said he ought to have done on December 24, 2001 (see Appendix).

Endnotes

1.   As Panday whinged, "my understanding of the Constitution is that where there is a tie, the President must call on the incumbent Prime Minister to form a government" (*Express*, December 11, 2001).

2.   Mr. Sat Maharaj claims that he was. As he said in an interview, "Mr. Panday negotiated badly. But I was told - and I am not saying by who Mr. Panday was told - and I am not saying by who: 'You could afford to be generous, because you are in the driver's seat.' If he was told that, he was deceived. He may have negotiated on some kind of promise" (*Guardian*, March 17, 2002).

3.   Mr. Panday praised his MPs for standing with him like the "rock of Gibraltar." He warned them that the PNM would throw as much mud as they can. He noted that so far, "Manning had not proven one single allegation against them, but I think Manning is going to try and charge and arrest some of us. But he will make sure we are not tried before the election. He prefers that we face the election with criminal charges hanging over our heads like in 1995." But, he warned, whatever the PNM did the UNC was going to beat them whenever the election was called (*Newsday*, April 15, 2002).

4.   Mr. Robinson did not agree with the view that being a former politician prevented him from being an effective and fair President. As he reflected following the election of his successor:

> I do not believe, as many are advocating, that a former politician should never be the President of the country. Experience gained through active politics was an inestimable value in enabling me to take some of the decisions that I took.... That experience contributed to my being able to manage some of the extremely difficult and extraordinary situations I had to manage... (*Express*, February 21, 2003)

5. *Newsday* frowned on the proposed power sharing plan thusly: "At the end of the arrangement, what next? An election campaign with both sides attacking each other again? Goodness Gracious!" *Newsday* speculated, editorially, that Panday's offer was driven by a sense of impotence (December 13, 2001).

Chapter 7

THE EBC IMBROGLIO

One of the vexed questions separating the parties throughout the period related to the role of the Election and Boundaries Commission, the regulatory body which superintends elections. This body had over time been the subject of much controversy, but never more so than in the elections of 2000, 2001 and 2002. While the Boundaries Commission was justly accused in the post-independence years of being pro-PNM in terms of how boundaries were constructed, the voters list had never been the subject of sustained criticism. The most that was said of it was that it contained the names of many who had died, who had migrated internally or externally, or who were illegal residents from the Eastern Caribbean. Few seriously argued that the list was padded to favour one party or another. And indeed, given the ease with which the PNM had won its victories in the sixties and seventies, there really was no need on its part to tamper with the voters list.

The list however became a *cheval de la bataille* when it was realised that elections were actually decided by a few thousand votes in a few swing or marginal constituencies where neither the PNM nor the UNC had an unchallengeable majority as was the case in the others. In these latter seats, victories were achieved with substantial majorities. These excess votes were "wasted" which would not have occurred if a system of proportional representation had been used. Constituencies like Arima, Arouca North and South, Caroni Central, East, North, and South, Chaguanas, Diego Martin Central, East and West, Fyzabad, Laventille-Morvant, Laventille West, Naparima, Nariva, Oropouche, Pointe-a-Pierre, Princes Town, San Fernando East, Siparia, St. Anns

East, St. Augustine and Tabaquite were won by margins of 4,000 votes or more. These were ethnic bastions which "belonged" to one party or another, and it would have taken an electoral revolution such as occurred in 1986 for them to change hands (Ryan 1989).

The competitive constituencies included the two in Tobago. Only 289 votes separated the NAR from the PNM in Tobago East in 2000. In Trinidad, the marginals included Tunapuna (336), San Fernando West (943), Ortoire-Mayaro (1,620), Barataria San Juan (1,977), La Brea (2,125), Toco-Manzanilla (2,243) and St. Joseph (2,366). In all of these 9 seats, which constituted 25 percent of the total, the losing party gained at least 40 percent of the votes cast. A minor political tremor such as occurred in 2000 could result in political change. Both parties thus accused each other of gerrymandering or list tampering. The PNM was accused of having "scientifically" gerrymandered the constituencies in 1961 (Ryan 1972; 1989:80). The PNM's claim was that the UNC was seeking to counter gerrymander the system by shifting hundreds of voters to neighbouring constituencies where their votes were needed more.

In the battle for the marginal seats, the PNM had certain advantages and the UNC others. The PNM's advantage had to do with the ethnic make up of the constituencies. The ethnic patterns in the five most marginal constituencies were as follows:

Table 24. Ethnic Composition of Marginal Constituencies (%)

Constituency	Ethnic Breakdown		
Tunapuna	Indians	9,995	38.6
	Others	15,875	61.4
St. Joseph	Indians	10,784	42.5
	Others	14,594	57.5
San Juan/Barataria	Indians	10,878	43.8
	Others	13,984	56.2
San Fernando West	Indians	10,051	41.0
	Others	14,434	59.0
Ortoire/Mayaro	Indians	13,140	46.9
	Others	14,874	53.1

Despite the fact that the demographics favoured the PNM, it lost 3 of these seats in 1995. What happened in 1995 was that the turn out rate among Indo-Trinidadian voters was higher than that of Afro-Trinidadian voters by about 20 percent (78% to 58%). This differential voting helped to close the demographic gap between the two communities. The UNC could not however assume that these differentials would hold in the 2000 elections. What if the UNC had "maxed out" in 1995, and there were "reversals" and "stay at homes?" What if the PNM, having learnt the hard way that it could not afford to be complacent as it was in 1995, managed to awaken ethnic pride among its supporters, bring out the young, and took its turn out tally to say 65 percent? The UNC would then become history as had the NAR.

This was a prospect that the UNC backroom boys in the so called "G13" group could not easily accept since millions of dollars were riding on the outcome of the election. The UNC money men had to make sure that nothing was left to chance. Thus the decision to create a Special Field Operations (SFOps) Unit to target the five key marginals. The declared objective of the operation as was defined in a document which was leaked to the PNM, was to transfer 1000 voters to each marginal constituency. The methods for executing the operation included identifying the constituencies from which the transfer of voters was to take place, and the voters who would agree to be transferred by signing Form 22. The receiving marginal constituencies were to provide legitimate addresses for transferees through persons who would not violate the top secret nature of the exercise. Persons in the information loop included MPs from the donor constituencies, councillors, constituency executives, candidates, *bona fide* field officers of the Party Administration Support Unit (PASU), and other persons known to SFOps. To guarantee compliance, proper introductions were said to be necessary.

The completed Form 22s were to be submitted to registration officers at the relevant registration offices "in bulk." These officers were to sign the reverse side of the forms indicating that they were satisfied that the transfer was valid. Care was to be taken to "win the loyalty and cultivate the trust of the EBC registration officers in all marginal constituencies and their superiors through extensive lobbying, lunches, dinners and 'power' meetings." There was also need to secure 6000 Form 22s since photocopies were not acceptable to the EBC and only a limited number were given to any one person. The exercise was to be done without raising suspicions. As such, only some 250 persons a week were to be transferred over a four week period. The exercise, which was said to require an unusual degree of confidentiality and compliance from all the parties involved, was to be completed by September 30, 2000. The author of the document warned that any breach of confidentiality would lead to investigations by the EBC which could have "severe legal implications." The help of four sitting UNC MPs from donor constituencies were sought, three from safe seats, (St. Augustine, Oropouche, Naparima) and one from a marginal seat (San Juan/Barataria). Their help was however not readily forthcoming since at the time they were approached, their status as candidates was not yet determined. They expected to be by passed. It was also said that they had expressed concerns about their integrity and about the "violations of the sanctity of democracy."

What was interesting about this document, was that it was detailed, and contained names and initials that were easily recognizable. Taken together with a tape which was published in the *Sunday Express*, (October 15, 2001), what one had was an elaborate plan to steal the election. When challenged, UNC leaders denied the allegations, and saw it as yet another occasion on which Mr. Manning was crying "wolf." When it was realised that there was proof that a wolf in UNC clothing was actually at the door, Messrs. Panday *et. al.* could do no better than claim that the PNM had done it before, and that Mr. Chambers and Mr. Manning had also used dirty electoral tricks to win elections. The PNM however never padded electoral lists though it did "scientifically gerrymander" the boundaries in 1961. This was however not illegal. It was part of the electoral game. There were also persistent allegations that the voting machines which were used in 1961 and 1966 had been rigged. No proof has ever surfaced that they were. Even if they were, however, it was disingenuous for the UNC to argue that this justified what they were attempting to do forty years later.

The "voter padding" scandal loomed large over the elections of 2000, and led to several investigations and searches of the offices, homes, and computer files of UNC officials including at least one minister, and the laying of charges against several other UNC activists. No one was successfully prosecuted before the Courts, mainly because the prosecution was either unwilling or unable to bring forward justiciable evidence. The matter was "lawyered" to death. PNM supporters were however firmly of the view that the 2000 election was stolen and that the UNC had used the fact of its incumbency to deter or derail police investigations and to protect elements within the EBC. Note was taken of the fact that a Task Force which had been appointed to pursue the matter had been demobilised. Mr. Manning claimed that at least 2000 voters were moved illegally. "Voter padding is not fictional; it is very real. PNM is in opposition today for one reason only, voter padding" (*Guardian,* November 31, 2001). Manning also claimed that the PNM knew the names of the persons within the EBC who supported the UNC and who were acting in a manner that was prejudicial to the interest of other political parties and to the constitutional status of the independence of the EBC" (*ibid.*).[1]

The EBC in its official post-election report, admitted that the UNC had attempted to steal the election. To quote the Report:

- Two aspects of the election process ... became major issues in the campaign of the December 2000 election. One was the issue of alleged "voter padding' in certain marginal constituencies, and the other was the allegation that two candidates had false declarations during the nomination process.

- On October 6, 2000, allegations of a plan to 'pad' the electoral lists in marginal constituencies were made to the then Chairman, the late Sir Isaac Hyatali, at his office by the Leader of the Opposition. Support for the allegations was furnished in the form of a series of photocopied documents said to have been handed to the Leader of the Opposition by a person whose name it was said could not be disclosed as he was in hiding. The Chairman undertook to advise the other Members of the Commission and to investigate the allegations.

- Almost immediately thereafter, the leader of the Opposition reported his allegation to the Press and then to the Police, and the Press promptly published the same under banner headlines while the Police prepared themselves to investigate the allegations.

- It is important to point out at this juncture that in order to preserve the integrity and validity of the electoral list, particularly in the face of the pending election, the Commission had redoubled its efforts to improve the surveillance of registration system by initiating at the beginning of the year 2000 a monitoring exercise to oversee transactions dealing especially with applications for across-constituency transfers. This was done with particular reference to the so-called marginal constituencies.

- Arising from this monitoring exercise, it was in late September 2000 that two bundles of fifty-three (53) and forty-nine (49) notifications of change of addresses were received for transfers to the marginal constituencies of Ortoire/Mayaro and Tunapuna, respectively. Field investigation thereafter revealed that the information supplied in support of all but seven notifications was inaccurate and consequently, ninety-five (95) notifications for transfers were deemed invalid and rejected.

- In the face of the allegations and the above invalid notifications for transfers, the Commission decided that all such notifications in the marginal constituencies from July 1, 2000 and including the period of Electoral Registrations, October 3-11, 2000, would be subjected to special scrutiny. This was done in order to ensure:

  1. The rejected notifications for transfers lacked bona fides or were untruthful; and

  2. The acceptance only of those that passed the test of accuracy and satisfied the statutory requirement of at least two (2) months' residence at the changed address preceding the qualifying date of the Electoral Registration, October 12, 2000.

- As a consequence of such scrutiny, the Commission rejected altogether 252 notifications for across-constituency transfers into the marginal constituencies. (Report *of the Elections and Boundaries Commission on the Parliamentary Elections* held on December 11th 2000, vii-viii).

Following the 2000 election, the EBC admitted that it had "lost credibility," and undertook a comprehensive nationwide survey to sanitise the voters list. The aim of the house to house exercise was to delete the names of voters who were dead or who had migrated, as well as to ensure that persons were registered in the constituencies in which they now lived as opposed to where they had lived previously. It was also assumed that the exercise would identify and correct such illegal registrations as had taken place. As with any such exercise, there were numerous cases of persons whose names were deleted or transferred to other constituencies in error because of the incompetence or carelessness of field workers, or because the latter had been given incorrect information by neighbours or villagers. PNM elements were however of the view that the deletions and transfers were deliberately effected to weaken its support in the marginals.

The EBC however insisted that the 2001 list was as clean as was humanly possible, and that it was 95 to 98 percent accurate. Many however remained unpersuaded. The President was likewise convinced that something was wrong, and that the list was not in sufficiently good order to guarantee a free and fair election as the EBC claimed. Following the Prime Minister's advice to him to dissolve Parliament and call fresh elections, the President formally took the unusual step of inquiring of the EBC as to the state of readiness of the list. The EBC gave the assurance that it would be "ready" by October 31, 2001, an assurance that neither the President nor much of the electorate felt had any credibility. The President in fact chided the EBC for giving conflicting information about its state of readiness, an accusation which the EBC denied. The EBC was in fact known to be in a state of administrative confusion having regard to the work which was being done on the house to house survey, but took the view that it had to declare itself "ready" whenever the date for elections was proclaimed. To do otherwise would give it *defacto* power to determine whether or not the President should heed a Prime Minister's advise to dissolve Parliament and call elections. Its definition of "ready" was thus technical rather than actual (*Express*, October 13, 2001).

The confusion that occurred in polling stations on election day suggested that the EBC was not in fact "ready." The Commission however put the blame on voters whom it said did not heed its insistent call to ascertain that they were properly registered. Of the 5,168 persons who visited polling stations on election day and were unable to cast their votes, 1,814 were said to have gone to the wrong polling station, 2,701 had had their names deleted (in their view wrongly so), 225 were under age, and 401 did not provide sufficient information to allow the Commission to undertake an appropriate investigation. While the EBC was not entirely to blame for all that occurred, the EBC had released lists to the public which led those not on it to believe that their name was still on the list when in fact it had been deleted or transferred to some other polling station without their knowledge. The EBC claimed that the cost of publishing the full list was prohibitive and denied that the deletions were deliberate. PNM voters however believed otherwise and took the view that a Commission of Inquiry was required to determine what took place in 2000 and 2001. They also insisted that a sanitised list had to be put in place before any further elections could take place, however long that exercise took. The UNC, for its part, denied that there was any significant "padding" or "deletion" phenomenon, and felt that the PNM was fabricating reasons for its defeat in 2000 and its showing in 2001. The party bluntly refused to endorse the call for a Commission of Inquiry which it felt threatened the independence of the Commission, but in the end agreed that there were systemic problems which needed to be put right. The party felt that these could be done within a short space of time.

The question as to whether the PNM lost the 2000 elections and tied that of 2001 because of manipulation of the list remained an issue in 2002. It is clear that efforts had been made by the UNC to contaminate the list in 2000, and that they were able to secure the assistance of elements within the EBC at its staff level, reportedly for considerable sums of money. The EBC conceded that such efforts were made, but claimed that prophylactic steps had been taken to break up the networks that were involved by massive staff reassignments. It had also determined that applications for transfers from one constituency to another had to be effected by individual voters rather than by party officials acting on their behalf. In its view, the damage done was negligible and had been contained.

Public Opinion and the "Voter Padding" Issue

In a national opinion survey conducted by SARA in October 2001 on the "voter padding issues," 39 percent of our respondents believed that there was a "great deal" of voter padding, 15 percent felt that there was a "fair amount" of it, while another 17 percent felt that there was padding but not enough to affect the overall result. In sum, 71 percent were of the view that the UNC cheated in the 2000 election. Only 17 percent disagreed. Indo-Trinidadians were less inclined to this view than Afro-Trinidadians. Despite what the UNC leadership claimed, 52 percent of them agreed that there was some voter padding, compared to 88 percent of the Afros, 66 percent of whom felt that there was in fact a "great deal" of it (Table 25).

Table 25
How Much Voter Padding Took Place in Last Election (2000)
(%)

Response	National	Indo	Afro
A great deal	39	11	66
Fair amount	15	13	16
Some, but not enough to make a difference to the result	17	28	6
None	12	23	2
Uncertain	14	10	10
Refuse to say	3	5	0

Seventy percent of the Afros agreed with Mr. Manning's charge that the PNM did not lose the 2000 election and that it was stolen. A significant minority of Indos, 12 percent, also believed that the PNM was robbed. Equally significant is the fact that 75 percent of Indos in the sample refused to offer an opinion in respect of this question. They saw refusal as the preferred alternative to admission or denial (Table 26).

Table 26
PNM Lost 2000 Election Due to Voter Padding
(%)

Response	National	Indo	Afro
Agree	42	12	70
Disagree	7	5	8
Uncertain	8	8	8
Refuse to Say	43	75	14

During the crisis, the Commissioners of the EBC came under a great deal of pressure from sections of the public. It was alleged that they either sanctioned or condoned the irregularities which took place during the conduct of the 2000 elections, and there were calls for their resignation and the appointment of a Commission of Inquiry to investigate what had gone wrong. The President also asked one of the Commissioners to resign on the ground that there was a conflict of interest in his role as a member of the Commission and that of the presidency of the Chamber of Commerce.

When asked whether the EBC Commissioners should resign, 31 percent felt that they should. Afros were more inclined to be critical of them than Indos by a whopping margin of 46 points. Fifty-four percent of the former felt that they should resign compared to only 8 percent of the latter (Table 27).

Table 27
EBC Commissioners Should Resign
(%)

Response	National	Indo	Afro
Yes	31	8	54
No	41	64	20
Do not know	21	22	20
Refuse to say	6	5	7

Following the 2001 elections, a Commission of Inquiry chaired by retired judge Lennox Deyalsingh was appointed to enquire into the functioning of the Elections and Boundaries Commission. The Commission however failed to settle once and for all the question as to whether there was massive voter padding in the 2000 election and politically inspired deletion of voters names in the election of 2001. Both parties and their supporters continued to make claims and counter claims about the integrity of the two elections. The Commissioners correctly noted that the electoral process was the bedrock of parliamentary type democracies, and that the integrity of the voters list was crucial to free and fair elections. It thus found that the EBC's policy of putting the burden on the elector to keep his registration status up to date was ill advised having regard to the laid back culture of the society. The Commission was of the view that the EBC should have adopted a more pro-active approach to keeping the voters register as accurate as possible. As the Commission opined:

> It is not good enough to formulate and rely on rules and regulations which ignore reality and which result in the disenfranchisement of voters and then blame these voters because they have not adhered to the rules. There will always be people who will wait until it is too late but the system must be such that their number is minimized. (Deyalsingh 2002: 12)

During the course of the Inquiry, the general impression given was that the PNM had presented little hard evidence to support its claim that ghost voters had been added to the list of electors for the 2000 election, or that the names of many voters had been unfairly deleted from that of 2001. The Commissioners however found that notwithstanding some egregious errors made by PNM witnesses, the data presented by the PNM was "generally reliable" or "substantially correct." To quote the Commissioners, "we are satisfied that the results of their [the PNM] monitoring can be regarded as generally reliable. There would of course be, and there were in fact mistakes and oversights, but on the whole, we are satisfied that we can use their evidence to draw broad conclusions as may be necessary" (*ibid.*: 18).

In respect of the evidence submitted by the PNM in four marginal constituencies, the Commission, after due deliberation, had the following to say:

> On the review of all the evidence relative to the PNM's claim for Barataria/San Juan, Diego Martin East, San Fernando West, and Tunapuna, we conclude that the errors on the electoral lists were such as to affect the accuracy of those lists. Further, the EBC's responses were not always clear, and even with the corrections it made, we cannot say that we are satisfied that the final lists were accurate (*ibid.:* 36).

The Commissioners were not impressed with the House to House Survey that was conducted in 2001 to clean up the electoral list. They observed that the process of recruiting itinerant registration officers and temporary field officers raised serious questions about their suitability. The Commissioners were equally critical of the manner in which deletions were effected following the Survey. It was noted that between July and December 2001, 132,000 deletions were effected, 57,000 of which were due to deaths (10,000) or migration (47,000). This meant that 85,000 could not be found at the addresses which the EBC had on their data system. Twenty-three thousand (23,000) of these were advised that they were to be deleted in a single advertisement in a newspaper which had the lowest circulation.[2]. The others were notified by post at addresses where they were unlikely to be found. The Commission felt that these cancellations, which could have led to constructive disenfranchisement, should have been undertaken with greater caution.

The Commission of Inquiry expressed the view that the 2001 list was "seriously compromised." To quote the Commissioners:

> Preparing for the Election would itself have been a full-time job for the EBC. The final phases of the House to House Survey, with its demands on staff must have imposed an extra heavy burden. We got the impression of a staff,

working under intense pressure, taking short-cuts wherever possible and trying desperately to keep on top of the situation. This was, in our view, trying to accomplish miracles, and not surprisingly, the system could not cope. We would not go so far as to say that the system crashed, but it came near to doing so. It is not surprising therefore, that so important a function like "field-checks" in the House to House Survey suffered and the Electoral List for 2001 was seriously compromised. Considering all the evidence, both oral and documentary, we have come to the conclusion that the figures emerging from the House to House Survey are flawed. Since those figures were reflected in the 2001 Electoral List, we conclude also that that List was likewise flawed and in need of immediate review. (*ibid.*: 67)

The Commissioners recommended that there should be a review of the list, beginning with those in the five marginals, a process which it believed could be completed within 3 months if there was proper planning and funding. The Commissioners deemed this a reasonable course to follow, and warned that failure to adopt it would give rise to disaffection among significant sections of the electorate. To quote the Commissioners, "persisting with the existing list would be very unwise and could present dangers to this country which [it] has so far been very fortunate to avoid" (*ibid.*: 83).

The Voter Padding Issue

When the Inquiry began, it was assumed that the issue of voter padding would be one of the issues that would be thoroughly ventilated. It was widely assumed that it was the very *raison d'être* of the Inquiry. That was not to be. In one of his key rulings, the Chairman of the Commission of Inquiry declared that the PNM witness who had leaked PASU's plan to tamper with the list would not be allowed to testify. Deyalsingh noted that the evidence that might be led would be the same as that which would be used in the pending criminal trial, and that allowing the witness to testify would transform the Inquiry into a criminal trial. Pre-trial publicity would also contaminate the pending trial. Deyalsingh ruled that

> ...the Commission's terms of reference does not include an
> Inquiry into whether or not there was any plan or attempt
> by any person to pad the election list. Further, parallel
> investigations into a criminal issue both by a criminal court
> and a Commission of Inquiry are undesirable both in
> principle and practice. (*Express*, May 3, 2002)

Deyalsingh further amplified his statement, noting that "the alleged UNC plan to transfer voters illegally from one constituency to another was not admissible as "evidence" before the Inquiry unless it could be shown that the plan was put into effect in such a way as to affect the accuracy of the voters list And we have no evidence that such a plan translated into action that affected the accuracy of the voters list" (*Guardian*, May 8, 2002). The Director of Public Prosecutions (DPP) also advised the Commission that calling witnesses who were also due to appear in pending criminal proceedings to testify could prejudice those proceedings. Since the PNM called no other witnesses, the Commission concluded that "*there was no evidence of voter padding before the Commission* on the issue of voter padding." The PNM's Attorney shared the Commission's view, though he told the Commission that "voter padding has been very much in the air, very much with us."

But were there other "clues" that there was such a plan afoot? The EBC's Chief Executive Officer told the Commission that prior to the year 2000, "bulk" transfers of voters from one constituency to another were allowed, and that he had come to the view that the system could be abused; as such he had begun monitoring transfers. It was found, for example, that 53 applications were made by party activists to transfer voters from Nariva to Ortoire-Mayaro by way of bulk transfer. All were deemed invalid by the EBC. The EBC thereupon decided to stop accepting bulk transfers on October 3, 2000, the date when election registration officially began (*Guardian*, May 8, 2002). Voters were required to apply in person.[3]

The Commission sought to find answers to the voter padding question by looking to see whether another type of evidence would throw light on the problem. It looked at the number of transfers of registration that had been made into the five marginals to see whether there were any unusual patterns in the year 2000.

Table 28
Transfers into the Marginal Constituencies, 1994-2001

Years	1994-1995	1995-1996	1996-1997	1997-1998	1998-1999	1999-2000	2000-2001
Total Transfers	4005	7195	5894	6562	17583	10919	16007
Transfers: Marginals	649	1620	810	958	2464	1711	3721
% Increase	16%	23%	14%	15%	14%	16%	23%

The data did reveal an increase in transfers into the marginals in election years from an average of 15 percent in non-election years to 23 percent in the election years 1995-96 and 2000-2001. The evidence seemed even clearer in the battleground seats of Tunapuna and San Fernando West. In San Fernando West, there were 1204 inward transfers in the year 2000 compared to the 233 which took place in 1994-1995, an increase of over 400 percent. The pattern was the same in Tunapuna where the comparative figures were 892 and 107, an increase of over 700 percent. One cannot however be certain that all of these transfers were illegal or that if they were, the UNC or its supporters were the only ones responsible, but the presumption was that the latter was more than likely.

In their comment on the possible significance of these figures, the Commissioners were harsh on the EBC. They noted that the EBC Commissioners had told the country that they had been "monitoring" transfers into the marginals, and that they had found nothing unusual. No details were however provided as to what formula was in place to monitor such movement. The Commissioners were chided for not mounting a "special inquiry" to keep track of what was taking place given the fact that there were persistent allegations that there were rogue elements within the EBC who were facilitating illegal transfers. As the Commissioners wrote:

> The Commissioners should have seen the need to assure
> themselves and the public that there was not a "facilitating
> network" within their organization, allegations of which had
> been brought to their knowledge. In a context where there
> were serious allegations of a breach of the EBC system,
> and where police cases have resulted from the alleged breach,
> it is unacceptable that the Commissioners of the EBC did
> not see the need to mount an internal investigation into the
> allegations. In the face of what might have been a serious
> assault on the Electoral Process, the Commissioners of the
> EBC adopted what we consider to be a position of aloofness
> (*ibid.*: 56).

The Chief Elections Officer however told the Inquiry that every request for a transfer was checked by Field Officers and that of the 3000 or so applications which were received, only 252 were invalid, and these had been referred to the Police (*Newsday,* March 20, 2002).

One of the Commissioners, Dr. Noel Kallicharan, dissented from the majority view with respect to whether the pattern of transfers into the marginals was significantly different from what obtained in the other constituencies. His claim was that the data showed greater movement in some of the latter. Table 29 reveals that there was greater movement in constituencies like Arima, Arouca North and South than there was in some of the marginals.

Table 29. Voter Transfers by Constituency, 1994-2001

Constituencies	1994/97	1998/01	Ratio
Arima	146	524	358%
Arouca North	218	844	387%
Arouca South	246	882	359%
Barataria/San Juan	167	472	282%
Caroni Central	306	631	207%
Caroni East	160	402	252%
Chaguanas	231	530	230%
Couva North	205	404	198%
Couva South	207	377	182%
Diego Martin Central	125	372	297%
Diego Martin East	103	315	305%
Diego Martin West	128	406	315%
Fyzabad	149	391	262%
La Brea	132	297	226%
Laventille East/Morvant	111	368	331%
Laventille West	92	266	288%
Naparima	109	254	234%
Nariva	130	299	231%
Oropouche	123	360	293%
Ortoire/Mayaro	156	374	239%
Point Fortin	98	201	205%
Pointe-a-Pierre	178	381	213%
Port of Spain Nth/St. Anns West	165	368	225%
Port of Spain South	126	277	220%
Princess Town	157	313	200%
San Fernando East	215	560	260%
San Fernando West	302	714	237%
Siparia	109	291	267%
St. Anns East	98	322	330%
St. Augustine	151	396	262%
St. Joseph	228	463	203%
Tabaquite	119	274	230%
Tobago East	55	175	317%
Tobago West	91	269	296%
Toco/Manzanilla	188	453	241%
Tunapuna	173	609	353%

Dr. Kallicharan's comparison were however based on "ratios" (the second average as a percentage of the first) and not percentage increases which other Commissioners used (*Sunday Guardian,* June 23, 2002). Dr. Kallicharan's general argument was however supported by other data which looked only at transfers effected during the actual election period in question, i.e. 2000-2001. What the figures in Table 30 show is that while as a group, movement into the marginal constituencies was generally higher than was the case in the others, especially in Tunapuna and San Fernando West, there were other constituencies which displayed comparably high inward transfers. These included Arouca North, San Fernando East, Caroni Central, Chaguanas and Arouca South.

Table 30
Transfers to and from Selected Constituencies
July to July 2000-2001

Constituencies	Transfers In	Transfers Out	New Registration
Arima	542	450	626
Arouca North	1116	396	647
Arouca South	654	584	675
Barataria/San Juan	566	639	445
Caroni Central	678	426	487
Chaguanas	611	350	474
San Fernando East	776	520	446
San Fernando West	1204	466	620
St. Joseph	656	547	529
Tunapuna	892	497	628
Ortoire/Mayaro	403	425	425

New registrations also showed a mixed pattern. While there were more of these in Tunapuna and San Fernando West, there were comparable numbers in Arima, Arouca North and Arouca South.

It is not possible to draw unequivocal conclusions from these aggregate ιdata as to whether there was voter padding in the 2000 election. The figures could be the result of increased party activity in constituencies which were deemed competitive or reflect movement to new residential communities such as those which have been created in Arouca. All we do know for certain is that 252 persons sought to defraud the EBC by making false claims about their residential status and that these were rejected by the EBC and their names turned over to the Police. We also have the allegation made by "secret witness" Richard Bickram that he was part of a UNC scam to transfer 1000 votes from safe seats to marginal seats. Bickram was however widely regarded as someone who was not a credible witness. It is also believed that he might well have been a mercenary who was working for both the UNC and the PNM.

While the jury is still out as to whether the UNC won Tunapuna and San Fernando West fairly in 2000, Mr. Manning's claim that "2000 votes were moved illegally" and that "the PNM is in opposition for one reason only, voter padding," remains unproven and perhaps exaggerated. The numbers do not add up. The available "evidence" such as it is, indicates that an effort to "pad" was certainly made, but that it was foiled before it gained significant momentum. As Mr. Deyalsingh himself observed, "we have no evidence that such a plan translated into any action that affected the accuracy of the voters list."

The Commission of Inquiry also recommended that the EBC Commissioners should resign with immediate effect. The recommendation was based on their view that the EBC had not performed competently under their watch, the deficiencies in terms of human resources and the funding necessary to improve its capacity notwithstanding. As the Commissioners concluded mournfully:

> The EBC we found, sees itself as an autonomous body circumscribed by an Act and the Rules appended thereto. It is not prepared to venture outside the Act (and rules) except where it is absolutely necessary to do so. It does not see itself as a pro-active institution. It sees itself more as a

Government Department rather than an institution which is the Guardian of the Electoral Process and therefore, in a sense, a Guardian of Democracy in Trinidad and Tobago. This being so, it has no vision. It is content to preside over the Electoral Process purely as a mechanical exercise. Notwithstanding what has been said above, the fact is that the EBC has not performed efficiently and effectively over the last two election periods and this has led to great public unease and concern and a loss of confidence by many people in the electoral Process. The EBC cannot be heard to say that it was not responsible for this state of affairs, that it was due to the failure of Government to provide adequate resources for its effective operation. Independent persons who accept appointment to independent constitutional commissions and upon whom vital constitutional and legal functions are imposed, *must* carry out those functions efficiently and effectively. If they cannot do so, whatever the reason, they must resign. Public morality and public responsibility require no less (*ibid.*: 84, 85).

Somewhat contradictorily, the Commissioners conceded that the EBC was a victim of circumstances beyond their control. As they declared:

It must not be assumed from what has gone before that the EBC has been totally responsible for the obvious short-comings of the electoral process. Culpable it has been in several respects, but it was operating with limited resources under intense pressure within the last three years. It embarked upon the 2000 General Election with an inaccurate Electoral List. It tried to correct the situation with a House to House Survey in 2001 and everything may have worked out well if it had been given sufficient time to verify the data collected in the field and produce an updated and accurate List. But, it was suddenly confronted with the announcement of the 2001 General Election and decided to go along with the decision of the Political Directorate. And now, to make things doubly worse, it faces the prospect of another general Election, perhaps later this year. The

> EBC must be given some time to take stock and to fix the flaws in the System and in the Electoral Lists. Without this, we fear that our democracy will be the loser. (Deyalsingh 2002:85-86)

The Commissioners nevertheless remained convinced that the EBC and its executive officers had developed and displayed a "mindset" that was not compatible with the role which it was required to play as the guardian of the country's electoral system. As such, they recommended that the EBC should employ a full time Chairman and a Chief Elections Officer who had the expertise required to manage a complex institution. In terms of the latter, it recommended that such an officer should be recruited on contract from the private sector if necessary, a recommendation that invited the legitimate concern that someone who was partisan to the ruling party could be recruited, which would compromise the independence of the EBC.

The EBC challenged the findings of the Commission of Inquiry and some of its key recommendations, especially that relating to the resignation of the Commissioners and the replacement of the Chief Election Officer by a contract officer. In respect of the latter, it was noted that the CEO was a public servant and removable only by the Public Service Commission in accordance with Section 129 of the Constitution. In terms of the recommendation that the Commissioners should tender their recommendations to the President, the EBC noted that

> At no time during the Commission of Enquiry were any allegations made against any Commissioner of the EBC; nor were any of the Commissioners required by the Commission of Enquiry to appear before it to answer any allegations. The Commissioners of the EBC were given no opportunity to correct or contradict any prejudicial statement or adduce material which might have deterred the Commission of Enquiry from making the first recommendation. The Commissioners of the EBC were never told that there was any risk of an adverse finding

being made against them by the Commission of Enquiry. (*Express*, June 13, 2002)

In terms of the complaints about the inaccuracy of the list, the EBC's reply was that the strictures made pertained to the Annual list and not the Revised or Supplemental list. It noted further that if the statistical formula used by the Commission's Report in respect of the four marginal constituencies, which were analysed in detail, the 2000 and 2001 lists were more than 99.4 percent accurate. It noted that the Report itself was equivocal about the extent of the inaccuracy. As the Report had stated in paragraph 4 of its executive summary:

> On the question of the Electoral Lists: While the Commission has arrived at a definitive answer with respect to the 2001 General Election, the same cannot be said for the 2000 Election.... In respect of the 2000 List, there was not much evidence before the Commission relating to the compilation procedures adopted. With respect to this List, the Commission cannot state as a finding of fact that the Electoral List for 2000 was inaccurate, although it appears that the probabilities point in this direction. (*Express*, June 14, 2002)

In respect of the allegation of incompetence, the CEO of the EBC noted that the regulatory body was under-resourced in terms of both material and human resources. It was noted, *inter alia*, that

(a) ... its computer system was obsolete and that in 2000 it requested $3.9m to upgrade its system, but was only allocated $1.5m. It never received the latter. It was also noted that the EBC had only one qualified person in its entire computer department.

(b) it was under-resourced with respect to field officers and space in sub-registration offices to cater to the public's needs. The EBC had 11,084 polling divisions and only 10 Registration Officers. Its permanent full time staff was a mere 300.

(c) following the 2001 General Elections, the EBC was in the red to the tune of $3.9m.

EBC Commissioner Raoul John also challenged the view that the EBC was aloof or not sufficiently pro-active. He likewise rubbished the widely held view that the EBC's computer base had been tampered with. Not only was there no evidence that it had been attempted, but it would have been difficult to conceal such penetration. As he noted:

> Suppose someone wanted to either create 1,000 fictitious names in, say, a particular constituency, or maybe transfer, illegally, 1,000 persons to that constituency, do you see how difficult it would be to conceal such a plan? Remember, not only would the central register here in Port of Spain have to be changed, but also the unit registers at all the district offices involved. In addition, we would either see an abnormal jump in the number of voters in that constituency, an abnormal amount of requests for transfers or, on investigating complaints sent to us, we would not have found a person's name in the binder or, perhaps, unauthorised changes on registration cards. The evidence would show up. (*Guardian*, February 28, 2001)

John also noted that the PNM's complaints that the names of 763 persons had been deleted from the 1995 list in the Tunapuna constituency had been investigated. It was found that 68 percent were still on the 2000 list but had changed heir names or addresses, 26 percent were deleted due to death while another 6 percent were deleted because of dual or incomplete registration. In terms of the 603 persons whose names were added but whom it could not find, the EBC found 55 percent to be still residing at the addresses on the list, 24 percent had moved to unknown addresses, 6 percent to known addresses, while 11 percent had migrated or died. Thirteen percent had moved so long ago that no one in the immediate vicinity had any information on them. Similar findings were made in respect to queries about other constituencies (*Guardian*, February 28, 2001).

All kinds of dark motives were imputed to the Chairman and members of the Commission and the PNM. There were even allegations of bribery. Attorney at Law Russell Martineau, who represented the EBC at the Inquiry, accused Prime Minister Manning and the Attorney General of applying "executive pressure" on the EBC Commissioners to resign. He in fact deemed the Commission of Inquiry "very near unconstitutional" in terms of what it recommended (*Newsday,* June 21, 2002). Attorney at Law Anand Ramlogan went further and accused the Commissioners of being part of a strategy to demonise the UNC. As he wrote, "the Commission couldn't take a swipe at the UNC's jugular because the PNM's case of voter padding had fallen flat on its face. The Commission was faced with a dilemma: How to justify the millions of taxpayers money that was spent on the fiasco? The obvious answer was, of course, to jam the EBC, evidence or no evidence" (*Guardian,* June 18, 2002).

The Commission was accused of failing the test of fairness when it called for the resignation of the EBC Commissioners without first advising them that they ran the risk of being deemed guilty of mismanagement or some other offence if they failed to testify before the Inquiry. The complaint was that far from being told that this possibility existed, the Chairman specifically advised that his Commission was "not there to find guilt or innocence or even impropriety on the part of anybody." Mr. Martineau was of the view that the Commissioners would have pursued a "MacKay kind of approach,"[4] and limit themselves to making recommendations to improve the electoral system in ways that would enable the EBC to recover the credibility which it had clearly lost.

Other critics of the Commission's Report were of the view that the prescription of natural justice and the right to notice and fair hearing required that the EBC Commissioners be told that the "evidence" seemed to indicate that they were incompetent and unfit to occupy posts of such importance, and that they should have been given an opportunity to comment on or contradict the evidence that seemed to be pointing to that conclusion. They should not have been "ambushed" in the Report. The Privy Council's (per Diplock) dictum that "persons who came before tribunals had a right to know what procedures would be used, and a legitimate right to expect that when a public authority promised to follow a particular procedure, it [was] in the interest of good administration that it should implement its promise so long as implementation did not interfere with its statutory duty," should apply. Lord Denning also opined that "if the right to be heard is to be a real right which is worth anything, it must carry with it a right in the accused man to know the case which is made against him. He must know what evidence has been given and what statements have been made affecting him and he must be given a fair opportunity to contradict them" (Kanda *vs* Government of Malaya [1992] AC 322).

One can have little argument with these nostrums about how tribunals ought to proceed. There are however two questions that may be relevant. One had to do with whether the EBC Commissioners were actually accused of any impropriety or misconduct and therefore entitled to be given notice that they had a case to answer. Incompetence is arguably quite different from impropriety or wrong doing, and no one publicly accused the EBC Commissioners of wrong doing though imputations were frequently made in private. The other question related to the practicality of providing the EBC Commissioners with an opportunity to contest the findings of the Commission of Inquiry, especially if the latter's judgement was formed after the hearings had been concluded. Should one have resumed hearings to reventilate the issues? Could this have been done within the time frame allowed?

There were however legitimate concerns about the advisability, constitutionality, and political wisdom of the recommendation that the EBC Commissioners should all resign, and that the Chief Election Officer should be replaced by a human resources expert on contract, especially if these were all to be done prior to the 2002 general election. Problems would certainly have arisen if all the Commissioners were to go at the same time. Organisations have memories, and it is bad administrative practice to take actions which cause that memory to be completely erased, especially if the organisation in question was as pivotal as was the EBC. Reappointing all the members of the Commission could also have posed delicate problems for the President given the temper of the times and the fact that Mr. Panday had refused the President's invitation to serve as Leader of the Opposition. How would one have satisfied a querulous public that the new appointments were not partisan? Pro-UNC Attorney Anand Ramlogan in fact alleged that the Deyalsingh Report was intended to "clear the way for political interference with the EBC" (*Guardian*, June 18, 2002). As Ramlogan continued:

> ...forcing the EBC commissioners to resign is both dangerous and wrong. Recommending contracting out the Chief Elections Officer's position is suicidal; we might as well move the EBC's head office to Balisier House. If these recommendations are implemented, it signals the beginning of the end of democracy and free and fair elections in our beloved country. It opens up a door that leads to the Guyanese experience of rigged elections, genuine voter padding and Burnham-style dictatorship. We are going down a dangerous road that transcends the narrow politics of both the UNC and PNM. (*Guardian*, June 18, 2002)

The Attorney General's attack on the EBC for its refusal to accept the Government's recommendation that a Human Resources expert be appointed to advise the Chief Elections Officer was also bothersome to many. The Attorney General accused the EBC of maintaining an attitude of "arrogant aloofness" and of allowing their "personal view to interfere with their duty to the population," which was to have an organisation which functioned in an efficient and effective manner. The EBC's concern was that the Government wanted to control the EBC, which is an independent and not a main line Government Department. The EBC Chairman in fact expressed the view that the Prime Minister and the Attorney General wished to have a "PNM Commission."[5] The PNM, for its part, claimed that it wanted to ensure that those elements in the EBC who were partisan to the UNC did not use their strategic positions to subvert the electoral process. They wanted free and fair elections. The PNM's insistence on the appointment of a cabinet approved (and possibly selected) adviser was however unwise, and fortunately was not pursued. (see Reginald Dumas, "The Attorney General and the EBC," *Express*, August 29, 2002).

Speaking on behalf of the EBC, Mr. Martineau accused the PNM leadership of mobilizing the media and half the country to discredit the EBC and possibly subvert the Constitution (*Newsday*, June 21, 2002). Martineau argued that the "EBC was constitutionally accountable to no one." As such the Commissioners could not tell the EBC how to do its work (*Guardian*, June 21, 2002). Martineau drew parallels with the McKay Commission into the Administration of Justice by asking what would have happened if McKay had recommended that the Chief Justice should resign (Ryan 1999b).

There is however no evidence that Deyalsingh *et. al.* collectively intended to effect any constitutional *coup*. One however admits that there was need to tread warily on the matter of restructuring the EBC. For this and other reasons, it was inadvisable that any attempt be made to invoke the provisions in the Constitution which related to the removal from office of the EBC Commissioners. Mr. Manning's statement that "the Government was moving to implement all the recommendations of the Commissioners" [so] that "when Trinidad and Tobago next goes to the polls, the elections will be free and fair and free from fear" was certainly ill advised, especially seeing that the Government did not have the constitutional power to do so (*Express* June 10, 2002).

The findings of the Commission notwithstanding, the operations of the EBC still hung like spectre over the campaigns (short and long) for the 2002 elections.

Endnotes

1. The person who functioned as the "whistle blower" in this matter was spirited out of the country to a safe house in a neighbouring Caribbean island. He "surfaced" in June 2002 and gave press interviews in which he claimed *inter alia* that the main aims of PASU were to:

   (a)   turn the PNM constituencies of Toco-Manzanilla, Arouca North and South and San Fernando East into marginal constituencies.

   (b)   pad five seats - Tunapuna, San Juan-Barataria, San Fernando West, St. Joseph and Ortoire-Mayaro by transferring 1000 voters to them.

   (c)   that he and his conspirators were to be paid $250,000.

   (d)   the Plan collapsed when the PNM exposed it and turned the information over to the Police. The DPP gave the witness immunity from prosecution.

   The frustrated whistle blower complained that he had been ignored by the state and the PNM and was no longer interested in testifying (*Newsday*, June 17, 2002). He also complained that the PNM had promised to pay him $100,000 for agreeing to take his evidence to the police but he had only been given $20,000. UNC spokesmen counter-charge that the whistle blower was in fact a PNM member who pretended that he had defected to the UNC, but was in effect a plant.

2. The EBC noted that the cost of publishing the names was $160.000 and that if it had published the entire list of 127,000 in all three newspapers, the cost of doing so would have been about half of what was spent on the entire general election (*Express*, May 4, 2002).

3. One Commissioner found it "worrying" that none of the persons cited as references on the transfer application forms were contacted by the EBC. He noted that of the 56 persons who responded to queries, 42 were aware that their names were on the form, nine were not aware, and two did not know the persons whose names were on the form (*Newsday*, May 9, 2002).

4. This was a reference to the approach used by Lord McKay in the Commission of Inquiry which was appointed by the UNC in 1999 into the functioning of the Judiciary (see Ryan 2001).

5. In a fit of exasperation about the Prime Minister's remark that "the EBC must be responsible to someone," the Chairman remarked that: "He wants to change the Constitution, well let him go ahead and change it. I suppose he wants a PNM Commission. The PNM wants to control the EBC by seeking to force the Commission to hire an adviser" (*Guardian*, September 21, 2001).

Chapter 8

THE ELECTIONS OF 2002: THE LONG CAMPAIGN

*T*he collapse of the power sharing negotiations led inevitably to the launching by both parties of the "long campaign" for fresh elections. Despite seemingly exaggerated hopes that some UNC MP would cross the floor and give the PNM a majority in Parliament, Mr. Manning was fully aware that the PNM would have to return to the polls to resolve the question as to who would govern the country. From time to time, the Prime Minister spoke as if he was certain that he would be in power for an extended period, and his strategy was to govern as though he in fact had an unequivocal mandate for a full five year term. Whether this posture was informed by arrogance, stubbornness, utopianism, or by delusion is not clear, (perhaps it was a mixture of all) but Mr. Manning sought to project the view that he was not a pro-tem Prime Minister. Win or draw, as Prime Minister, all the power of the incumbent belonged to him. Manning was aware that extended incumbency would give him a tactical edge in the coming election, and he was determined to use it to consolidate his grip on the reins of power.

Mr. Manning however begun his Ministry by making several unforced errors. To the chagrin and consternation of many friends of the PNM, and to the ridicule of his detractors, he appointed an extraordinarily large Cabinet of 29 ministers which unbelievably, included his wife as Minister of Education and a number of ministerial hold overs from the 1991-1994 administration whom many thought were beyond recycling. While it is true that some had worked hard for the party and had to be offered rewards for their loyalty and effort, some were literally prised out of the interstices of the woodwork, much to the embarrassment, consternation and disappointment of those who knew how important it was for the PNM to show that it was indeed a renovated outfit that had something to offer to the young and to detribalised elements. The feeling was that the Party had to put its best foot forward to convince those who believed that it was beyond redemption, especially since all were aware that new elections would soon have to be called. The popular canard was that the PNM was the party of the "mooks" and the "blunderers" while the UNC was the party of the "crooks" and the "plunderers."

The PNM team not only seemed old and tired looking, but was also unambiguously Afro-creole. Of the 29 ministers, only three were Indo-Trinidadian, a fact that invited comment from friend and foe that unlike the UNC, the PNM remained ethnically exclusionist. Part of the problem was that the society had become so polarised and the PNM so demonised in the Indian community, that few Indo-Trinidadians were willing to make themselves available for consideration to high office. That apart, Indians could be forgiven for believing that Mr. Manning had not tried hard enough, particularly in terms of ministers who were brought in *via* the Senate. Needless to say, Mr. Panday was at pains to tar Mr. Manning with an anti-Indian brush.

The PNM's strategy for dealing with the UNC was to interrogate the UNC to demonstrate that it was indeed grossly corrupt as alleged, that it had governed wastefully and partisanly, and that its claim that it had performed was without foundation. The CEOs of many state owned companies were accused of squandermania, either for personal enrichment or as political milch cows of the former ruling party. Mr. Manning told executives of the companies that his government was "extremely uneasy about the level of total internal contingent indebtedness among the agents of the state. A number of agencies have incurred significant liabilities of the Central Government and even to suppliers and contractors from the private sector which they seek to have settled by the central governments." The Prime Minister noted that the contribution to the debt generated by state companies had risen from 11.1 percent of GDP in 1995 to 20 percent of GDP in 2002. Mr. Manning reminded the directors that good governance required that they be guided by principles of fairness, transparency and accountability" (*Guardian*, June 20, 2002).

As had been promised in its manifesto, Commissions of Inquiry and forensic investigations were mounted into several projects, foremost among which were the allocation of contracts for the construction of the new Piarco Airport which was said to have cost TT$1.6b, the construction of a secondary school which cost TT$30m, but which could not be opened because it was built against professional advice on terrain that was geologically unstable and through which there were gaseous and other liquid emissions, and the construction of an electricity co-generation (Inncogen) plant which the country did not need and which had saddled the country with an onerous and fraudulent "take or pay" energy consumption contract. Investigations were also conducted into road paving projects undertaken by The Tourism and Industrial Development Co. Ltd. (TIDCO), the Water and Sewerage Authority, the Regional Health Authorities, and the National Maintenance Training and Security Company (MTS).[1] Many of the projects inquired into had been identified by the PNM in the Crowne Plaza Agreement. Needless to say, the PNM was less than eager to investigate those contracts or projects which were undertaken between 1991 and 1995 which the UNC had identified as being in need of investigation. Specially targeted were deals where it was suspected that the former Prime Minister was a pecuniary beneficiary. The PNM's aim was to discredit the UNC and its leader and to reduce its attractiveness to its hardcore supporters, and swing voters whom it believed had been misled by Mr. Panday's rhetoric about performance.[2]

Mr. Panday unequivocally refused to occupy the post of Leader of the Opposition, and campaigned incessantly for new elections which he insisted must be held by July 2002 or September 2002 at latest. His anxiety to provoke early elections was informed by his hope of frustrating Mr. Manning's strategy of marshalling evidence to show that the UNC regime in general and Mr. Panday in particular were venal and incompetent, and that they had left the country wallowing in debt and sleaze. The UNC had refused an European union loan of TT$250m at three percent with a 5 year moratorium and an IDB loan for TT$150 million at 6 percent and instead chose to borrow from a local bank at 11 percent. The local loan had no conditionalities attached in respect of tendering, and allowed the regime to pick its preferred contractor without competitive tenders. The loan was to construct a fly-over to alleviate traffic congestion on a major arterial highway.

Mr. Panday portrayed the Government as being racially driven and exclusionist in terms of its personnel policies. The PNM was likewise accused of seeking to impose an "executive dictatorship" on the country, of trying to govern without the benefit of Parliament, of employing friends and cronies, and of replacing UNC appointees with its own "boys" and "girls." The PNM was also accused of misgovernance and of taking postures which alienated and drove away potential foreign investors. It was alleged that the economy had virtually collapsed because of the prevailing mood of uncertainty, a comment that had some merit even if it was much exaggerated.

Mr. Manning was charged with using the Police Service to engage in witchhunts, and that his aim was to embarrass him and some of his ministerial colleagues for alleged offenses in order to gain parliamentary ascendancy or to discredit the UNC electorally. As the UNC complained, "it appears that the emphasis is on making humiliating arrests rather than on ensuring that the cases be determined. There is a deliberate attempt to intimidate and destroy the leadership and administrative capability of the party" (*Guardian,* June 18, 2002). The latter was certainly true, but it was disingenuous and self-serving of Mr. Panday to deem the investigations a "witchhunt" unless he assumed that he should be allowed to do whatsoever he wished with public funds without having to give an account to anyone as to how they were spent or misspent. The PNM denied that they were victimising UNC members and reminded the party that the investigations were sanctioned by them in the Crowne Plaza Agreement. They noted that the PNM would have been on the receiving end if the UNC had been called upon to form the Government.

The emotive phrase "ethnic cleansing" was also bandied about by Panday and UNC supporters to describe some of the resource allocation and recruitment policies of the PNM. The term was no doubt employed as part of a strategy to give a racial dimension to the campaign against the UNC. The PNM was accused of systematically purging the state enterprises and public utilities of Indo-Trinidadians simply because they were Indo-Trinidadians. Mr. Panday himself used very strong language to describe what he claims was taking place. As he said in relation to reports that squatters were being evicted from lands that they had been allowed to occupy, "this PNM Government is acting with vengeance, spite, ferocity and malice" (*Guardian*, May 2, 2002).

Spokesmen for the PNM predictably denied that the Government was systematically cleansing public sector offices of people merely because they were Indo-Trinidadian. They counter claimed that during the six years that the UNC held the reins, there was a deliberate policy of "overstuffing" state offices with Indians, either because it was felt that "it was Indian time now" and that historical wrongs had to be put right, or because it was felt that if one was going to use public office as a mechanism for group or individual enrichment and aggrandisement, certain strategic positions of authority had to be filled by co-ethnics upon whom one could rely. The circle had to be closed.

Over the 1995-2001 period, there were in fact persistent complaints that selection processes were rigged to ensure that certain persons got appointed or promoted, regardless of merit, that the tendering processes were rigged, and that all sorts of other irregularities took place, the full details of which were only discovered when the PNM regained power. It was also said that the guilty parties were using the fig leaf of race to conceal their crookedness and their shame. As Mr. Manning opined, what was taking place "has nothing to do with ethnic cleansing. There are those among us who the minute things do not go their way, they fall back on the race card, and that's what they are doing now. They don't care if they fracture the society in so doing" (*Newsday*, May 16, 2002).[3]

The UNC, for its part counter claimed that whatever it did when in power was done on the basis of politics and performance rather than on race. Race was incidental. A former UNC Minister of culture, Daphne Phillips had in fact justified the UNC's policy in the following terms: "if we had 100 percent African CEOs or people of any race, if you had a majority of one race and there were circumstances that (because of their performance or whatever), they have to be dismissed, then it would be people of that particular group being dismissed" (sic). And there is no doubt that following the coming to power of the UNC, several CEOs and managers of African descent were made to "bite the dust." The list was a long one, and some of the victims were immortalised in calypsoes. It is also a fact that persons of Indian descent who were parachuted into these offices, either on contract or through regular appointment, were being replaced by persons of African descent in what some regard as a legitimate case of "tit for tat." This was particularly so where contract officers were involved. Minister of Public Administration Lenny Saith noted that there were some 2,400 contract officers in the public service, and that when contracts came up for renewal, or when there were reasons to take action, "then obviously it'll reflect what is there now." In sum, if most of the contractees were Indian, the "firees" will be Indian.

What one was witnessing, however, was not "ethnic cleansing," a term that had a very specific meaning, but the operation of a spoils system that was a normal feature of the "winner takes all" paradigm that was characteristic of American and Westminster type political systems. These personnel turnovers take place routinely in all Caribbean political systems and have been repeatedly criticised as being wasteful of scarce human resources and inimical to orderly public policy making and implementation. It is also destructive of community in that it pits winners against losers, sometimes violently so. We have seen the effects of this in the inner city areas of Kingston, Jamaica, where people do whatever is necessary, including maim and kill, to ensure that their party wins, since one could starve if it failed to do so (Ryan 1999b).

The problem existed not only in terms of jobs and contracts, but also in respect of invitation lists to state sponsored social functions. Certain people were excluded to "make room" for others who were seen to be part of the new in-group. Former UNC Minister of Finance, Brian Kuei Tung, argued that this game of musical chairs was understandable in the context of adversary type party politics, and correctly observed that both parties were guilty of the practice. As he remarked, "I have seen both sides, and the policy has been consistent. We want the best people, but we also want people, unfortunately, who would support our policy and philosophy. The PNM did it when I was in a PNM Cabinet, and the UNC/NAR is doing it now that they're there; and there's nothing wrong with it. It so happened that the majority of support [for the UNC] seems to have come from a particular ethnic group."

But there is much that is wrong with the system, especially in countries like Guyana, Suriname and Trinidad and Tobago where the problem is compounded by the emotive factor of ethnicity. The "cleansing" was not merely driven by party, but was also perceived as being ethnically motivated. This of course made it doubly dangerous. The country becomes divided not only on the basis of party related tribalism, but also on some assumed or imagined ethnic criteria. There was thus genuine cause for concern that this "in and out system" which began in 1986-1988 with the coming to power of the NAR after 30 years of PNM rule, and which now routinely surfaces when administrations change, would become deeply entrenched, and would come to have consequences for the society that all will come to regret. One could be sure, for example, that if the UNC had regained power in the 2002 election, they would do precisely what they were now piously and hypocritically accusing the PNM of doing. Clearly, one should reject the view that a changing of the guards and gatekeepers should automatically follow after every change of administration. Such changes as are necessary should be limited to those appointees whose positions were obviously political and meant to be linked to the tenure of the party in power.

Team Unity

Mr. Panday also trained his political guns on Team Unity and its leader, Ramesh Lawrence Maharaj. Urged on by the party's financial backers, the two men discussed a reconciliation in the interest of reuniting the tribe for the coming electoral encounter. Both publicly indicated that they did not consider themselves permanent irreconcilable enemies. Both men however had differing agendas. Mr. Maharaj hoped to secure Panday's blessing for the succession while Panday needed Maharaj's legal skills and his neutrality in the legal battles which he was facing in respect of his false declarations to the Integrity Commission. He also hoped that the voters who supported Team Unity in the 2001 election would return to the UNC fold. The talks however collapsed in part because several UNC MPs made it clear to Panday that they would have absolutely nothing to do with someone who had betrayed their trust and who had caused them to lose office. Some in fact threatened to resign from the party, a warning that Mr. Panday at first brushed aside but eventually chose to heed since a resignation would have upset the parliamentary balance. Maharaj's "asking price" for the deal was perhaps too high for Panday. Many in the party rank and file were also opposed, and were not convinced that the prodigal son *(neemakharam)* was in fact an electoral asset.[4]

Following the collapse of the proposed entente, Mr. Panday renewed his attacks on Maharaj. He argued that both the PNM and Maharaj were hostile to his efforts to unify the country. As he clearly put it:

> The PNM realised the philosophy of unity of our people was going to be a dagger in the heart of racism, and all those who depended on racism for political power.... It would appear that our efforts at uniting our people have taken a beating. Those in the party who depended upon the old system of living, started to get frightened. Those who

were looking for position of leadership started to get frightened. The party and the nation suffered when those frightened people left the UNC. We in the UNC have paid the supreme price for trying to unite our people. We lost the government, but we were not broken. And where are they now, they who tried to carry us back? They are in the wilderness, wearing sackcloth and ashes and living off of the locusts that sit on the plate of Patrick Manning. (*Guardian,* June 23, 2002)

As we shall see attempts would later be made to bridge the chasm, but these would also prove unavailing.

One of the controversies that erupted following the change over of Prime Ministers had to do with whether religious icons that were implanted by Mr. Panday at the official residence of the Prime Minister should remain where they were. Following his return to the residence, Prime Minister Manning had the *jhandis* (Hindu prayer flags) removed from where they had been implanted (Ryan 1999). This act was seen by the Hindu community as an act of disrespect and intolerance and as evidence that the Afro-creole or Afro-Christian community were not yet prepared to recognise that Hinduism and its icons were an essential part of the Trinidadian mosaic, and that room had to be made for them in the national iconic complex.

Mr. Panday accused Mr. Manning of the "worst kind of bigotry" and said he was "unfit to be Prime Minister in a plural society." "If the *jhandis* offended against your religion, would you not also be offended by those who planted the *jhandis*?" And if the people who plant the *jhandis* offended you, how can you be fair to them in matters of governance?" As Panday moaned further, "the *jhandis* were out of sight unless you were looking for these harmless flags. The mere presence of the *jhandis* on the compound of the Prime Minister's residence offended Manning. He is offended by the presence of somebody else's religion. I have never seen such bigotry in all my life." Panday nevertheless warned Manning that while "he may have uprooted the *jhandis,* what [he] does not know is that before I planted those flags, I poured *dhaar* (milk, flowers, coins etc.) into the earth. That is still there. The coins, flowers, and milk have consecrated the very earth into which those *jhandis* stood. Those coins are like eyes and they watch Manning everywhere he goes. They watch every move. I dare him to go near the mango tree. I dare him" (*Express*, May 25, 2002).

Sat Maharaj, Secretary General of the Maha Sabha also advised Mr. Manning that when Mr. Panday became Prime Minister in 1995, Hinduism and Indians generally had become mainstream. There was no way to erase that fact. We roast *baigan* (melongene) and make *choka* and we plant *jhandi, paan* trees and did pooja at the Residence at St. Ann's. No matter what happens, that cannot be replaced any more. Those are sacred Hindu grounds" (*Express*, May 31, 2002).[5]

In response, one PNM minister argued that the former Prime Minister should not have erected *Jhandis* or any other religious icon at the official residence of the Prime Minister, a state building, since by doing so, one excluded every other accepted faith in the country. As the Minister Regis chided the former Prime Minister:

> If you say rainbow, and you have opportunity, you should show the colours; if you failed to do so, then you have forfeited your moral authority to pronounce on approaches to piecing the colours together. That is my contribution to the debate. The *Jhandi* should not have been erected in isolation. That itself was a blatant disregard for unity, harmony, and diversity. (*Express* May 31, 2002)

Mr. Manning's response to the controversy was that he was a Christian, and that the display of Hindu symbols at what was now his home was incompatible with his religious beliefs and practices. He however insisted that no disrespect was intended to any religious group, all of which he tolerated. As evidence of his concern, understanding and sensitivity, he noted that he had not rooted out the prayer flags in a cavalier fashion, but had requested a pundit to do so after having done the necessary rituals. The counter comment to this assertion was that one was not interested in being merely tolerated; one wanted to be "appreciated," which was a more positive response to the fact of cultural diversity. Both Mr. Panday and the Secretary General of the Hindu Maha Sabha insisted that they wanted "respect" and appreciation and not passive tolerance, which they deemed condescending. Complained Panday: "I do not want to be tolerated by anybody in the rest of the society. I want to be appreciated for who I am and for what I am" (*Express*, May 31, 2002).

Interestingly, some reform minded Hindus, especially the Arya Samajists, argued that too much "fuss' was being made about the *jhandis*. In their view, the prayer flags did not have the imagined religious significance as identity markers which the Sanatanists deemed them to have. It was also observed that *jhandis* were rarely found in contemporary India. They were virtually obsolete. Some Christians and secular minded analysts however felt that Mr. Manning should have shown greater flexibility and political savvy by leaving the *jhandis*. The Inter Religious Organisation however deemed the Prime Ministers' handling of the matter "reasonable." To quote IRO President, Noble Khan, "as far as we know, it was handled properly, and within the protocol of the Hindu faith" (*Sunday Express*, May 26, 2002).

Endnotes

1. In respect to the Airport, 8 executives, 3 of whom were major financiers of the UNC, were arrested and charged for conspiring to defraud the Airports Authority of TT$19.7 million and to launder millions of dollars. In terms of the Inncogen inquiry, forensic investigations were undertaken to determine if any official benefitted from the onerous and fraudulent contract which required the state owned electricity generation company T&TEC to "take or pay" for electricity whether it was needed or not. The contract was supposed to be part of a package that would have led to the construction of 4 industrial plants which were to consume the bulk of the energy generated with T&TEC taking the remainder. The other plants were never built and were never intended to be. It was a scam to bypass tendering rules.

    In respect of the Biche School, the allegation was that the school was built as a political showpiece inspite of warnings from technical agencies and the IDB that the site was unsuitable. Mr. Panday was reported as having said: "Build the damn school" and then "open the damn school," so anxious was he to showcase his regimes performance (*Newsday*, March 2002).

    Allegations were also made about corruption in the Miss Universe Pageant which was said to cost TT$100m. Inquiries revealed that most of these allegations did in fact have an evidential basis and that very senior ministers were involved.

2. The Auditor General's Report into the procedures used in the $1billion pre-election National Road Paving Programme in 2000 and 2001 revealed gross irregularities and fiscal irresponsibility in the award of the various contracts. The Programme was facilitated by The Tourism and Industrial Development Company (TIDCO) and the state owned First Citizen's Bank, both of which had a common chairman. The Bank released $583.5m without proper

documentation being in place, inviting the accusation that it was being used as the source of a *"slush fund"* to facilitate the ruling party's reelection campaign. The Report revealed that work was executed and payments made before contracts were signed or submitted to counsel for vetting. Board or Ministry of Finance approval for the projects were also not in evidence, even though the contracts exceeded the $5m limit which was stipulated by the rules.

The Report also revealed that the projects involved huge overruns and that monies were diverted to other unauthorised purposes. It also revealed that moneys were arbitrarily paid to public servants as bonuses and for other unauthorised expenses which were not permitted under the rules of the public service and which exceeded their normal salaries.

Carlos John, the Minister of Infrastructure and Development who was responsible for the project, insisted that he had Cabinet authorisation for whatever he did and that he had done nothing wrong even if bureaucratic rules were broached. Boasted John: "I sometimes swim against the tide and I make no apologies for that. The way I run my business is procedurally [different] and can surpass anybody in the [existing] Cabinet in terms of how I do business, particularly in terms of delivery. I challenge anybody to say otherwise." John insisted that he would do what he did again if he was the responsible minister.

John also defended the payment of bonuses to ministry officials. "You cannot ask the officers to work beyond the call of duty and not be prepared to compensate them. I reward people for their performance." What was done did not constitute a "dangerous precedent."

Both John and the Prime Minister justified using TIDCO as the executing agency saying that it was their way of circumventing an injunction filed by a contracting company against the Central

Tenders Board, inviting the accusation that the Government was in contempt of court (*Newsday*, August 8, 2002; *Sunday Express*, August 4 2002; *Guardian*, August 6, 2002).

What the Report made evident was that the UNC was determined to provide evidence of "performance" even if all the rules were violated. The UNC clearly felt inhibited by the protocols and rules of the public service. Some saw their behaviour as evidence of "executive lawlessness" while others saw it as evidence of a new public management style.

The construction of a controversial desalinisation plant by a UNC crony was also savagely criticised. While the construction of the plant increased the available water supply to domestic users by releasing that which was provided to industrial users, the cost of production far exceeded that which obtained from the state owned Water And Sewerage Authority. WASA produced water at about TT$1 per gallon while that produced by the desalinisation plant was TT$ 4.50 per gallon. WASA's expenditure thus increased by TT $15.5 million per month. As WASA's CEO noted, "prior to desalination coming on board, we did not have to pay $15.5 million a month for that water so the revenue that we were getting was based on water that we were producing from our existing facilities which had a much lower cost. So, in fact, we have a greater burden on our accounts as a result of desal coming on stream. Prior to the desalination plant, WASA's revenue was between $32 and $35 million a month and its expenditure was $40 million. With the commissioning of the plant, WASA's expenditure is likely to increase to $55 million with its revenue staying the same. While contributing water to the grid, desalination has widened WASA's operating deficit to $120 million onto which WASA must add the cost of servicing its loans" (*Express*, September 11, 2002).

3. Speaking about the state owned oil company Petrotrin, Manning noted that employees referred to it as "Petrosingh." "When the UNC was putting its people there, they justified it as putting their

people in place. It was not a question of ethnicity or race."
(*Newsday*, May 20, 2002)

4. Mr. Gerald Yetming, the former Minister of Finance, accused
    Mr. Maharaj of betraying him and indicated that he could not
    bear to be in the same room with him. "He could not be trusted"
    (*Newsday*, June 2, 2002). Some MPs however preferred to leave the
    matter for the leader to decide. Others said they would relent if
    Maharaj apologised to them publicly. Team Unity member Trevor
    Sudama however opposed any move towards reconciliation. As
    far as he was concerned, both the PNM and the UNC were
    "locusts." "Some locusts prey on the tax payers and deposit their
    eggs in banks in London and elsewhere while there are other locusts
    who make holy gestures to distract people from their true
    intentions." Sudama accused both parties of practicing exclusion
    for the purpose of political mobilisation (*Newsday*, July 9, 2002).

5. Mr. Maharaj however applauded Mr. Manning's indication that he
    was giving consideration to replacing the Trinity Cross, the nation's
    highest honour, with a secular alternative that was more appropriate
    to the country's religious diversity. Mr. Maharaj noted that Mr.
    Panday did not have the strength to do it (*Guardian*, July 31, 2002).

Chapter 9

THE ELECTIONS OF 2002: THE SHORT CAMPAIGN

For most of the year 2002, the UNC demanded that elections be scheduled as early as possible. For obvious reasons, Mr. Panday wanted elections earlier rather than later, while the PNM wanted them deferred for as long as possible to give it time to undermine the UNC's electoral credibility in general and Mr. Panday's in particular. The PNM also wanted to make as much use of the resources of incumbency as were available to it. The leader of Team Unity also demanded that elections be held by October 8th, and went so far as to take legal action to force the Prime Minister to call them. Mr. Manning was accused of creating a "galloping dictatorship" in Trinidad and Tobago. Mr. Manning's response was that elections would only be called if Parliament was summoned and failed to elect a Speaker. This would mean that no budget could be presented, a development which would mean that no funds would be legally available to the Government to provide for salaries, goods, and services.

Not unexpectedly, the Court rejected Mr. Maharaj's application that it should declare the Office of Prime Minister vacant and that fresh elections be called. The Judge found no evidence of an abuse of process in the Prime Minister's retention of office after a Speaker was not elected in April 2002 and took notice of the fact that another attempt was to be made on August 28, 2002. "Dependent on what transpires, the House of Representatives may become constituted or the Prime Minister may be left with no practical choice but to call elections - a matter for his political judgement and strategy. The matters raised are premature, hypothetical and academic in nature." It was clear that the Court felt that the request was frivolous and that Maharaj was asking it to act unconstitutionally (*Express*, August 28, 2002).

The Prime Minister's response to Maharaj *et. al.* was that the Government would act within the framework of the Constitution. If a Speaker was elected, so be it. If no Speaker was elected, "crapaud smoke they pipe" (colloquialism "for they will have to pay the price"). Manning told his supporters that the PNM was "ready to take on all comers, collectively or otherwise. If it is elections they want, they would get it. But let us go to Parliament first.... The PNM is [committed] to properly governing Trinidad and Tobago" (*Newsday*, August 26, 2002). Predictably, Parliament failed to elect a Speaker and the President was advised to dissolve Parliament and schedule elections for October 7, 2002.

Five parties entered the fray, the PNM, the UNC, the newly formed Citizens Alliance led by former PNM Minister of Finance, Wendell Mottley, the Democratic Party of Trinidad and Tobago (DPTT), and the National Alliance for Reconstruction (NAR), which campaigned mainly in Tobago. Team Unity, for strategic reasons, chose to withdraw from the race. The leaders of Team Unity were aware that on its own, the party would make no impact on the election and had sought to forge alliances with any party other than the PNM. It quite rightly calculated that any alliance with the PNM would make it "untouchable" in the eyes of the Indian community which they still hoped to lead once Mr. Panday was off the political scene. Maharaj was however aware that he would have had a credibility problem if he rejoined an unreformed UNC. Thus his assertion that an alliance with the UNC could only occur if the UNC promised to investigate corruption, initiate systems for the equitable distribution of wealth and to prevent big business from manipulating the government (*Express*, September 9th 2002).[1] This was a price which Mr. Panday found to be much too high. Moreover, many within his team objected to reconciliation. By September, Mr. Panday had come to the conclusion that an alliance with Team Unity was not politically cost effective though he was still open to "listening to what anyone had to say." The collapse of the reconciliation talks with the UNC left Team Unity with the option of either contesting on its own, or withdrawing. Maharaj admitted that Team Unity could not win any seats, but did not want to be accused of again splitting the Indian vote. As he asserted, "if we contested, we run the risk of extending the deadlock" (*Express*, September 15, 2002). Thus the decision to stay out and play for the long run in the post-Panday era.

There was a great deal of chatter about the nature of the deadlock facing the society and what had to be done to break it. There were those who sought to deal with the problem by institutional innovations which they hoped would result in social retrofitting. Change the electoral and constitutional institutions and the society would reconstruct itself to accommodate the new changes. A variant of this view was that the institutional changes should reflect the social landscape: they should be made more relevant to the social realities of the society which was plural (or dual) depending on one's point of view. Whatever the prescription, the view was that the existing constitutional and electoral arrangements were dysfunctional and ought to be radically altered.

Some who held this view wanted yet another 18 - 18 tie. They believed that neither party could speak for a majority of the population and that a victory for one would traumatise the other to the point where the society could be destabilised. This view was articulated by the NAR and by some independents in the Senate. Senator Ken Ramchand spoke for this element when he said:

> ...if that [a tie] happens, the politicians may at last recognise that the country is calling upon them to form an integrated government, that is to say, a kind of coalition government truly representative of all groups and interest in the country. It is with such a government in place that steps can be taken to reform the Constitution and the electoral laws, and prepare for a form of governance shaped by the particular needs of the society and the people of Trinidad and Tobago. (*Express*, August 29, 2002)

Citizens Alliance

Another option offered was that of the Citizens Alliance which felt that neither the UNC nor the PNM had the legitimacy to govern. The Alliance profiled itself as something that was qualitatively different form the old line parties. It claimed that its politics constituted a break with the old divisive politics, and that it held a different view of government and governance. Mottley argued that Trinidad and Tobago had reached a sorry pass and that things had to be done differently, both with the economy and with respect to race relations. "Fear stalks the land, fear of each other. What a horrible place to have reached. There is decay in our institutions and in our society. Only Citizens Alliance [has] the hammer to break the padlock on the old deadlock" (*Express,* October 3, 2002). The Alliance argued that one must not deal merely with the symptoms, but the real underlying issues that contribute to things like crime ... we have to do something radical. We are too polarised and too politicised (*Sunday Guardian,* March 17, 2002). The Alliance promised that instead of being driven by the game playing of professional politicians, its "servant leader" would take its directives from the people. "Maximum participation would replace maximum leadership and the phenomenon of the 'safe seat.'" In pursuit of this agenda, Mottley held talks with all groups and parties. Many however noted that he spoke mainly to the UNC and reserved his critical comments for the PNM. Nearer the end of the campaign, Mottley did however speak out against corruption, which he described as "an acid that has dissolved our institutions... It has made the country virtually ungovernable" (*Newsday,* October 6, 2002).

Mottley's problem was that he could not decide whether he wanted to be seen as standing for something that was different, or whether he wanted to make opportunistic deals in the interest of winning a share of the power. UNC financiers, convinced that the UNC would lose the election if it went into the fray alone under Panday's leadership or in alliance with Team Unity, lobbied for a strategic alliance with Citizens Alliance. Panday was allegedly offered the Presidency if he agreed to cede the Prime Ministership to Mottley. It was also alleged that he was promised a generous financial settlement, (TT$25 million) if he agreed to the deal. The new grouping was to be called the United Citizens Alliance. Other parts of the alleged deal involved funding for Citizens Alliance to build up its image precedent to the alliance and a safe seat for Mottley (*Newsday*, August 24, 2002).

To many, Mottley seemed inclined to play the very games about which he accused others, his denials notwithstanding. Many were convinced that his initial thrust into formal politics and his advertising campaign was in fact funded by UNC financiers who hoped that if he made a credible showing early in the campaign, he might succeed in forcing the UNC political leader to agree to forge a strategic alliance with him. Whether true or not, the wheeling and dealing was costly for the Citizens Alliance. As *Newsday*, August 28, 2002 put it editorially, "an electoral partnership with the UNC will be seen as nothing but another of the old political games, a marriage of convenience arranged in order to achieve some political objective, in this case electoral victory."

Given the seeming closeness of the likely outcome, supporters of Citizens Alliance hoped that their party would make the difference. As Mottley himself put it dreamily, "all we have to do is to elect Wendell Mottley and perhaps win another seat or two, and Citizens Alliance will lead the government. I will seek to become Prime Minister in a government that will focus on new politics and new principles of transparency, accountability and character" (*Guardian*, September 21, 2002). Mottley was however not naïve, and clearly did not expect to "win" the election. Thus his talk of a "niche party." His hope was that Citizens Alliance might win about 3 seats and force one of the two major parties to bargain with him as James Mitchell did in St. Vincent in 1972. One recalls that following that election, there was a tie between the St. Vincent Labour Party (SVLP) and the People's Political Party (PPP), and that Mitchell, then an Independent, bargained for the Prime Ministership and secured it in a deal with the PPP. Few however expected the Alliance to win even one seat. Many doubted that Mottley had the "charisma" to mobilise the inert "none of the above" constituency. There was however concern that the party could draw away sufficient votes to hurt one or other of the parties in the marginal seats that were closely contested. PNM supporters feared that the Alliance would attract the mixed and white upscale middle class voters whom they hoped would vote for the PNM and therefore hurt it more than the UNC, a fact that led some to allege that the Alliance was a Trojan Horse.

Paradoxically, far from providing a predisposing environment for the success of a new third party, gridlock seemed to have made such a development impossible. Both ethnic groups wanted the tie broken in their favour. What was historically necessary did not seem to be politically possible or practicable. Mottley however claimed quixotically that Citizens Alliance had already "won" the election "by showing what politics ought to be about." He however denied that he ever proposed that he be made Deputy Political Leader of the UNC. "We are fighting the election alone." Mottley however complained that money was a serious problem for the party. "We are a new party. We do not have the power of the state behind us, nor long-established business associations as the other parties. But elections cost money, and we need money." The party's treasurer said they were soliciting donations of not more than TT$100,000 from individuals and TT$500,000 from corporations (*Newsday*, September 15, 2002).

Panday's Predicament

Whatever Mr. Mottley's hopes or that of the UNC moneymen, Mr. Panday had other thoughts. He told party supporters that he had indeed promised them that he would go at 70, "but I cannot leave without completing the task which I began some 36 years ago." That task involved "finishing the job of training and educating the people to fit into any kind of job in this world." His vision was that 75 percent of the children of Trinidad and Tobago would get a tertiary education:

> We have the brightest children. We could beat the best of
> the world with brains. The society I dream of for you is to

> develop our children intellectually so that Trinidad and
> Tobago will not only be a consumer but a producer of
> technology. (*Express*, September 26, 2002)

He could not withdraw "now, when the party is on the eve of elections. We want to win the elections from jail" (*Guardian*, August 7, 2002). Panday dismissed as rumor the claim that he had been offered TT$25 million to withdraw from the leadership. Some of the principal financial backers of the UNC had however concluded that Mr. Panday was an electoral liability, and that he should step down to make room for either Mr. Mottley or Mr. Dookeran, the former Governor of the Central Bank, both of whom it was felt, could "bleach" the UNC and attract the middle and upper middle sectors of both ethnic groups who were turned off by the corruption within the UNC in general, and Mr. Panday in particular. The UNC financial elite however had no choice but to go along with Panday, but they were not sanguine about victory, and donated much less to the party than they had previously done. Other UNC parliamentarians were also relieved, since many did not want to be led either by Maharaj or Mottley both of whom, they felt, carried too much baggage (*Newsday*, August 24, 2002).

Mr. Panday's political predicament took a turn for the worse when he was called upon by the Integrity Commission two months before the elections to account for moneys that were in an account in a London Bank (Acct. # 89036189 in the Natwest Bank in Westminster) which had not been declared as part of his assets as required by the Integrity in Public Life Act. No. 83 which came into effect in November 2000 as a replacement for the 1987 version. That Act required all holders of public office to declare their assets and those of their spouses and children under 18 years of age within 3 months of the assumption of office. The Act provided that failure to declare one's assets or the making of a false declaration constituted a breach of the law which was punishable by a fine of TT$250,000 or 10 years in prison. The offense was a summary one triable by a magistrate. The sums involved were said to be of the order of TT$5.5 million and information about its existence was secured *via* the British Government under a Mutual

Legal Assistance Treaty designed to curb money laundering. It later turned out that the regulations and forms for giving effect to the 2000 Act had not been made ready, and Panday thus had to be charged under the 1987 Act.

Panday gave a number of explanations as to why the account was opened, and why he had failed to declare the balances as part of his assets, not all of which were consistent. Panday first denied that the account existed, and then said it was his wife's money. He later said it was opened when he went to England for heart surgery in 1999 and that the balances, "a little money," were left to take care of his children's education. His basic claim however was that the money belonged to his wife and was put there to service the expenses of his children while they were at school in London. That function, he said, was performed by his wife, and was nothing unusual in Indian families. "In most Indian homes, the wife is in charge of such matters. Praise God for such wives!" His name was subsequently put on the account for convenience in case anything happened to Oma who was the beneficial owner of the money. "I did not regard it as part of my assets and therefore I did not indicate it as part of [my] assets to the Integrity Commission.... I make no apologies for caring for my family. If for that I must go to prison, then so be it" (*Express*, July 21, 2002).

Although a few UNC MPs affected to believe Panday's risable apologia, it was generally seen as an unbelievable "cock and bull story" put out to give him deniability. It was clearly an appeal for ethnic sympathy. Panday also sought to project himself as an ethnic hero who had been wronged by the PNM, whom he accused of colluding with The British High Commission, whom he claimed had sourced the information, and the Integrity Commission or elements close to it who had allegedly leaked details of deposits and withdrawals to the media. An examination of the account showed substantial deposits of £119,000, £150,000, £100,000, £60,000, £40,000, £25,000, £20,000, £10,000, £5,800, £5,000, and that the deposits were made between November 1997, a year after the UNC assumed office and October 2001, a few months before the election that was held that year. The deposits originated in Guyana, Trinidad, London and Canada (*Express,* July 21, 31, 2002).

What was revealing about Mr. Panday's various statements was that at no time did he indicate how his wife, who was known to be unemployed, was able to amass TT$5.5m in the six years when her husband, an MP, was earning an income of TT$1 million. One PNM MP described the feat as a "miracle of biblical proportions, one that rivals the feeding of the multitude with five loaves and two small fishes." Mr. Panday was savagely lampooned by the media editorially and by columnists (*Express,* July 26, 28, 2000) some of whom thought he was either "losing it,' or deliberately encouraging his followers to pull his chestnuts out of the fire by engaging in questionable tactics such as threatening to transform Port of Spain into the largest car park in the world.

Mr. and Mrs. Panday also felt the wrath of the calypsonian's lyrics. The attack on Mrs. Panday by "Marvellous Marva" was particularly savage. The lyrics of "Oma's Secret" composed by Kurt Murphy sum up the things the general public was whispering. The calypsonian wanted to know her secret for making money. Did she earn her income by selling Indian delicacies, winning the lottery or did she get it from her "nani," which could mean either her grandmother or through sexual work? The full text of the calypso is as follows:

"Oma's Secret"

When town hear de rumour,
John public was surprised,
Oma, Oma
Some swear is bout ten million,
somehow ah doubt de size,
Oma, Oma,
And gal, yuh know dem macco,
dey peeping now because,
Yuh husband who reveal it... de paisa, all is yours,

According to de bible, you are de perfect wife,
To save up such a bundle without wukking in life!

Chorus

So please tell me your secret, dear Oma,
Ah want to know you secret - eh Oma,
Yuh make it selling barra - Oma gal
Saheena with cucheela - Oma gal,
Yuh make it dancing chutney - Oma gal,
Yuh make it through yuh Nani - eh, Oma gal;
Ah want to hear yuh secret, dear Oma,
Why won't yuh share yuh secret, eh Oma,
Because so long I wukking, meh pocket have a hole,
Gal, tell me yuh secret, ah wouldn't tell ah soul.

Yuh husband he start crying,
de commission have a leak,
Oma, Oma
But how come yuh ent talking,
gal why you wouldn't speak,
Oma, Oma
If we had yuh answer, de nation wouldn't sink,
forget bout oil and sugar, for you are de missing link,
Maybe you were a model, you used to walk de ramp,
I disagree with Aloes, dis lady's not a tramp

Chorus

So tell me yuh secret, dear Oma,
I want to know yuh secret, eh Oma,
Yuh invest in stock market - Oma gal,
Yuh dowry, gal, yuh bank it - Oma, gal,
Yuh win it in de Lotto - Oma gal,
De mark yuh play was lolo - Oma gal;

So let me hear yuh secret, dear Oma,
Why can't you share yuh secret, eh Oma,
Yuh husband isn't Ishwar, yuh not married to Dole,
So gal come on and whisper, ah wouldn't tell ah soul!
Come do de dollar wine, like Oma,
Come make yuh dollar wine, like Oma,
No cent, no five cent, no quarter,
Only dollar, dollar, dollar, dollar, etc;

I hope I don't seem pushy,
I hope yuh husband name is Bas,
Oma, Oma,
They say yuh have duty to talk and clear de air,
Come clean and tell de country,
you earn it fair and square,
And on all dis paisa, you even pay yuh tax,
Doh leave no one to ponder,
we need to know de facts.

So let me know you secret, dear Oma,
Ah want to know de secret, eh Oma,
Yuh make it selling roti - Oma gal,
Yuh make it washing dhoti - Oma gal,
Yuh are a big exporter - Oma gal,
Yuh import rice from India - eh Oma gal,
Maybe yuh pawn yuh diamonds, yuh sequins,
all yuh gold,
Gal if ah learn yuh secret, ah wouldn't tell ah soul!

Team Unity

The members of Team Unity denied that they were responsible for the collapse of the UNC and placed the blame squarely on Mr. Panday's shoulders for refusing to discipline his errant financial "boys." As Mr. Maharaj noted:

> Mr. Panday has said I have caused his head to be in water,
> but it is Mr. Panday who immersed his head. Other people
> around him helped to do that. I was telling him that some
> of his financiers would push his head down in the water,
> but he did not believe me. He did not accept my advice.
> (*Sunday Guardian*, August 25, 2002)

Maharaj also chided Mr. Panday for not speaking out against
ministers and associates who plundered the Treasury. He openly
chastised Panday for turning a blind eye to corruption, knowing full
well that Mr. Panday could not take the high ground on this issue. As
he told a party meeting:

> Where members of a political party are perceived by the
> public to have done wrong, it is the duty of the party to
> investigate these matters and to give answers to the
> population. The party must condemn the irregular practices
> which the member was guilty of and must condemn these
> irregular practices in the strongest possible terms. That is
> what is meant by enforcing sanctions against such conduct.
> Where a member of the party breaks the law or the rules, he
> must be condemned, instead of being praised, especially
> where the member said he would do it again. (*Newsday*,
> September 13, 2002)

Maharaj said that he joined the UNC in 1990 as part of a "historic
crusade to create a society based on quality, honesty and high moral
principles and fairness, but that the party had "now" lost its way." Were
it to be provided with good leadership, it could however be a strong
party.

Team Unity's deputy leader, Trevor Sudama, also accused Mr.
Panday of bringing shame and disgrace to the Indian community, of
being a dictator, and of taking decisions unilaterally without reference
to the party. He was especially critical of the decision to move Carlos
John from the "safe" constituency of St. Joseph to the pivotal Tunapuna
seat in the hope that John would do what Mervyn Assam could not do

in the 2000 election. Sudama observed that dark clouds hung over the head of John as they did over Panday's, and that he could not evade the issue by claiming that no one had been found guilty. Asked Sudama:

> What is the perception? How long can we hide behind the legality that since there has been no conviction in a court of law there has been no wrongdoing? A former minister of government who had difficulty meeting his debt since 1995, had the colossal sum of $52 million pass through his account. A man of highest integrity, such integrity, second only to Jesus Christ. (*Newsday*, September 14, 2000)

Feeling ensnared, Mr. Panday countercharged that he was the victim of a "witch hunt" and blamed the PNM for persecuting him. He was however reminded that he had urged those who accused the UNC of corruption to take the evidence to the police. Now that they had done so, he sought to project himself as a helpless victim.[2]

The PNM also advised Panday that the charges laid against him had nothing to do with his ethnicity, but with the imperative of accountability. The PNM denied that it was persecuting Mr. Panday. It was the police and the Director of Public Prosecution's who felt that there was enough evidence to charge Mr. Panday, and had done so. The fact that the charge came in the middle of an election campaign was not relevant. Few agreed. PNM supporters however breathed a sigh of relief when the UNC leader was formally charged.

Mr. Panday's strategy for dealing with the corruption issue was to insist that he and the other eight persons who had been arrested and charged in the Airport scandal would be exonerated. As such, he demanded that he should be tried before the elections. As he told supporters, "I did not hide, I did not run. I co-operated with the police and the Integrity Commission. I am being attacked by wolves on all sides. They are doing everything to devour me.... I say to you now emphatically that there is not one iota of truth in the allegations that have been made against me and my colleagues. I do not want to be charged on November 27th, I want to be tried now, before the election"

(*Newsday*, September 25, 2002). "The last time when charges were over my head, we won the election" (*Newsday*, October 6, 2002). "My cell is reserved for me. I've been there so many times and I hope they have the same one for me. If they do, it is the first time in Trinidad and Tobago somebody is going to win an election from inside the jail" (*Express*, June 13, 2002). Panday, who was clearly courting political martyrdom insisted that only a "bullet" could stop him from fighting for the people of Trinidad and Tobago in general and particularly to ensure that the educational revolution which he envisioned was brought to reality.[3]

Panday claimed that the UNC left a booming economy, and an enormous inflow of jobs creating investment. "When we left office, the economy had expanded by 5.2 percent, poverty was reduced, inflation was lowered and foreign exchange was stable" (*Newsday*, September 11, 2002). Panday's bag of goodies for the election included a pledge that the old age pension of $1,000 per month would be paid from age 60 instead of age 65, a $1500 kickstart for every newborn baby deposited in the Unit Trust, but accessible only at age 18,[4] reduced duty on car parts, tax free supplies for taxis (tyres and batteries), a 5 percent tax cut on personal and corporation tax, reductions in VAT, fully developed land for the landless, and a traffic interchange for North South East-west traffic.

It was an attractive package, but the corruption issue refused to go away. Businessmen were known to have openly told him that the public's perception was that he was a "crook." It was in fact widely believed that much more was stashed away abroad than what was said to be in the Westminster Bank Account. It was alleged that he also owned a flat on Campden Hill Road in the posh South Kensington residential area of London in which his two daughters lived, and which was said to be a 1998 gift of the Ispat Steel Company. He was also said to own accounts and properties in the Isle of Mann, the Cayman Islands, Miami and Toronto collectively worth over US$100 million. Panday's wife was also described as "Kali Mai," and regarded as a bag woman of no mean competence and wealth.

Reports abounded that the US Drug Enforcement Agency was monitoring the movement of substantial amounts in various regional accounts. Under the Mutual Assistance in Criminal Matters Act 1997, the United Kingdom government was also known to be helping the Government of Trinidad and Tobago track down deposits belonging to various politicians and businessmen (*Mirror,* June 9, 2002; *Newsday,* May 24, 2002). In the pursuit of their inquiries, a transfer of £20,000 from the account of Carlos John to Mrs. Panday's account was discovered. John was at the time Minister of Infrastructure (*Express,* June 18, 2002). The transfer was said by a spokesman of John to have been sent to facilitate the resettling of John's daughter who was at school in London. Few believed that explanation.

Panday denied that he owned the flat estimated to be worth £800,000. A rental of £1,000 a month was in fact paid from the account, but investigators hired by the government estimated that rents for premises in that area for such upscale units was £1,500 per week, which was what the former renters paid. The allegation was that the rental was a formula designed to disguise true ownership of the flat which was managed by a blind trust registered in Guernsey in the name of St. Sampsons Management Ltd. (*Express,* May 20, 2002). The report of the investigators, which was leaked to the media, stated *inter alia,* that having regard to the fact that St. Sampsons Management Ltd. paid the annual Council Tax of £6,000, the real rent was in fact £500 per month, which was much too low to represent a bona-fide rental arrangement. The report also indicated that employees of the Ispat Steel Company were instrumental in helping Mrs. Panday "choose" the property and in effecting improvements to it (*Newsday,* May 26, 2002). The allegation was that the house and other payments made by Ispat were *quid pro-quos* for low energy costs paid by Ispat in Trinidad and Tobago.

Aranguez *vs* Macoya

Both parties waged an intense battle for the peoples minds and their vote. In its glitzy air war, the PNM told voters that they were the party of the saintly, and portrayed the leader of the UNC as the party of amoral crooks, plunderers, and kleptocrats who, over the past six years, had engaged in an unseemly and shameless scramble to sack the Treasury and transfer public wealth into their own bulging pockets. The bigger the project to which they pointed as evidence of performance - the Airport, Inncogen, the Desalicott, road paving etc. - the bigger the piece of cheese which they nibbled off for themselves. The PNM also projected itself as a party that had delivered on its promises to aged pensioners, the youth, steelbandsmen, public servants, students at all levels of the educational system, the poor and the unemployed. It had not only delivered, but had done so without becoming enmeshed in the web of corruption that was characteristic of the UNC robber barons.[5] The Party boasted that it did all that in just 8 months, and could have done a lot more if it had had the benefit of the extended term which would have been available had Mr. Panday kept his word solemnly given at Crowne Plaza.

The UNC for its part, claimed that it was a reincarnation of the NAR and had recreated the ethnic ecumenism of 1986. In his closing campaign speech at the Aranguez Savannah which he said should be called "National Unity Park," Panday remarked that while he might never lead another election campaign, he had no intention of abandoning his campaign for "true inclusion, economic justice for all, social conclusion and a better life for all…" He also claimed that whatever he had struggled for was not for Basdeo Panday, but for "the dispossessed of the country" (*Newsday*, August 28, 2002, *Express*, October 6, 2002). Panday seemed to be begging for understanding and forgiveness.

The UNC counter accused the PNM of moral self-inflation. It depicted the PNM as a party of "blunderers" and "mooks" whose historical record on the issue of corruption was blemished. What was more, far from being a party which had given the country the good governance about which it boasted, the PNM was accused of having divided the society along ethnic lines as it had never been divided before, of having governed dictatorially and lawlessly, of having spent billions without parliamentary approval, of having used the prosecutorial arms of the state to harass and victimize its political opponents, and of having installed known terrorists in the corridors of power. The UNC's strategy was to use attack advertisements to frighten the population, especially the Indians and the middle class minorities, with the spectre of terrorism and violence which it hoped would serve as an override to the corruption issue.

On the question of corruption, Mr. Panday's position was that it was not as bad a thing as alleged, provided the people got collateral benefits. As Panday put it, "they say we tief, but your child going to secondary school; 22 police stations built, though. But you have 4,000 kilometers of road, though; you could see water in your pipe, though." It was a cynical position to take which he hoped would buy him some badly needed support. The Deputy Leader of Team Unity, Mr. Trevor Sudama, did his best to prevent Mr. Panday from taking that escape route. He complained that Indians were paying too high a price for Mr. Panday's indulgences. Panday's actions, he moaned, had led to the "wholesale condemnation of an entire race," a fate which they did not deserve. Sudama accused Panday of giving people the impression that the entire ethnic group was corrupt, when only a few persons, many of whom were PNM imports into the UNC, were responsible (see Chapter 10).

While the aerial war was seen to be necessary to soften up the population, the political combatants knew that in the final analysis, victory would be won by the party that best mastered the "guerrilla" warfare that was being fought out in the darkened caves of the marginal constituencies. In this clandestine war, PNM supporters believed that the UNC had more guile than the PNM. It also seemed to have less scruple when it came to pushing at the limits of the rules. In the year 2000, it attempted "voter padding." In 2001, the strategy was "voter deletion." In 2002, it was "voter frustration." The latter reference was to the tactic of making frivolous objections to a large number (2,118) of voters whose names appeared on the preliminary list in marginal constituencies. It was a brilliant trick meant to frustrate the unwary.

Fortunately, it was detected and scotched by the EBC whose field officers established that the persons objected to did in fact live at the addresses given. The EBC refused all 860 objections filed in Barataria-San Juan, allowed only 53 out of the 345 filed in Tunapuna, and 165 of the 426 filed in Ortoire/Mayaro. The UNC disingenuously claimed that it's actions were preemptive and intended to counter what was being done by the PNM which it accused of padding the voters list. The UNC's ground war strategy also involved the massive use of money to bribe and seduce young blacks into voting for the UNC.

For its part, the PNM as the incumbent party, used the resources of the state to dispense patronage to encourage its potential supporters to turn out and vote. Mr. Manning was in fact quite open with his pledge to "look after his supporters." He told them that he had made an "error" while in office in 1991-1995. "The error I made was that I did not spend enough time thinking about you. I plead guilty. I'm a good student and I do not intend to make the same mistake." In short, while some might think him a "mook," he was not. Asked whether he felt the campaign was more racially divisive than any other as many believed, Manning felt that 1995 was worse. "This one was more subtle. The same games are being played, but underground. Every now and then you get a lapse from Mr. Panday, and he allows it to surface; but the fellas have become quite crafty. They're saying things to people, but you wouldn't see it in the newspaper (*Guardian*, October 6, 2002).

In response to UNC accusation that his government was giving "handouts" to young "dependent" minded blacks as part of its strategy of maintaining power, Manning noted that 40 percent of the population was living below the poverty line, and that no self-respecting government could ignore that. Manning argued that his social policy had two purposes. One was to target the poor, needy and vulnerable from depressed communities, both young and old, who were not benefitting from the gains being made as the economy expanded and who needed to be made more secure economically. The other goal was transformational. The need was to equip the young with skills and tools for self-development to get them out of "make work" activity. Thus programmes like The National Enterprise Development Company Ltd. (NEDCO), The Civilian Conservation Corps (CCC), Youth, Training, and Empowerment Partnership Programme (YTEPP), Social Help and Rehabilitation Effort (SHARE), Community Education and Support Programme (CESP), Youth Apprentice Programme in Agriculture (YAPA) and the Community Environmental Protection and Enhancement Programme (CEPEP). While the programmes were national in scope, the evidence suggests that they targeted young black youths who did not normally vote unless paid to do so.

In response to opposition complaints that elections were being delayed. Manning opined that the PNM stayed in office for as long as it did in order to allow the population to come to some conclusion as to whom they were, and what they were capable of if given an extended term of office. "The possible consequence of going to the polls too early would have been an 18-18 situation which would have been worse than what some people considered to be too long" (*Guardian*, October 6 2002). Manning was also calculating that the PNM needed the time to delegitimise the UNC as well as to put projects in place to attract and lock in the black underclass vote. The principal "fronts" in the war against the UNC were in San Fernando West, Ortoire-Mayaro and Tunapuna.

The Battle for Tunapuna

While all the marginal seats were closely contested, Tunapuna, for long considered a safe PNM seat, had become *le cheval de la bataille* in the past three elections. The seat, which straddled the "port" and the "plantation," and in which once lived the likes of Afro-creole notables CLR James, George Padmore, Sylvester Williams, and Learie Constantine, was ethnically mixed, but always had a larger Afro-creole population which normally returned PNM MPs. But the contests were at times close. In 1956, Constantine narrowly defeated Surujpat Mathura by a mere 179 votes (6,622 to 6, 443). The other votes were won by Afro-creole parties and an independent. Other PNM candidates who won the seat were Alfred Thompson, who defeated the DLP's

Rampersad Bholai, 6,690 to 4,901 in 1961. In 1966, Thompson again prevailed over the DLP's Ashton Chambers 5,134 to 3,901. The seat was won comprehensively by the PNM's Hector Mc Lean in the boycotted 1971 election. Mc Lean got 4,594 votes to 145 for Ashton Chambers. In the pivotal election of 1976, Bertie Fraser convincingly trounced both David Abdulah of the United Labour Front and "home boy " Tapia's Lloyd Best. Abdulah got 2,377 votes and Best a humiliating 1,131. In 1981, the PNM's John Scott again defeated Lloyd Best, 6,290 to 4,168, as well as Rhona Baptiste of the ONR who secured 1,642 votes.

The PNM lost Tunapuna for the first time in the 1986 electoral earthquake which changed the whole template of politics in Trinidad and Tobago. The NAR's Emmanuel Hosein gained 10,684, nearly twice as many votes as the PNM's John Scott, who secured 5,565 votes. In 1991, Eddie Hart regained the seat for the PNM, but only did so because the NAR and the UNC split the anti-PNM votes. Hart got a plurality of 6,872 votes, the UNC got 4,173, Hosein 3,266 and Ayegoro Ome of NJAC, 257. In 1995, Hart again won by a plurality defeating Mc Lean by a mere 244 votes. The NAR picked up 368 votes.

The message was clear. If the anti-PNM vote was solid, the tables could be turned, which is precisely what occurred in 2000 when Mervyn Assam defeated Hart by 336 votes. What the results over the years showed was that the constituency was an electoral "swinger," one of the few that was winnable by either of the major parties depending on turn out and who else was in the race. Both the PNM and UNC had assets that favoured them. Demographics favoured the PNM in that the mixed and Afro populations were in the majority by margins of approximately 14 percent. The UNC however compensated for this by having higher turnout rates.

It was also worth noting that while the constituency was one of those that most closely mirrored the national population in terms of ethnic composition, there were communities in the eastern part of the constituency that were heavily UNC and those in the centre and west that were heavily PNM, a fact that the electoral data made clearly evident. Those areas nearer the University of the West Indies on its northern side were more or less equally divided in their support for the two parties.

Both parties lavished a great deal of attention on Tunapuna and used every trick in the book, and some that were not, in order to prevail. Both claimed to be using "scientific strategies" to get out the vote. The main plan was to cut losses among voters who were not likely to offer support while devoting resources to clusters that promised to yield "ballot fodder" at the margins. The UNC, which was actively supported by the Hindu Maha Sabha, mounted a heavy campaign to register Indo-Trinidadian university students who were not ordinarily resident in the constituency in apartments belonging to a well known sports official. A determined attempt was also made by the UNC to frustrate and constructively disenfranchise legitimate voters by falsely claiming that they were either dead or had moved. The UNC made counter claims.

The PNM knew that it had to retain the seat to be in contention for Whitehall. The UNC likewise knew that it had to recapture it to avoid defeat, with all that this could mean in terms of the relationship of certain persons in its leadership ranks with the law. Thus Mr. Panday's decision to parachute so called "wonder boy" "honest" Carlos John into the constituency on the assumption that he would prove more attractive to the "rank and file" (translation - young black men) than the incumbent Mervyn Assam allegedly was. As Panday declared, "it is because Tunapuna is so crucial and so critical and so important, that I thought in my mind that I could not afford to make a mistake. That is the reason why I took the hard decision of asking Carlos John to give up his safe seat in St. Joseph and to give me a safe seat in Tunapuna. The future of this country will depend on what happens in Tunapuna on October 7, 2002" (*Express,* September 9, 2002). The UNC in fact conducted private polls before it decided to sacrifice Assam, who bitterly resented being cast aside to make room for a blemished John. Assam would later blame the UNC's defeat on what he deemed this "tactical error" on Panday's part.[6]

Panday had in fact made an error when he chose to parachute John into the Tunapuna constituency. There was a widespread view that John had won the St. Joseph constituency in 2000 and 2001 because of the appeal of his brash action oriented style to young black youths whom he had promised to look after. In fact, as subsequent events showed, St. Joseph had become a safe UNC seat, winnable even by one of its least telegenic candidates.

By placing John in Tunapuna as the UNC's "rabbit" in its attempt to win Afro-Trinidadian votes, Panday made it clear that he did not take the corruption issue as seriously as he ought to have done, since to many, John had come to objectify UNC arrogance and sleaze. John claimed otherwise, and proclaimed that he was a man of principle and of the highest public integrity, someone who was above board and could stand scrutiny. According to John, "I have nothing to hide. I have never taken a bribe. I don't know how to start" (*Guardian*, September 11, 2002). John also rubbed salt in the public wound by boasting that what he did in relation to the National Road Enhancement Programme, *viz.* violate several protocols of public sector procurement and governance, he would do again if given another bite at the cherry.[7] John claimed that his aim was to bypass the bureaucracy to get the job done, but that every tendering procedure was adhered to, a claim which was denied by the Joint Consultative Council of the Contractors Association who accused John of ignoring all their recommendations for competitive tendering and quality control (*Newsday*, August 18, 2002).

There were not many people who believed John's statement that he had nothing to hide, and that the TT$52m that flowed through his account in the years that he served as a minister was due to his astuteness as a businessman. That statement was disingenuous and only made sense if one assumed, as some obviously did, that politics is a business as any other, with perhaps one of the highest rates of return for any business in the world![8]

Both parties claimed that they had done what was necessary to win Tunapuna. Eddie Hart, the PNM incumbent, boasted that he had done a great deal to satisfy the needs of his constituents for water, roads, electricity, and other community services, and that the youths of the constituency were firmly behind him and unlikely to be easily won over by UNC largesse. Hart claimed that his main fear was that the elections would not be free and fair. John's claim was that Hart had done nothing for Tunapuna, and his boast was that he was an "action man" with an "action plan." He in fact brashly predicted that he would win the seat by 1,500 votes, failing which, he would retire from politics for having wasted the last four weeks of the campaign (*Guardian*, September, 13, 2002). As we shall see, John secured more votes than his predecessors had done in previous elections, but lost the seat nevertheless.

The Unholy Alliance

The PNM seemed to many to have come pretty close to "losing" the election before a vote was cast when Prime Minister Manning, seemingly quixotically, publicly indicated that the Government had agreed to settle the long outstanding "land" issue with the Jamaat al Muslimeen which had given rise to the latter's abortive coup attempt in 1990 (Ryan 1992). According to Mr. Manning:

> .... steps are being taken to make the entire parcel of lands at Mucurapo Road available to the Jammat al Muslimeen consistent with our decision in 1995 that the time had come to put an end to an issue which was a source of unnecessary anxiety to sections of the national community. [In 1995] we took a decision in a certain direction which we did not have a chance to implement. We are now back in the office, and the matter was still outstanding. Just as we anticipated in 1995, the matter led to great anxiety between the Jamaat and the Government. We thought it was time to put this thing behind us, to remove it from the national agenda.

Manning was roundly condemned by PNM supporters and called all sort of unprintable names. The hysterical reaction to the announcement indicated that the broad public, and the middle class in particular, were still profoundly traumatized by the events of 1990 and were firmly opposed to any deal which would have the land issue settled in favour of the Jamaat in return for any promise of electoral support. Phones and alarms bells jangled loudly nationwide. A majority of Manning's Cabinet colleagues, many of whom had not been consulted, also forced him to back pedal. The PNM leader eventually signalled that he got the message. There could and would not be any "unholy alliance" with Abu Bakr and the Muslimeen.

With a keen eye to what he fared could happen in the marginal constituencies where support for the two parties was believed to be evenly balanced, Manning nevertheless openly welcomed the electoral support of the Jamaat. As he declared:

> As a political party campaigning in an election, we solicit the support of all citizens in the national community, and if Imam Abu Bakr (leader of the Jamaat) and his group are prepared to support the PNM, I accept that, and 'am very pleased with it.

Told that it was alleged by the FBI and a US Congressional Report that the Jamaat al Muslimeen was linked to Bin Laden's *al Qaeda,* Manning indicated that he was the Chairman of the National Security Council, and was unaware of any such link. Even if the report was correct, he would nevertheless not refuse their electoral support. "In an election, you do not refuse any votes" (*Express,* September 21, 2002).

Clearly, Manning felt he could not risk alienating the Jamaat's support and possibly have them transfer that support to the UNC which was not beyond doing a mercenary deal with them as had been done before. Indeed, Manning's courting of the Jamaat may well have been designed to preempt such a development. In close elections, one has to win at the margins. Each extra incremental vote counts, especially if it is attracted away form one's rivals. His gamble was that the support gained in the marginals amongst young under class blacks would count for more than that which might be lost as a result of middle class hostility. Those who questioned Manning's logic felt that he was behaving like the proverbial dog which dropped the bone into the water which was reflecting that which was already in his mouth. He was accused of being "mad" and of "digging his own grave." Manning however noted that when the Jamaat openly supported the UNC in previous elections, he did not detect any equivalent alarm:

> When he [Yasin Abu Bakr] was supporting the UNC, I did not get the impression that there was all this concern. The Jamaat al Muslimeen has supported various organizations over the years. He has announced that he is supporting the PNM on this occasion, and we welcome their support. (*Express*, September 21, 2002)

Those who defended the deal argued, with merit, that the Jamaat had acquired prescriptive rights to the land under the squatters regularization programme. They were also the persons who had transformed what was essentially swamp land into valuable real estate. Both Manning and Bakr would later claim, inexplicably, that no deal had been entered into (*Express*, October 10, 2002) but there was clearly some sort of deal, and Bakr must have been told *via* back channels that given the likely electoral backlash, the PNM could not deliver on the promise of the land. Manning however publicly signalled that consultations would be held to see whether the Government and the Jamaat could arrive at some kind of settlement on the issue that was acceptable to all concerned, including the people of Trinidad and Tobago. As he put it, "giving the land is not a course of action that we can now pursue, and we'll do something else, and that stands."

Notwithstanding much noise that the land was theirs and talk about "betrayal," the Jamaat supported the PNM in the crucial marginal seats of Tunapuna, San Fernando West, Ortoire – Mayaro and San Juan-Barataria which they boasted they would win for the PNM. The UNC's claim was that in doing so, they harassed and intimidated voters, some of whom were prevented from exercising their franchise. That the Jamaat openly threatened UNC voters is incontrovertible. Bakr told UNC supporters that they should be "careful how [they were] voting because if you vote for the UNC, you going to get locked up. Everyone who votes for the UNC, [is] an accomplice to thievery; so you corrupt... Anyone is entitled to their political preference. I have no problem if an Indian wants to vote for an Indian party, but plenty people going to get lock up." Bakr also went on to add that he was going to see that certain changes were made in the country. "Don't worry," he boasted: "there is a new Minister of National Security ... I going to fix that" (*Guardian*, September 27, 2002). It was an idle boast. Bakr said that it was Panday who had alleged that he would be made Minister of National Security, and that he had merely confirmed his fears, but the UNC seized on it and used much of their campaign funds and platform time trying to convince the electorate that if the PNM were to win, Bakr, a "terrorist," said to be wanted by the FBI, would become the Minister of National Security.[9] As Panday warned "we will never know if he is effectively in charge of the Ministry of National Security."

Needless to say, Bakr denied that he was a terrorist, and saw himself as a patriot, a lawmaker, and a kingmaker as well.[10] "The Jamaat supported the UNC [but], they denied it was our support that made them win... they treat[ed] us real bad... if you know the things I [did] for Ramesh Lawrence Maharaj and Panday!" (*Guardian*, October 11, 2002). Panday accused the Jamaat of using "kidnap money" and muscle to campaign against the UNC. He in fact alleged that kidnapping was started by a "group of debt collectors," a clear allusion to the Jamaat. "When they failed to collect the debt, they kidnapped the fellas. That is how kidnapping in this country began, and the Government did nothing about it" (*Express*, October 14, 2002).

Panday made a number of other allegations designed to show up the close links between the PNM and the Jamaat. He claimed that the PNM had not taken resolute steps to collect the TT$15 million which the Jamaat owed the state for damages awarded to it by the Court, and that most of the short term pre – election jobs had been given to Afro – Muslims. Panday warned his followers that if the PNM came to power, it would share it with the Jamaat. "If Bakr gets control, you would not be able to practice your religion, have a free press, or travel freely abroad since the world is now afraid of terrorists." Panday predicted that the latter would call for their pound of flesh. As he warned, "payback will be demanded because greed has no limit."

We can never be certain how significant the Jamaat's support was, but one expected them to make exaggerated claims that it was, and that they expected to be paid back, as the UNC had in fact warned they would. Bakr in fact threatened that he would move against anyone who sought to block his efforts to secure the land (*Express*, September 27, 2002). Following the elections, there were many allegations about "payback," and it is clear that hundreds of young black Muslims were employed in the empowerment projects undertaken by the PNM prior to and following the elections. Many of the "community leaders" who organised the projects were Muslims. Hundreds of names of "ghost" workers also appeared on lists to be paid. Reports are that each "ghost" paid TT$200 to the influentials, many of whom were Muslims (*Newsday*, November 28, December 3, 2002).

One aspect of the Jamaat matter that caused controversy in the closing phases of the campaign was Bakr's claim that he had brokered a peace in the ghetto designed to bring to an end to the spate of kidnappings that was causing grave concern to the country generally, and to Indians, Europeans, and Syrians in particular. The latter groups felt that they were the chosen targets because they were business persons and assumed to be able to meet ransom demands. Bakr boasted that he had brought together rival gangs and community leaders who had agreed, *inter alia*, to stop the spate of kidnappings and other types of criminal activity which many in the PNM feared could cost the party the election. Given this, it was believed by some that the pact was part of a "land for peace deal." The Minister of National Security however denied that the abrupt cessation of the kidnappings was in any way the by-product of any deal with Bakr, and ascribed the halt to the work of the Anti Kidnapping Squad and not to any deal that Bakr had negotiated. The police also dismissed Bakr's claim that he had engineered gangland truce. Their view was that the pre-election lull in activities was due to increased police patrols and hard police work. Their prediction that "there never will be any truce between these gangs" would prove to be very accurate.

Gang warfare in fact increased dramatically in the weeks following the election (*Newsday*, October 10, 2002).[11] The Prime Minister however endorsed the claim made by Bakr that he had negotiated an arrangement that would reduce crime in certain communities, though he insisted that the agreement between the groups was a private one, and not between the Government and the Muslimeen. The Prime Minister in fact acknowledged that he had seen the agreement and welcomed it (*Express*, September 21, 2002).[12]

While all the facts on the Jamaat matter, are not yet publicly known, it is clear that the Political Leader of the PNM and some of his close political advisers believed that the Jamaat had a measure of influence over a group that they were courting politically, but quite incredibly, had not calculated that the deal would be made public by the garrulous Bakr who clearly saw himself as a "Don" in the Jamaican mould. As it turned out, the PNM may not have needed the Jamaat at the margins as Mr. Manning believed, since its supporters badly wanted "regime change."[13] The UNC was seen by them to be the "axis of evil," and not the Jamaat. The PNM did not therefore have to "steal" the election as Mr. Panday asserted. Many believed that the country and its regional and international reputation was in grave danger, and rallied to the PNM banner. It is worth noting that the PNM increased its share of the vote in every single constituency, and not only in those in which the Jamaat intervened.

Endnotes

1. Deputy Political Leader of Team Unity, Trevor Sudama, blamed his former leader for the proliferation of white collar crime which he claimed was having a "field day" under the UNC. He also charged that crime increased when Mr. Panday took over the National Security portfolio (*Newsday*, January 2, 2003).

2. Mr. Panday took note of Manning's ill advised statement that more UNC financiers would be arrested in the matters involving the Airport, a statement that provoked a stern rebuke from the Director of Public Prosecutions who insisted that he does not take orders from the Executive. Mr. Panday affected to believe otherwise. "It is not for the Prime Minister to determine whether people are locked up or not. But the Prime Minister's statement indicates that he is influencing who will be locked up. That is a clear indication…. He will either direct people to be locked up or influence those who give the people direction to cause people to be locked up" (*Express*, March 26, 2002).

3. Panday expressed confidence that if he was sent to jail, "the people will protect me, and if I'm not, then I ought not to be protected anyway." Panday said his supporters "are rational and reasonable people and know what they have to do. My instructions are: Do not engage in violence. If I am in jail, don't take me out; just do what you have to do" (*Express*, July 20, 2002).

4. Panday denied that the plan to give parents TT $1500 would encourage promiscuity. He noted that the funds would only be accessible at age 18, and would be available for tertiary education. It was intended to encourage saving.

5. Manning boasted that "my hands have been clean for all my 32 years as a Member of Parliament… The whole world knows that" (*Guardian*, October 6, 2002).

6   Panday was aware that the Tunapuna arm of the party was badly divided. He called on them to close ranks and heal the cracks. "Tunapuna is the best example of how to lose an election by division, in fighting and indiscipline" (*Express,* April, 2002).

7.   According to John, "I sometimes swim against the tide, and I make no apologies for that. The way I run my business... can surpass anybody in the [PNM] cabinet right now.... Particularly in terms of delivery... The cabinet approved all the expenses" (*Guardian,* August 8, 2002).

The auditor General's Report on the accounts of the NREP was full of details of gross financial improprieties in the multimillion project which was effected by TIDCO, and the state owned First Citizens Bank which advanced TT $538 million to TIDCO, and the Ministry of Works and Infrastructure (*Newsday,* August 4, 2002, *Express,* August 4, 2002). Moneys were paid to the 13 contractors before some of them had signed agreements or the worked assessed, all in the interest of executing the projects before elections some feared could might result in a change of government. One assumes that some of the moneys paid were rechannelled into the UNC's election campaign.

8.   John's account at a local bank, which was leaked to the media, revealed that monies totalling TT $52 million were credited to him and his wife in the 19 month period between June 1999 and December 2000. John became a Junior Minister in May 2000 and a Senior Minister in October 12, 2000. Prior to that, he was Executive Chairman of the Tourism and Industrial Development Company (TIDCO) which organized the Miss Universe Pageant and which also handled road paving on behalf of the Government. John argued that the monies in the account were proceeds of investments that he had made while employed with CL Financial, a private sector conglomerate, the result of hard work and prudent investments and not anything done since he took up public office.

Newsday, which broke the story and published photocopies of John's accounts sought an explanation from him. John's first reaction was to deny that he had ever seen that much money. When told that they had documentary evidence, John claimed that some of the deposits were loans and some referred to times when he was not in Government. Some were said to be proceeds of investments he made in conjunction with the Executive Chairman of Colonial Life Financial. The monies did not all remain in the account which led some to believe that John was a conduit. Mr. Panday dismissed the allegations as "PNM propaganda" (see *Newsday*, August 18, September 1, September 4, and September 11, 2002; also *Guardian*, September 11, 2002, *Express*, August 29, 2002).

The PNM savaged John during the campaign. As Mr. Manning declared at a campaign rally:

> Some of them are shouting from the roof - tops that they are men of integrity... Tell the nation how $52 million were deposited in your bank account in just over one year as a government official. Say where it came from and let the nation judge whether you are angel or scoundrel. And please don't say it's your wife's account. That has already gone down in history as the most scandalous utterance that any Prime Minister could make .... Tell us why your fortune only started to flow when you got access to public office. Tell us the secret of moving from bankruptcy to boom in two quick steps. The people of Tunapuna are anxious to find out about this amazing miracle. (*Newsday*, September 16, 2002)

9. It is well known that the UNC itself had a close working relationship with the Jamaat during the 1995 - 2000 period, and that the latter had played pivotal roles in the management of the Unemployment Relief Programme (URP) on behalf of the UNC. Panday had also suggested that the Jamaat should be given the

land. As he said in 1990, "let us give the Jamaat a deed for a piece of the land... we would have been heroes..." (Siewah *et. al.* 1991:462).

10.   The UNC candidate for Arouca North, himself linked to the Jamaat, denied that Bakr was a terrorist. As he declared, "in my dealings with the Imam, I have never found or seen anything which could make me consider him a terrorist" (*Express*, October 3, 2002).

11.   One of the gang leaders, Sean Francis, the so-called "don" of Vegas, Morvant, blamed pro-PNM elements and the Jamaat al Muslimeen for the killing spree. Francis alleged that a certain well known religious group wanted to control the entire East-West Corridor so that when elections were called they could "ring the bell and swing the vote." Francis, a former UNC election candidate, alleged that he was being targetted by the Jamaat because he "took millions of dollars from them" when he was running the URP programme on behalf of the UNC and gave it to the "people." He claims he cut out 7,000 ghost names from Laventille in 1997. Francis claims that the Jamaat was now in charge of the programme, and that thousands of "ghosts" had returned to the list in the run up to the October elections. Some community leaders were said to be taking home as much as TT$200,000 a month. "Is them who killing one another for greed. Is a NHA turf war going on in town .... Who feeding the "hood" control the crime, and these people will make the government fall. Crime have a propeller on it now" (*Express*, December 17, 2002).

Two weeks after making these statements, Francis claimed that he was shot at and harassed by the Police whom he accused of working closely with a "well known religious sect" (*Express*, January 5, 2003). Francis also alleged that the attack was "political" since the other party to the gang war was not raided. "My information is that the plot to kill me comes from within the PNM and the people in charge of the NHA and URP who have police friends" (*ibid.*).

12. The document was never made public. A Jamaat official claimed that it was not published for "security reasons." One needs to protect certain individuals since "some of them are felons. Some have warrants. They came in under the red flag. We have to guarantee their protection" (*Guardian,* December 20, 2002).

13. On the eve of the election, a former PNM activist flew in from the United States, held a press conference, seemingly with the assistance of the UNC, at which she declared that Prime Minister Manning had fathered her child, whom she had named Destiny, while on a fund raising trip to Miami. The woman denied that she had been induced by the UNC to embarrass Manning in the hope that it would cost him support among women. Given the mood of the Afro - creole electorate, the gambit backfired. If anything, it enhanced support for the PNM leader who had a reputation for not being sufficiently "macho" for a Caribbean electorate. The woman, Angela MacMillian, was virtually run out of town. She however denied that she was a UNC mercenary or mentally ill. She in fact claimed that she was not hostile to Manning, but did what she did because she was concerned about Bakr's growing influence on him.

Chapter 10

ETHNICITY, CORRUPTION AND PARTY CHOICE IN THE 2000-2002 ELECTIONS

Corruption is the
only constant in the Universe

- Salman Rushdie

Corruption is their only strength, their only
defence for the performance of the UNC.

- Basdeo Panday
(*Newsday*, September 3, 2002)

*O*ne of the more unfortunate things that happened to the Indian community during the various election campaigns was that many in the general community had come to believe that Indians as a group were either ethically challenged or prepared to tolerate corruption in the interest of maintaining political power. The wide spread complaint was that Panday and his cronies had severely embarrassed the Indian community and had tarnished the image which it had of itself and which it wished to project, especially in relation to its significant ethnic "other." Among the few who gave public voice to this sentiment was *Express* columnist, Indira Maharaj. As she wrote: "Panday is a lost cause, totally irretrievable. He is a political corpse and must be got rid of. Panday has outlived his usefulness; his historical possibilities having been fulfilled, it is time for the UNC to move on" (*Sunday Express*, July 28, 2002).

On the very eve of the 2002 election, a spirited denunciation of Panday and the UNC came from the pen of Dr. Anand Chattergoon, a devotee of Bhagawan Sri Sathya Sai Baba, which was obviously intended to sway Indian voters, perhaps those in the middle class. We quote extensively from Chattergoon's full page advertisement:

> Basdeo Panday and the United National Congress should take note of the fate that befell the evil King of Lanka, Rawan, and his demonic horde. Many of the Hindu members of the UNC seem to be ignorant of the spiritual principles and precepts of the Holy Ramayana. For God has said: "Rawan, the evil King of Lanka, ruled over a kingdom and his capital could compare well with heaven. But because of his bad qualities, he lost his own happiness, his Kingdom and even everything that he had. He destroyed his own dynasty and family. He knew all the codes of conduct of a King and yet he was behaving like a monkey. A leader of any sort should set an example to his followers and serve as an ideal to them. Trinbagonians must be ever mindful of and never forget what God-on-earth has said about the UNC regime: "Too much corruption from top to bottom!" Should the citizenry of a country vote for a political party that boldfacely and unashamedly employs corrupt means to achieve the desirable goal of performance? Panday's refusal to explain about his London Bank Account, Sadiq Baksh's disconcerting reluctance to appear before the Commission of Inquiry and to account to the population, Carlos John's explanation about the alleged sum of 52 million dollars, all amply demonstrate scant respect and scant regard for the spiritual teachings of supreme Spiritual Masters. (*Guardian*, October 6, 2002)

The UNC was accused of pursuing politics without principles. The statement ended with a clear Don't vote UNC incantation "May God… protect us all from ever having a Prime Minister like Basdeo Panday again (*Guardian*, October 6, 2002).

For those who could not bring themselves to vote PNM, other options were suggested by Ishmael Samad who entered the race as a candidate for the Citizens Alliance but had had his candidacy withdrawn because of his criticism of Panday. Samad's suggestion to the voters of Couva North was that they should spoil their ballot:

> Panday has rubbed salt into the gaping wound he has inflicted on the East Indian community, his very involvement being an act of obscene defiance against the shared morality that binds and holds our society together. The candidacy of Basdeo Panday is a calculated assault on the moral order. It is an act of contempt for all that we consider decent and right. It is an absolute abomination. I hereby appeal to the electorate of North Couva to cast their ballots in my favour as a mark of protest against the despicable behaviour of Basdeo Panday. It is the least they can do to remove some of the shame he has smeared on their faces. I shall not settle for less than 10,000 spoilt ballots. (*Newsday*, September 28, 2002)

These criticisms led some to believe that their was a strong silent majority which would disavow Panday and withhold their vote or vote for the PNM. Others however questioned the assumption that disenchantment with Panday was widespread among Indians, and that this would lead to a significant withdrawal of support for the UNC. They observed that inspite of the vigorous anticorruption campaign mounted in the 2000 and 2001 elections, the bulk of the Indian electorate remained with the UNC. Only a small critical fragment switched to the PNM, Team Unity, or abstained.[1] One could not therefore be sanguine that the pattern would be very different in the 2002 elections, even though the evidence that Mr. Panday had in fact been accumulating funds which he could not credibly explain had become more compelling.

There was much debate as to whether the Indo-Trinidadian community in Trinidad and Tobago generally or sections thereof had a different political morality to that of the Afro-Creole community and that their voting behaviour was evidence of such a difference. This controversial view was asserted by the author. As I argued, "the Afro-Creole model punishes leaders if they are politically deviant. The other tolerates them in the name of the tribe and sees virtues in their excesses... The current crisis is really a long-postponed collision of visions, epistemologies, of political cultures, indeed of worlds" (*Sunday Express*, January 14, 2001). This view was savagely criticized by several Indian commentators.[2]

Four broad responses to the question were forthcoming from Indians. One denied with a great deal of indignation the allegation that Indians in general and Hindus in particular were more tolerant of leaders who were corrupt than were other groups. In their view, the behaviour of the UNC political class had merely shown that Indo-Trinidadians were neither more nor less moral than their Afro-Trinidadian counterparts, and that neither could meaningfully criticise the other. Indira Maharaj in fact conceded that Indians could no longer claim the high moral ground as they did during the PNM era. "Indos and Afros now stand on the same ground, as it were." Another variant of this response was to say that both PNM and UNC political elites were equally culpable of having been corrupt while in office, and that one should not assign blame to either ethnic group for the crookery of the political class, whatever their political affiliation. It was also argued that the voting behaviour of the Indian community was not an endorsement of UNC corruption but a vote against the PNM which was seen as the greater evil.

Another view held that there were in fact differences between the two communities, and that Indians brought certain cultural habits with them in their "Jahagi bundles" when they came to the Caribbean which remained embedded in their psyches, particularly among the folk who live and work on the plantations and in the rice and vegetable fields of rural Trinidad.[3] This view was often expressed by middle class Christian Indians and upwardly mobile Hindus and Muslims who freely used the formally proscribed *"C"* word to describe those attitudes and behaviour which they found embarrassing in much the same way as creoles use the "N" word (*vieux Nègre*) with all its qualifying expletives to characterise gross and unseemly behaviour on the part of errant co-ethnics.

Yet another view held that there were indeed attitudinal differences, but that these were nurtured in the Caribbean as indentured immigrants sought to come to terms with the existing host society. According to this point of view, Indian immigrants encountered a hostile host society which they had to navigate and propitiate as a condition of survival and advancement. To do so, they not only had to work hard and save, but also to dissemble and engage in various kinds of deviant behaviour to make the great social ascent. What was once instrumental behaviour had now become a learned characterological trait, a *habitus* that was not easily shed.

This behaviour was however not peculiar to Indian indentured labourers. The same argument was advanced by American sociologists to explain deviant behaviour among immigrants into the United States. Robert Merton theorized that in societies in which pecuniary achievement was deemed to be an all important badge of success, ambitious people were driven to use any means necessary to achieve it. "The moral mandate to achieve success... exerts pressure to succeed, by fair means if possible, and by foul means if necessary" (cited in Lipset 1996:269). The temptation to violate the established rules of the game increased if the social structure and the dominant cultural norms of the society made it difficult for the aspirant groups to achieve social and economic mobility. The higher the hurdles, the greater the temptation to find ways to vault them. Seymour Martin Lipset agrees. "The pressure to succeed may lead individuals and groups from deprived social backgrounds to serve social needs through employment *outside* the law...." (*ibid.*: 270). These patterns of functional, but extra-legal behaviour, may remain part of the group's repertoire even after they are no longer treated as pariahs.

A fourth view on the subject took serious issue with the assumption that the *whole* Indian community was prone to extra-legal behaviour. Those taking this position included former UNC Minister, Trevor

Sudama, who asked whether Indians were the only immigrant groups who resorted to extra-legal behaviour to cope with marginalisation in colonial society (see "Ethnicity and Corruption," *Newsday,* September 8, 2002). And it is a matter of record that Afro-Trinidadians and Afro-descended persons from the Eastern Caribbean inhabited an underworld in urban Trinidad in which they had to flout the law and established norms in order to survive and get ahead. The calypsoes of the era have detailed the various ways in which these elements sought to deal with their exclusion from established society and harassment by the forces of law and order.

But while some of what was said about the deviant behaviour of the Indian community was also true of "Afro-Creole" elements in an earlier era, the Indians were the last to seek to cross the social borders into the dominant creole host society and the hurdles were higher than that for earlier immigrant groups. The methods used to do so inevitably came to be viewed as being more questionable and less acceptable, in part because their religious and other cultural patterns of behaviour were sharply different from those of the host group. Whether correctly or not, the general society perceived that there were two codes of behaviour, the Afro-Saxon and the Indian with that belonging to Indians being viewed as being "oriental," "pagan" and unchristian.

Needless to say, there was much stereotyping, and members of the entire group were stigmatised when only some exhibited deviant and anomic patterns of behaviour. It is however quite normal for a group to be labelled in accordance with behaviour displayed by a criminalised subset. Thus the fervent attempts on the part of others in the group to disassociate themselves from the deviants, and to do what they hoped would purchase them acceptability by the established elites whom they used as their points of reference. All pariah migrant groups behave in this way, though the patterns of behaviour may differ.

While corruption is a global phenomenon that transcends all cultures, there is little question that its incidence is greater in certain societies than in others, and that at certain times, it is more virulent than at others. The behaviour of leaders is crucial in setting the tone of the regime. If they condone gross corruption or are seen to be participating in it, others assume that it is legitimate for them to follow suit. In Trinidad and Tobago, the incidence, scale and ubiquity of corruption was greater under the Panday regime than it ever was under the PNM, and Mr. Panday's own behaviour contributed mightily to what occurred. Instead of policing the feeding pond, and closing it down, he seemed to have been the baddest shark therein. This was clearly seen in his refusal to rein in the greed of those who build or benefitted from contracts to built the new Piarco Airport, persons whom his Minister of Transportation later described as "maggots who were feeding on the Treasury."[4]

But Who we go Put?

During the three elections, UNC supporters generally claimed that the PNM had been corrupt during its period of ascendancy between 1956 and 1988 and that Afro-Trinidadians continued to support the then ruling party rather than the opposition or any of the third party alternatives that appeared on the scene from time to time. The elections of 1981 were often cited as evidence that Afro-Trinidadians also condoned corruption, given the way they voted. Afro-Trinidadians were indeed equally cross pressured 20 years ago when they had to decide whether to vote for the PNM, the Organisation For National Reconstruction (ONR), or the United Labour front (ULF). The problem however began long before 1981. Many Afro-Trinidadians had become openly critical of the PNM in the sixties, and had left its ranks for Tapia, the Liberals, National Joint Action Committee (NJAC), the Democratic Action Congress (DAC) and the ONR (Ryan 1972). Many however stayed with the PNM, asking rhetorically, "but who we go put?"

It was widely believed that with the death of Dr. Eric Williams in 1981, thinking PNM supporters would consider themselves absolved from their feeling of loyalty and gratefulness to him and vote for the morality in public affairs and good governance platform which the

PNM had abandoned and which was now being offered by the ONR. The electoral data show that many of them did so. The ONR secured 91,704 or 22.08 per cent of the votes. The PNM was nevertheless returned to power with an increased majority in terms of seats won. It won 26 seats even though it lost the two seats it previously held in Tobago. ONR leaders and their supporters were aghast. So too were ULF supporters. Both parties felt that the PNM had stolen the election and that the Afro-creole electorate had voted for continued corruption. But did they? Were there other factors which help explain the way in which they exercised their franchise? Could UNC supporters use 1981 to justify voting for the UNC on the ground that all governments steal?

ONR leader, Karl Hudson-Phillips, was stunned at his party's loss, and blamed this on systematic electoral fraud and bribery. According to Hudson-Phillips, "the government was not properly and fairly elected and therefore does not represent the will of the majority. It is a most dangerous situation for democracy in Trinidad and Tobago. The same inefficiencies and corruption will now continue unabated." Similar broadsides were issued by the late Dr. Patrick Solomon and Lloyd Best. Best whinged that "the country had returned to power the party which had governed us to the brink of revolutionary upheaval in 1970, which had been squandering a gigantic fortune of petrodollars since the end of 1973, and which by its errors of omission and commission, had converted our country into a virtual slum, into a den of ·corruption, indiscipline and immorality, into a desert of desperation and despair." ULF spokesmen echoed Best. Sparrow immortalised the feeling of despair felt by those opposed to the PNM whose supporters he said knew what was going on, but "liked it so." ONR supporters were told to take their party's symbolic "steel beam, and go."

But was that a fair comment about the mindset of the PNM voter in 1981 as UNC supporters claimed? Does 1981 provide a pretext for what they were minded to do 20 years later? The PNM's victory in 1981 was due to several factors. One was the "fraid Karl factor," the then equivalent to the "fraid Ramesh [Maharaj] factor" of 2001. Karl's image as an authoritarian leader of the ONR frightened many potential dissidents back into the waiting arms of George Chambers. The PNM had also waged a brilliant campaign. As Anthony Smart, then ONR secretary admitted, "the PNM fought well and won well. Their strategy was first class." As Smart also admitted, "the ONR's image was that of a brown skin socially upscale party. The ONR in fact never succeeded in penetrating the PNM base." It in fact never had a base. Plenty icing! Not enough black cake(!), a fate that had befallen all its predecessors, from the Liberal party to Tapia.

But the PNM's true trump card was George Chambers who succeeded Eric Williams as Political Leader of the PNM. Chambers stunned all by the excellence of his political generalship. His most brilliant thrust was to pose as a PNM reformer, someone who had come to clean up the mess that Williams and some of the PNM stalwarts had made. The "party was over," he told PNM supporters. It was back to work! He also promised to put right that which was wrong and keep right that which was right. Many who loved the PNM but who had left it out of scorn or hatred for Williams and his clique chose to run back to the old church which now seemed to have acquired a new presbyter.

The pro-PNM vote in 1981 did not represent an endorsement of freeness and corruption. That was a canard spun by the ONR/ULF myth makers to explain their comprehensive defeat, one that was being repeated in 2001-2002 by UNC apologists. Dianna Mahabir came closer to the truth when she wrote in 1981 that

> It is something of a disappointment to be greeted so often with bitter public statements, that by voting the PNM back in power, the public had voted for continuing corruption. The public have made it quite clear that change is necessary .... It is perhaps the insistence of the Prime Minister that we were going to have to get down to work, restore values of family life, tolerance, understanding and discipline that resulted in the PNM winning the election. It would be more accurate to say that by putting the PNM back in power, the public was indicating its belief that George Chambers has

the strength and the ability to effect those changes that
everybody wants. Whether that belief is justified, the next
five years will show. (See Ryan 1989: 287)

Chambers however failed miserably in the mission on which he
had embarked. The vested interests in the PNM and the wider society
were too powerful to be readily overcome. Thus the popular revolution
of 1986 which saw more than half of the PNM going over to the
NAR which was promising to do what Chambers hoped to do, *viz.,*
clean out the Augean stables of the nation. The UNC too had made
lavish promises on this score while in opposition, and by all standards
it fared even worse than the Chambers PNM.

It cannot however be asserted that by voting for the UNC in 2000
and 2001, Indians generally were condoning corruption among their
leaders though many clearly saw nothing unusual about what they did
or went into denial. The fact that they stained their fingers did not
mean that they were staining their characters. Many held their noses
and voted UNC because they saw the PNM as the greater of the two
evils. When people vote, they compress into one act a complex mixture
of opinions, practices, attitudes, and values. All of these form part of
a continuum. Opinions and practices may change in relation to contexts
and conjunctures. Attitudes and values are more stubborn, more abiding.
For many, though not for all, voting PNM or UNC was something one
did automatically or mindlessly, irrespective of the issues, or the opinions
one holds about the leadership and its probity or otherwise. For most,
it is an act of tribal affirmation, a way of life. This is especially so for
those of a certain age. It's the floaters or migrant voters who often
make the difference to the outcome of elections, the persons who give
flexibility to the system that we proudly proclaim as democratic.

Endnotes

1. Christian Indians in assembly type churches were openly and bitterly accused of sacrificing their ethical principles on the altar of tribal hegemony. In a full page advertisement, Pastor Amresh Semurath told Christians that as they contemplated their choices, they should keep the following in mind:

   > No pastor has the Biblical authority to dictate to you your political preferences and choices. No pastor must be allowed to lord it over your conscience and tell you who to vote for.

   > Your choice of political leader and party is not a question of right or wrong. If it was then, as a Christian, the dilemma you would face would be unsolvable and you would be forced to abstain from voting. Despite the perceptions that are begin created, there are no Christian (righteous) political parties in this country. Your choice is not between Christian (African) PNM and Hindu (Indian) UNC. Your choice is between PNM, UNC, CA and whatever else.

   > Your choice of political leader and party is not Biblical grounds for proving the genuineness of your Christianity. As a Christian, you should never think nor make the statement, "I can't understand how any Christian can support such and such a political leader and party" ("In Defense of Christian Indians," *Express*, September 27, 2002).

   It is clear that the campaign had created divisions in evangelical which had mixed memberships.

2. See Kevin Baldeosingh's, "Culture Trash," *Express*, January 25, 2001. Also Ken Ali, "Corruption, Sparrow and Ryan," *Mirror*, January 26, 2001.

3. In writing about Haitians, Melville Herskovits noted that they were characterized by a "socialised ambivalence." They inherited a dual cultural system that was part French and part African. The two traditions were often in conflict and had to be reconciled. The result was a bifurcated moral sense, one that was reserved for the family and another for the public realm (cited by Anthony Manigot 1996).

4. Evidence tendered by former UNC Minister of Transport, Jerlean John, made it all too clear that the new Piarco Airport was regarded as a "milch cow" by certain UNC financiers. John told the Commission of Inquiry that certain people acted as though they had an open cheque book to spend TT$1.6b, and that had she not tried to put a stop on it, the project would have cost TT$1.9b. "There seemed to be no fixed budget. It was basically a moving target and anybody could say we wish to do this or that, and it would be accommodated. People were just going and having meetings with whom they wished.... The greed was so palpable, it felt nasty." John estimated that change orders led to a 40 percent escalation in costs. Millions were saved when she insisted that modules of the project had to be tendered (*Guardian*, February 5, 6, 7, 2002; *Express*, 6, 7, 2002; *Newsday*, February 7, 2002).

    John told Panday that the project was indisciplined and without a fixed plan, and that too many persons were making self-regarding decisions. He acknowledged that the project was a "milch cow," and that there was a "feeding frenzy," and promised to disband the inter-ministerial committee which was managing the project. He also promised to provide security for John who complained that persons were threatening her. Panday however did not do much to stop what was taking place, and certainly did not discipline the ministers involved. Another witness, Noel Garcia, former chairman of NIPDEC and project manager of the Airport, also testified that he advised Panday about overbilling on the Airport project and other irregularities, but got nothing from him but promises to look into the matter. Garcia was subsequently relieved of his post as general manager (*Newsday*, September 4, 2002).

Chapter 11

ANATOMY OF AN ELECTION

> If you see me and a lion fighting,
> feel sorry for the lion.

> *- Basdeo Panday*

I

*T*he 2002 election was one of the most pivotal and stressful that the country had faced, and many prayers were offered up on behalf of the parties. Many saw it as a watershed election which would serve to determine the shape, the ethos, and political structure of the society for many years to come. The country was seen to be in a state of political emergency. Lloyd Best was among the few who did not agree that the election was pivotal. In his view, all Caribbean elections have been spectacular non – events which decide little. He however conceded that the 2002 election might well have been "the most sensational we've had in recent times even if there was no case for regarding it as the most important for the longest while" (*Express*, October 19, 2002).

Persons belonging to the cores of the two major ethnic groups had a vital stake in the outcome of the election. The UNC wanted to regain political power which it believed the President had illegally denied them. Black supporters of the PNM wanted the party to maintain its hold on power out of fear that a UNC victory would lock them out of power forever and that they would in time become a permanently marginalised underclass. Many supporters of the UNC were cross pressured. As noted in Chapter 10, they were ashamed of the involvement of their party's top leaders in corruption, but did not want to risk a return of the PNM. It was difficult for such persons to vote across family and community tradition. For many, voting was not merely an instrumental act, but one that was full of symbolism. Aisle crossing constituted "deviant" political behaviour which was difficult unless sustained by community supports or allegiances such as were provided by a change of religion, ideology, political affiliation, attachment to a cause of some kind, a change of residence or family identity. For many, voting decisions were not made on the basis of issues that were "rational," but in accordance with deeply embedded values. People vote "in" elections, but often do so on the basis of events that have occurred in the distant past. One voted automatically the way the herd and its validating elites "instructed" one to.

Even though the elections were expected to be a cliff hanger, and another tie not ruled out, the PNM was convinced that it would win. Most of the polls, SARA in particular, were predicting a likely PNM victory in at least three of the five marginals. Turnout and enthusiasm at PNM meetings were also clearly greater than in previous years, and comparisons were even made with the "one-love elections" of 1986 which had witnessed the 33-3 defeat of the PNM by the NAR. Young black voters were also very much in evidence at PNM meetings, and it was clear that that cohort was going to play a crucial role in the outcome of the election.

The figures tell the story. Some 70 percent of the electorate voted, the highest since 1961 when 88.11 percent of the electorate cast its vote. In 1995 and 2000, only 63 percent did so. One should however note that the total electorate had been reduced by 97,815 due to the pruning exercise which had been carried out in 2001. The PNM won 20 of the 36 seats, up from 18 which it had in 2001, and garnered 308,807 votes, an increase of 47,457 over that which it obtained in 2001. It was the largest number of votes which the party had ever received. In percentage terms, the ruling party obtained 50.7 percent of the votes cast, compared to the 46.2 which it had secured in 2001, a gain of 4.5 percent. It was the first time that the party had secured an absolute majority since 1981. The PNM also increased its share of the vote in every single constituency, including those controlled by the UNC, in some cases substantially. The percentage turnout in seats won by the PNM likewise increased from the 60.7 percent obtained in 2001 to 64.3 percent in 2002. The percentage increase in PNM votes in PNM held seats was 4.67 percent, from 68.6 percent in 2001 to 73.2 percent. The number of votes cast for the PNM also increased by an average of 1,575 in PNM seats, and 1,127 in UNC seats. Increases were substantial (over 1,500) in 11 constituencies.

Despite losing two pivotal seats, Ortoire-Mayaro and San Fernando West, and notwithstanding the anti-corruption campaign, the UNC increased its support nationally by 4,870. It received 283,656 votes compared to the 278,786 votes received in 2001. The percentages were 46.59 and 49.72 respectively, a loss of 3.15 percent. It should be noted that the UNC did not contest the Tobago East seat as it did in 2001. If one omits the two Tobago seats, neither of which the UNC contested, the overall PNM majority drops from 25,151 to 11,719, and the UNC percentage increases to 47.64 percent. The percentage turnout in UNC held seats increased from 69.4 percent to 72.7 percent, due mainly to the increase of support for the PNM in those constituencies. The percentage voting UNC in fact fell from 70.1 percent to 69.8 in UNC seats, a loss of 0.3 points. The percentage voting UNC fell from 27.5 percent to 24.2 percent in PNM controlled seats. The UNC also lost votes in 14 of the 34 Trinidad based constituencies. The PNM on the other hand gained in all 34, as well as in the two Tobago constituencies.

It is however in the 5 marginal seats that the battle was joined. As noted, both parties treated these constituencies as principal battle grounds and between them registered 5,440 new voters. Given the intense competition between the parties in these constituencies, it is not surprising that turnout was high for both parties. The average percentage turnout in the marginals increased from 73 percent to 77.3 percent, with a high of 80.4 percent in Ortoire-Mayaro. The average number of PNM votes in the marginals increased by 1,348 with an increase of 1,395 in Tunapuna, 1,331 in St. Joseph, 1,281 in San Fernando West, 1,143 in Barataria-San Juan and 1,592 in Ortoire-Mayaro. Interestingly, the UNC also increased its average vote by 590 in the marginals, and in Tunapuna by 985 votes, by 383 in Barataria-San Juan, 455 in Ortoire-Mayaro, 598 in San Fernando West, and 528 in St. Joseph. Of equal interest is the fact that a mere 565 votes (318 in Ortoire-Mayaro and 247 in San Fernando West) separated the UNC in these two constituencies. The result could thus have gone either way.

There was some concern that the focus on the 5 swing constituencies would have led to a decrease in voter turnout in the other 31 constituencies. The fear was that voters in the others would regard themselves as "orphans" and conclude that the election had nothing in it for them. This was not the case. Overall voter turnout was higher in every constituency than it was in 2001, but more so in constituencies won by the UNC by a margin of 8.4 (72.7 to 64.3). Turn out was however higher in the marginals than it was in the non-marginals by 9 percent 77.3 to 68.3 percent.

The Citizens Alliance, the party that had hoped to make a difference in the marginals, fared worse than many expected. All of its candidates, including its leader Wendell Mottley, lost their deposits. Mottley received a mere 734 votes in Port of Spain South, less than the 1,693 received by the UNC and the 9,080 received by the PNM. It was a slaughter. Only the candidate who contested the Diego Martin West Seat made a credible showing. He secured 1,267 votes, most of which came from the white/off white community which is heavily represented in the area. The Alliance as a whole only secured 5,955 votes. While the Alliance did not expect to win, it must have been mortified about its derisive support. It would nevertheless claim that its campaign raised the tone of the elections.

Reactions to the Outcome

The leaders of Team Unity felt that the country had handled the elections well, but that the results indicated that the country was split down the middle. As such, the deadlock crisis remained unresolved. As the party declared:

> The wounds which had been created during the campaign and the polarisation which has resulted from the electoral events of the past years must be healed. Very few countries with plural societies like Trinidad and Tobago and so polarised at election time as our country was during the campaign have the strength and capacity to produce peaceful elections. This is a tribute to the people of our country in not allowing ethnic and emotional considerations to hamper or disrupt this very important democratic process. (*Express*, October 9, 2002)

The PNM and its leader were pleased with their victory, but were generous in their post-election statements. Mr. Manning declared:

> We worked hard in the wilderness in the days between 1995 and 2001. We fought a formidable enemy. Today we take our victory directly from the people of Trinidad and Tobago so that we can no longer be accused of being a selected government. We are an elected government. Normalcy has been restored ... we now have a clear winner ... and a strong government to take us through the next five years and possibly beyond. I have no doubt that future generations will judge us favourably and will draw inspiration from the mature equanimity displayed by the nation in the face of an unusual political experience. Victory belonged to Almighty God. We fought a hard battle on both sides. But that battle has come to an end. Let us put the election differences behind us and move forward as one country. Remember, we all must live here together. Let us do nothing in our celebrations that would cause pain to our brothers and sisters. (*Express*, December 25, 2002)

Manning was also full of praise for the youth who supported the PNM in the elections. He however expressed concern that the election had revealed that the society remained segmented:

> We are not as terribly segmented as many other societies, but there can be no gainsaying that, as a nation, we have some distance to go, and that our social fabric is not as well - knitted as it should be. (*Express*, October 21, 2002)

Mr. Panday was also statesmanlike in his election night response to the results which he said indicated that an 18-18 tie again seemed likely. In saying so, Mr. Panday seemed to have decided to spare his followers the agony of defeat - at least for the time being. Panday praised the protective services and the Elections and Boundaries Commission which had "stuck to their guns and did all in their power to give us a free and fair election." He urged the nation to put aside all differences and to unite "since tomorrow we would all ride the same maxi taxis. We will all be walking shoulder to shoulder across the nation... Let the Ganges meet the Nile and the Nile meet the Yangtze - Yang. Let the rivers and the tributaries all over Trinidad and Tobago unite to form a mighty force...."

Panday also had some words for the President of the Republic on the question of what should happen if a tie were indeed to occur:

> If the elections turn out to be 18-18, as it seems to be, the President is faced with the same dilemma as the last elections. I am confident that he is wiser now as to the realties of our sociology, our morality, our values and our constitution. The logical option would be to bring together the competing parties in a government of national unity pending constitutional reform and fresh elections under a new constitution. Trinidad and Tobago must return to Parliamentary government immediately. We must return to normalcy and to peace. We must set the date now for fresh elections under a new system. We await his Excellency's guidance. (*Newsday*, October 9, 2002)

The statesmanlike statement barely concealed Panday's bitterness, and ere long, it was adversarial politics as usual. Mr. Panday in fact never conceded that the UNC had lost the election. In his view, it was stolen by the PNM and the Jamaat al Muslimeen, their partners in an "unholy alliance." To quote Mr. Panday, "this country knows that we did not lose the election. It was stolen from us by an unholy alliance of the PNM and Abu Bakr's Jamaat ... who terrorised UNC voters before, during, and after the election." As we have seen, the Jamaat did urge young blacks to vote for the PNM and did in fact attempt to prevent some UNC supporters from casting their ballots in the marginal constituencies. It does not however appear that that intimidation was as electorally significant as Panday charged. Panday claimed that the UNC did not retaliate against the Jamaat's tactics because it was not prepared. All it did was complain to the Police, who did not believe that the allegations had much substance. One of the Jamaat's declared objectives was to deter persons whom it believed would try to vote illegally.

Panday also alleged that the PNM bribed the electorate with billions of dollars worth of state resources. Young blacks, "persons born and bred in the syndrome of dependency," were said to have been paid $100 a day for several weeks to do nothing except vote for the PNM (*Newsday*, October 14, 2002).[1] Some were said to have been billeted and registered in the Tunapuna constituency before the election. State agencies, including the state owned TV station, were also said to have been used as a pivotal resource to win the election. Money was "spent like rain," complained Panday, who warned that "when the money runs out, as it is bound to sooner or later, the demonstrations and fires will begin. The kidnappings will be the new form of wealth distribution" (*Express*, October 14, 2002).

II

Much was said about whether the UNC lost or the PNM won the election, and whether the result was due to "swing" or to differential voter mobilisation. Whether one focuses on the performance of the UNC or on that of the PNM of course depends on one's conscious or unconscious biases and on one's hopes and fears about where the society is going. But in the final analysis, no single explanation would suffice for so multi-textured an event. The reasons are all interlocked.

Compared to what obtained in the 1995, 2000 and 2001 elections, the UNC's campaign in 2002 lacked focus, zest, and panache. The advertising and platform based campaigns were essentially negative, and focussed heavily on the spectre of the Jamaat al Muslimeen, the group which had unsuccessfully sought to overthrow the government in 1990 (Ryan 1992). The Jamaat was branded as a terrorist organisation with links to Osama bin Laden's *al Qaeda* organisation. Not being able to brag as effectively as it would have wished about its "performance," the myth of which had been challenged and eroded by the PNMs various exposés, the party attempted to scare the population into believing that a vote for the PNM was a vote for increased crime, kidnapping, and fiscal irresponsibility. The strategy clearly did not work as an override for the corruption issue which it was meant to be.

The party also seemed to be short of funds, at least when compared with what was available in previous elections. Following the election a top official was accused of having withheld some TT$7m that was given to the Party by its financiers for use in the campaign (*Newsday,* October 10, 28, 2002). The claim was that these funds could not be accounted for and were appropriated for personal use. It was felt that had they been employed for the intended purpose, the result in the critical marginal constituencies could well have been different. The Chairman of the Party denied the allegations, but the belief is widespread that they have substance. Whether true or not, one seriously doubts that insufficient money was a critical cause of the UNCs defeat.[2]

As we have seen, the Political Leader of the UNC, Mr. Basdeo Panday, did not concede defeat following the election. Panday told his dejected followers that the UNC was a government in waiting and that they "will not have to wait long.... Your chance will come again, and that will be sooner than you think. The PNM cannot last a full term.... The means by which they won will be the rope that will hang them." Panday in fact predicted that the collapse would follow the forthcoming local government elections (*Express,* October 14, 2002).

Panday, who displayed all the classic symptoms of "political tabanca" (colloquialism for unrequited love), clearly believed that he had to offer an explanation for the UNCs defeat that shifted blame away from him and his wife and cronies.[3] He also had to offer hope to his politically aggrieved following. At a religious function *(Divali)* held on November 3, 2002, he told the Hindu faithful that "we must never give up our struggle for unity and inclusion and for the removal of all forms of discrimination, alienation and marginalisation." Panday called on those assembled to resist the oncoming "PNM onslaught," and to "fight to take back 'our' country from thieves and terrorists." Panday was once more the ethnic hero. Some Indian critics however argued that it was he who had betrayed his co-ethnics while in office from 1995 to 2001 (*Express,* November 8, 2002).

In an address to the All Trinidad Sugar and General Workers Trade Union, the trade union which he had led before becoming Prime Minister in 1995, Panday repeated his call for civil disobedience. Workers were told to prepare to march into Port of Spain to protect their rights and to be prepared for "tear gas, baton and jail." A spokesman for the Sanatan Dharma Maha Sabha, the organisation that speaks for orthodox Hindus, felt compelled to object to Panday's call for civil disobedience. As he told Panday, "it is one thing for the UNC to claim that the PNM "stole" the elections by various means [but] to extend that to a call for civil disobedience as an alternative is not acceptable" (*Newsday,* November 26, 2002).

While the UNC and Mr. Panday lost the election, there was little gainsaying the fact that the PNM also won it through a combination of militant self mobilisation (the calypsonians were an important part of the process) and hard nosed party work in the marginals designed to turn back the UNC's triumphalism which Afro-creoles saw as a mortal threat to group survival. Many were also anxious to challenge the sanctification of corruption as a legitimate mode of public behaviour. It is however true that the PNM used the resources of incumbency to mobilise potential supporters, and that they targeted black youths whom they had identified as a ready reservoir of "ballot fodder." All political parties use the benefits that go with office, and the UNC was in no position to cry foul since it had done the same and much more in the elections of 2000 and 2001. One recalls the dictum of the former President of Guyana, Forbes Burnham that any party in office which loses an election was guilty of gross negligence! The PNM clearly heeded the Burnham doctrine this time round, and did what it felt it had to do, particularly in the marginal constituencies of Tunapuna, San Fernando West, and Ortoire-Mayaro where the Unemployment Relief Programme (URP), the Community Environmental Protection and Enhancement Programme (CEPEP) and several other youth oriented employment and empowerment programmes were systematically used to mobilise prospective voters.

The Swing Voter

There was much controversy as to whether the PNM's victory was due to "swing" or to enhanced mobilisation on the part of previously dormant PNM sympathisers who roused themselves from their political slumber or apathy and trooped to the polls to rid the country of the UNC. By "swing" here is meant the return to the PNM of persons who voted UNC in 1995, 2000, or 2001 but who switched back to the PNM in 2002.

In one of his analyses of the election, Lloyd Best waxed enthusiastically about the swing voter. As he wrote lyrically:

The most sensational development of all is that perhaps for
the first time in our recent electoral and political history, we
can identify a swing vote that has made its presence felt....
The real hero this time was the celebrated, unexpected, but
hitherto elusive voter swing. Those of us who had hitherto
seen an electorate wedded to tribal and primal voting were
surprised, to say the least. This is not only sensational; it is
downright subversive. (*Express*, October 19, 2002)

Best noted that the PNM had increased its support by some
50,000 votes, ten times the UNC increase. "This spells a remarkable
success at mobilisation.... Matters not whether the driving force was
a revulsion against UNC corruption or whether it was a response to
deep seated Afro fears of being relegated to the status of a permanent
underclass by the new dynamism of the Indos."

Best's arithmetic told him that if there were 31,000 first time
voters, 24,000 must have swung one way or another. Best also
calculated that the 7,000 voters who voted for the minor parties must
have swung if they had not abstained. This in his mind meant that no
less than 17,000 voters must have swung. "We cannot be sure exactly
how many of the 17,000 contributed to the PNM victory.... What is
clear is that a minimum of 12,000 deserted the UNC for the PNM,
while the number could be nearer 17,000" (*Express*, October 19, 2002).

Best opined that the behaviour of the electorate indicated a
"speeding up of the national process of learning and self-awareness."
"The adoption of genuine politics, implied by this new swing in the
vote, might well be the most subversive development of our times.
What it threatens to abolish is the slave and colonial culture."

Using the same figures, another analyst, Dr. Kirk Meighoo,
estimated that the number of swingers was about 19,000, and that it
was an inter-racial phenomenon. "Racial interpretations are simply
not sufficient to understand politics and society here." Meighoo would
later change his mind (*Guardian*, October 11, 2002). Meighoo later
abandoned this argument and admitted that he had not taken non-

voters, who numbered some 283,476 in 2001 into account. "It is therefore entirely possible that the 55,000 new voters could have come from this group…. Perhaps no swing occurred at all" (*Sunday Express*, October 27, 2002).

We should note first of all that the swing voter has always been a feature of modern Trinidad and Tobago, a fact which Best and Meighoo conceded. Voters swung from the PNM to a host of small parties in the sixties and seventies and to the ONR and the NAR and back to the PNM in the eighties and nineties. They also swung from the People's Democratic Party (PDP) to the Democratic Labour Party (DLP) and then to the ULF, the Alliance, and to the ONR and the NAR. In 1995, many swung from the PNM to the UNC. There has also been a great deal of swing in Tobago from the PNM to the DAC and to the NAR and back to the PNM. In 2000, there clearly was an element of swinging to the UNC from the PNM, and in 2002 from the UNC to the PNM, and in some areas to the Citizens Alliance.

Who were these swing voters? Were they indeed the heroes and torch bearers of the future that they were said to be? There is a notion that the swing voter is a detribalised, decolonised, and politically intelligent person who "toothcombs" manifestoes, seeks out information, weighs all the issues "rationally," and votes in an instrumental or utilitarian manner for one party or candidate on the basis of an issue or set of issues. Lord Bryce, author of the classic, *Modern Democracies*, mythologised the "average voter" in the following way:

> The man of broad common sense, mixing on equal terms
> with his neighbours, forming a fair unprejudiced judgement
> on every question, not viewy or pedantic like the man of
> learning, nor arrogant like the man of wealth, but seeing
> things in a practical, businesslike, and kindly spirit, pursuing
> happiness in his own way, and willing that everyone else
> should do so. Such average men make the bulk of the people,
> and are pretty sure to go right, because the publicity secured
> to the expression of opinion by speech and in print will

supply them with ample materials for judging what is best
for all... He may have limited knowledge and no initiative,
yet he may be able to form ... a shrewd judgement of
men.... What he lacks in knowledge, he often makes up for
by a sympathetic comprehension of the attitude of his fellow
men. (cited in Pulzer 1967: 96)

Some persons do vote in the way Bryce and other rationalist
utopians assume, but empirical evidence suggests that many do so for
reasons that are neither "principled" nor "intelligent." Among them
are persons who are bought or seduced with a job, a T-shirt, a basketball
outfit, a financial inducement, or some other material trinket. Some
switch for reasons that seem frivolous. Some, for example, are cross-
pressured between available alternatives and resolve their cognitive
dissonance by way of "vapse." Some also swing in response to polls
or subliminal advertising campaigns which target their fears,
insecurities, ambitions, or venality. Financiers also swing in response
to polls. The point here is that one should not romanticise the swing
voter as do many liberal utopians and make him/her out to be an icon
of democratic choice making.

We should also bear in mind that many persons make political
choices as part of socially homogeneous groups and not as individuals.
It may in fact make more sense to say that in most cases, it is the
group (whether inward looking or outward looking) that swings and
not the individual. Most voters, including swingers, are not desiccated
calculators, and take their cues from, or defer to opinion leaders in the
family, the church, the bloc, the club and/or the community generally.
This reality might help to explain why election outcomes are never
accurately predicted by analysts who regard the rational issue oriented
voter as the primary building bloc of democratic elections. It also
helps explain why third parties fail.

One analyst of politics in Britain from whence the concept of
the floating voter came, expressed regret that the term was ever coined.
As Pulzer (1967: 125) observed:

The word suggests that the electorate can be conveniently divided into two categories, on the one hand the faithful supporter of the big battalions, on the other, earnest individuals seeking after truth. All survey evidence suggests the contrary: that there is a relatively small core of 'thick-and-thin men,' shading off, through weak and conditional party-support into neutrality (or apathy).

One should also note that the concept of swing conceals the fact that there is often more volatility in the electorate than is evidenced by actual switching. Many swing between elections but return to base because of the pull of the tribe or group on election day in response to either class or ethnically based traditional signals. Those who do carry through with the decision to swing often do so with feelings of guilt or remorse. They feel a deep sense of betrayal.

It is often difficult to determine from consulting aggregate voting data who did the swinging and why. Polls however help us to make reasoned assumptions. In the 2002 election, pre-election polling data by SARA indicated that there would be some crossing of the political rivers, but that the "boat people" were not scrambling to get to the other bank in any significant numbers. Six percent of the Afro-Trinidadians in our sample said they were inclined to vote for the UNC, while 9 percent of the Indo-Trinidadians indicated a preference for the PNM, a net potential gain of 3 percent. This translates into an estimated 21,000 Afro-Trinidadians moving to the UNC and 26,000 Indo-Trinidadians moving to the PNM. Of the latter, 50 percent were Christian, 37 percent were Muslim, and 13 percent were Hindus. In sum, as in the previous two years, Christian Indians were more likely to vote PNM than were Muslims and Hindus. Even though the number of Indians who crossed over to support the PNM was not huge, they could have made a significant contribution to the outcome of the election, particularly in the marginal constituencies.

The Succession Crisis in the UNC

The defeat sustained by the UNC in the election raised profound questions about the nature of the party and its continued viability under the leadership of Basdeo Panday. In the immediate aftermath of the election, Panday indicated that he was approaching seventy, and planned to vacate the leadership on reaching that age. His plan was to devote his remaining time and energy to writing his memoirs and community work. Defeat was fortuitous, Panday seemed to be saying. He however made it clear that his decision to step down from the leadership did not mean that he was withdrawing from politics, which was "in his blood." To quote Panday:

> I want to move on to other things in preparation to meet my maker. That time is fast approaching, and I would like to keep the promise I made to myself. I would like to go now, [but] I want to make it absolutely clear that I am not getting out of politics. Politics is part of me, and politics would only get out of me when I die. I can't get out of politics, I am just changing my role. (*Newsday,* October 10, 2002, *Express* October 14, 2002)

Panday indicated that he would give up the leadership of the party, but remain an MP until he decided to quit in about three years (*Express,* October 8, 2002).

As expected, the UNC crowd, or the vocal parts thereof, implored Panday to remain as the party's leader, a reaction which Panday must have anticipated. Subsequent statements made it clear that he had no intention of giving up the leadership soon, let alone giving up his political career. He chided those who seem to have taken him seriously for their "political naivety," and accused them of making "reckless statements about successorship in the UNC which had the effect of weakening it and allowing the actions of the PNM to go unnoticed... They want to weaken us so that the PNM can keep us in bondage for the next five years" (*Newsday,* November 11, 2002). Panday reminded them that "I am the political leader. I have not vacated the seat, and until the transition team [which had been appointed to determine how a leader should be chosen] did their work, the question does not arise." Panday was known to have argued that leaders do not give up power. Power has to be wrested from them.

In an address to his followers on *The Way Forward*, Panday advised party supporters that there were still other critical battles to fight which required his continued leadership. There was first of all a local government election to be fought. He affected to believe that the government would inevitably fall soon thereafter, and that a general election would have to be called. "Why [then] give the enemy the impression that we are a splinter movement? We are united; we are a party. Forget who is leader and who is not" (*Newsday*, November 14, 2002). Panday was clearly telling all and sundry that he was still the leader of the party, and planned to remain such. As he once said, "I will die with my political boots on."

There was however a significant element within the party who believed that it was time for Panday to go, and who were prepared to wrest power from him and give it to someone whom they believed could rehabilitate the party. They felt that Panday was not giving leadership to the party and that it was slowly crumbling. Panday was angry with those who were holding discussions with Ramesh Lawrence Maharaj, whom he dismissed as "the political leader of another party which fought an election against the UNC and failed to get a single seat." Those who wanted Maharaj as their leader were advised to join Team Unity rather than disrespect the UNC, a party which "we built with our blood sweat and tears." Panday ordered that the "argument" as to whether there should be discussions with Maharaj "must come to an end, *finis, kaput*" (*Newsday*, November 19, 2002).

Most of the UNC MPs meekly obeyed Mr. Panday's order to cease and desist. One of the main dissidents, Fuad Khan, with tongue in cheek perhaps, remarked that: "Mr. Panday has made his decision clear, and I am a member of the UNC under Mr. Panday. That is where it is at this point. Maybe in the future other things may take place. What I was trying to show is that it may be time to introduce different approaches, but Mr. Panday says this is not the time, so that is where it is. I hope the UNC will grow from strength to strength because it will need a lot of strength to overtake the government (*Newsday*, November 11, 2002).

Maharaj's response was that the "argument" was far from over, and that Panday's stance, if adopted, ensured that the UNC would remain in opposition for a long while. He also confirmed what Panday had hitherto denied, that there had been serious discussions between himself and Panday prior to the elections, and that they had canvassed the possibility of reconciliation between the two parties. According to Maharaj, "When we met, Mr. Panday acknowledged that if the government had acted on corruption, the UNC would have won the elections. He expressed the view that unless a formula was found for there to be unity between members of Team Unity and the UNC, the UNC would lose the elections. A formula [was to] have been proposed at a later meeting" (*Newsday*, November 19, 2002). Mr. Panday has not challenged Maharaj's claim. Asked whether he would forgive Maharaj, he noted that he was not the Lord. "Vengeance is mine, says the Lord" (*Newsday*, November 16, 2002).

Maharaj confirmed that several persons, including MPs and party financiers had spoken to him following the election, and that there was a widespread view that Panday should give up the leadership and allow the party to grow. Asked why he did not transfer his loyalty to Team Unity instead of trying to effect a reconciliation between Maharaj and the UNC, one disenchanted financier opined that "the country only has room for two political parties, an African party and an Indian Party. You can't have two African leaders: neither can you have two Indian leaders: so the real problem is to get Panday to leave without creating too much bacchanal" (*Newsday*, November 18, 2002). The view was that Panday "had taken the party to the 'maximum' that he could, and that there [was] no further that he could take it." [*sic*]

Maharaj shrewdly observed that he could not just "walk in and take over the UNC. The UNC would have to be reformed first. If the UNC is not reformed, it is not politically worthwhile to take it over" (*Express* November 11, 2002). The leaders of Team Unity acknowledged that they would lose credibility if they returned to an unreformed UNC. Maharaj was however equivocal as to whether he wanted to return to the UNC, attract support away from the UNC to Team Unity, or whether he wanted an alliance of all opposition forces to challenge and eventually dislodge the PNM. For the time being, he was stressing the latter in the hope of achieving his ultimate goal, which was to capture the leadership of the UNC. As Maharaj declared:

> I am going to be the legitimate Opposition, the voice of the legitimate Opposition in the country. I am going to use whatever political clout I have outside the Parliament, and I am also going to use the law in order to make the Government account.... What is important now is for the membership of the UNC and the membership of all political parties to recognize that you have a strong and credible Opposition both in and out of Parliament. (*Newsday*, November 26, 2002)

His view seemed to be that what was needed in the short run was opposition unity and that he was the person best suited to lead that unified force.

The party was badly divided on the succession issue. Several MPs had very strong objections to Maharaj's re-entry to the party. They felt deeply aggrieved by what they saw as his "treachery" prior to the elections of 2001, and blamed him for their loss of office. Some of them also had leadership aspirations, and saw Maharaj not only as a rival for the throne, but as someone who would demand their heads if he were to become the leader. Candidates for the leadership included former Central Bank Governor Winston Dookeran (who clearly cleverly feigned disinterest), Kamla Persad-Bissessar, former Attorney General and Minister of Education, Ganga Singh, former Minister of Public Utilities, and new comer, Dr. Roodal Moonilal. Singh reportedly had the support of Persad-Bissessar and Panday, but was seen to be ethically vulnerable. According to Maharaj, "there are serious questions being asked about Mr. Ganga Singh ... [he] has to fight with his hands [and feet] tied behind his back ... he is afraid and has not been able to fight the PNM in Parliament" (*Newsday*, November 27, 2002).

The public line of the loyalists was to insist that Mr. Panday had to stay until such time as he himself decided that the time was right for him to go. That was seen to be his right, and as such he must not be forced out of the party. One MP noted that the UNC got 285,000 votes, and that was reason enough for Mr. Panday to stay. It was also argued that if one looked only at the 3 marginals, the PNM's victory was slim. Clearly, however, these MPs had come to the conclusion that Mr. Panday had no plans to leave soon, and that he was perhaps just testing his colleagues for their loyalty. Other MPs, and many supporters as well, felt that there was no one within its existing leadership ranks who had what was required to provide the UNC with what was needed at this juncture, and that Mr. Maharaj was the only person on the horizon who had the skills and will to rebuild the party. In their view, Mr. Panday was a liability, and either had to leave voluntarily or be forced to do so.

Maharaj was however clearly determined to succeed Panday as the new maximum leader of the Indian community and was not particular about how that succession would come about or what the new vehicle would be called. He reminded all and sundry that he had worked hard to build the UNC, and that he would work hard either to reinvent it, or build some other organisation. As he declared:

> I worked hard in the UNC since 1991. I built structures in the party and in government, and I gave it my all. The membership now sees certain qualities lacking [in the party], and they are entitled to protection and the security of their future in politics. It is important for a political party and its membership to examine what went wrong. The UNC needs added strength. When the PNM lost the election in 1986 because the party was perceived as corrupt and anti-people,

with nepotism and abuse of power for over 30 years, Patrick Manning created a new party, and got into office in 1991. But it was the abuse of power that caused his government to collapse. In 1995, the UNC was the hope of the people, but that changed. I did everything humanely possible to try to get the party and the government on a proper footing. There was no alternative but... to take the stand we did. If we did not do that, we would not have been serving the country and the membership of the UNC. Since then, it has been demonstrated that if we didn't take that stand, none of us would have had any credibility in Trinidad and Tobago. (*Sunday Mirror,* November 17, 2002)

Perhaps the most vocal spokesman of the "Panday must go now" view was the former MP for Tunapuna and Minister of Foreign Affairs, Mr. Mervyn Assam, who openly called on Mr. Panday to abdicate. "Mr. Panday must step down, write his memoirs, and enjoy his life." Assam felt that Panday had fought the good fight for over 36 years, and had given tremendous services to the country. He should be given a golden handshake and sent out to ride into the sunset. Panday should be told, "you have done well, but you have come to the end of your outstanding career; make way for others who have an input to make" (*Express,* November 21, 2002).

Assam openly accused the UNC leader of failing to take advice on the strategy that ought to have been pursued by the party in the election, and in fact blamed Panday for the UNC's defeat. He clearly felt that certain candidates were an electoral liability, and ought to have been made to step down. Others should not have been put in certain seats. Had that been done, the outcome might well have been different. "We wouldn't have lost the election. The UNC is a good party," Assam opined, "but decisions were made by the leadership which were not in its best interest" (*Guardian,* November 29, 2002). Interestingly and unbelievably, Assam felt that it was he who had won the St. Joseph and Tunapuna constituencies in the 1995 and 2000 elections respectively, and that he had "made Panday Prime Minister twice and put the UNC in Government twice." He, "who was once a star, had however been cast into the dustbin of history" (*Newsday*, November 25, 2002). He conceded that he had had his differences with Maharaj, but had since had a chance to hold discussions with him as a result of which his view had "changed somewhat" (*Guardian*, November 29, 2002).

Questions have been asked as to why Mr. Panday was so unwilling to regard Mr. Maharaj as his "rising son." One view was that he objected to Maharaj's constant injunctions to him to put an end to the corruption that was delegitimising the party. Since Panday was himself involved, he could not act on Maharaj's advice and clearly resented his moral posturing. One recalls that it was Maharaj who as Attorney General had advised the UNC Government that the Airport Contract was flawed and should be determined, and that this could be done without the state having to pay any penalty for default. One also recalls that Maharaj had hired a foreign forensic team to investigate allegations of corruption without obtaining cabinet approval or Mr. Panday's endorsement. There was also widespread concern that he was building up files on his colleagues, including Mr. Panday, which he hoped to use and to keep them enchained.

The other view was that Panday knew that Maharaj had a reputation for opportism and that he was not acceptable to either the Hindu base of the party or to the creole community which he felt the party had to cultivate if it wished to remain in power. He thus preferred someone who was easier to market. Yet another hypothesis was that Panday wanted a more pliable successor who would go along with his plan to accede to the Presidency (see *Newsday*, November 17, 2002). What is now clear, however, is that Mr. Panday was determined that Mr. Maharaj must not be his successor, and that he preferred to have the UNC split down the middle rather than have Maharaj succeed. Indeed, Mr. Panady's decision to remain leader of the party seems to be a deliberate strategy to deny Mr. Maharaj the leadership. It is also clear that Mr. Panday could not bring himself to walk away from the leadership. He in fact dared those in the party who wished to challenge him, to contest the leadership in the forthcoming leadership elections due in June 2003. As he said, "when the election is held, the party will have an opportunity to make known its views. That's democracy.... They have to contend with my decision [to remain as leader]." Panday was reacting to a NACTA mini-poll conducted in January 2003 which revealed that 53 percent of those sampled believed that he should give up the leadership of the UNC. Twenty-six percent disagreed. When the question was put to UNC supporters only, 61 percent felt Panday should resign, with 23 percent saying otherwise (*Guardian,* February 2, 2003).[4]

Endnotes

1. The PNM claims that it helped over 600 persons to register in the Tunapuna constituency. Both parties were involved in the exercise in Tunapuna and Ortoire-Mayaro where beach houses were rented to accommodate voters.

2. The allegation was made by the UNC's former treasurer who had broken with the party to join Team Unity. He broke with the latter party and is now a member of the PNM. While the allegation must be reviewed against this background, it is an established fact that a lot of money which is collected for use in election campaigns ends up in private pockets.

3. Panday's wife Oma was savagely criticised and scapegoated as being the source of his undoing. She was referred to as "Kali Mai" and said to have been largely responsible for a lot of the corruption that swirled around the UNC. She was also accused of behaving like a tin god and of only fraternising with the wives of the parasitic oligarchy and "a select few in the party" (see "Oma in UNC Doghouse," *Mirror*, November 1, 2002).

4. Panday has on more than one occasion made clear his view that true leaders do not give up power meekly. Power has to be wrested from them. As he once declared when arrested on sexual harassment charges, "they believe that I would lie down and die on the ground with my feet in the air. Old politicians never die; they become more sexy."

Chapter 12

PYRRHIC VICTORY?

*W*as the PNM's victory on October 7, 2002 a "Pyrrhic" victory? This was a question that many disillusioned PNM supporters asked themselves in the 100 days following the election. Some looked at the kind of decisions which were being made or not being made, and asked whether the country was better off being governed by "crooks" or "mooks"? Some argued that "mooks" can do more damage to a society than "crooks" in that the decisions they make or do not make could have structurally damaging effects on a society. Those who believed otherwise argued what ever the seeming benefits of corruption in the short-run in terms of getting certain things done, especially those that seem to promote growth, the impact of grand corruption was infinitely greater in that it could lead to long-term poverty, national indebtedness, fiscal collapse, political cynicism, and eventual state collapse. There is, it was argued, no such thing as "good corruption," as some analysts argued.

The agonising was a reflection of the fact that there was a great deal of anxiety and frustration in the country following the election. Many were saying that the PNM had "run out of gas." There was a widespread complaint that having run hard between January and September 2002 to create a record of performance to display to voters, the PNM seemed to have difficulty getting back on track. The frustrated believed that the victory seemed "pyrrhic." Several ministers were not performing as well as expected. While a few of them were in fact political novices, they were seen to be making too many unforced errors. Some were also taking too long to settle into their new portfolios.

The Government's reply to the criticisms was that projects had to be properly planned and phased to avoid over heating the economy and the kind of poor execution that was the hallmark of the UNC era.

Admittedly, some of the problems which the newly elected government had to face were difficult, and would have tested the mettle of any government. The problems with respect to restructuring Caroni Ltd., the nationally owned sugar company, and the Ministry of Health were recurrent ones which had defied several administrations, and were not easily fixed. The crime situation was also not one that could be made to go away by changing a minister, a Commissioner of Police, or indeed a government. Jamaica had thrown everything imaginable at its crime problem which had become progressively worse each day. Barbados and Guyana were also caught in the grip of crime, and seemed unable to identify a solution.

What was however clear was that the crime situation in Trinidad continued to spin wildly out of control. Much of the criminal behaviour that was being witnessed in Trinidad and Tobago and the Caribbean generally had its roots in the narco trafficking industry which was threatening to overwhelm the region. Drug trafficking constituted a seminal threat since it spawned the illegal possession of firearms, corruption, and turf wars. There was also a symbiotic inter-relationship between drugs and violent crime, and between drugs and party politics throughout the region, including Trinidad and Tobago. Drug money was in fact being used to fund election campaigns and to buy politicians.

One of the initiatives taken by the Prime Minister which led many to question his judgement was his decision to meet with self-confessed criminal elements in an attempt to restore peace and tranquillity to the embattled inner city areas of Laventille and East Port of Spain where 22 percent of the homicides that had been committed in the months immediately preceding and following the election had taken place. The Prime Minister justified his meeting with those whom he described as "community leaders" on the ground that the criminal activity which was taking a heavy toll on the affected areas in terms of lives, property, and community well being, was gang related, and one had to use unconventional dispute resolution strategies to bring the situation under control. To quote the Prime Minister who seemed to have been inspired by a deep conviction that he was being spiritually directed to pursue the path he was following, "we are taking an approach that recognises that there are specific individuals involved in it, and there might be an opportunity for some alternative dispute resolution that may have a great measure of success" (*Express,* December 22, 2002).

Those who supported the Prime Minister's initiative defended it on the ground that his prime consideration was humanitarian. The Director of the Laventille Outreach for Vertical Enrichment (LOVE) felt that while the Prime Minister might not have been "politically correct," he was seeking to save lives. Manning, he said, had more to gain politically by waiting until the gangs "cancelled each other out," but chose to put the country first (*Express,* December 26, 2002).

The well meaning attempt on Manning's part to play the role of "honest broker" however provoked a storm of hostile criticism and allegations about his tactlessness, especially when it was discovered that the carrot which was being held aloft to pacify the warring groups was a more "equitable share" in the URP and National Housing Authority Refurbishing programmes. Many of the killings were known to be the result of turf warfare between "community leaders" for shares in these projects.

Criticism of the Prime Minister's unorthodox intervention strategy was forthcoming from the Police who felt that he was undermining their authority. Criticism likewise came from media editorialists, columnists and many in the general public, all whom warned the Prime Minister that he was compromising his office and other national institutions. As one editorial asked:

...Is he not giving recognition to individuals who, if they are known to the police for illegal activities, should be subject to the courts? Is he not compromising the office of Prime Minister and also putting the police at a disadvantage in doing what in effect is their work, and not the Prime Minister's? Is Mr. Manning not head of the National Security Council? How can "leaders" who have been a part of creating the horrendous situation in which we find ourselves, now be asked to advise the Prime Minister on how best to deal with it? What's in it for them? What absolute nonsense is this? Can Mr. Manning be really so naïve as to believe that these leaders would give him hints as to strategies the Government could adopt to effectively clamp down on crime which has the whole society living in fear? Is Mr. Manning hoping that these meetings would provide information which he would then pass on to the Protective Services enabling an expansion of their intelligence gathering to deal with the crime situation, including forestalling the spate of killings? (*Newsday,* December 29, 2002)

The Prime Minister was warned that it could well happen, as it did in Jamaica, that the so-called community leaders would come to regard themselves as untouchable "dons" who not only controlled their garrisoned communities, but influenced public policy in other sensitive areas as well. In Jamaica, the dons have become independent of the politicians and better armed than the Police. The latter in fact often cannot maintain peace and order unless they can secure the cooperation of the area dons who rule these shanty states with an authoritarian hand, determining who eats, works, gets welfare, or conducts business or who is to be punished, and indeed who lives or dies.

Not surprisingly, the UNC blamed the Government for mollycoddling the Jamaat al Muslimeen, claiming that it was clearly "pay-back time for the services which the latter delivered to the PNM in the October election." The government was said to be incapable of handling Muslim aggression. Gang leaders were in fact known to have threatened that if they were not given jobs, there could be a reign of terror and that they would resort to "subtle extortion tactics" (*Newsday*, November 21, 2002).

The Anglo-American "war on terrorism" also featured prominently in the post-election contestation between the UNC and the PNM. Both the British and the Americans were nervous about reports that there were terrorists in Trinidad and Tobago linked to *al Qaeda*, and that British and American personnel and property could be at risk. The British Government in fact issued an advisory to the effect that Trinidad and Tobago might be "one of a number of countries where there may be an increased terrorist threat," and that "British nationals should exercise vigilance in places frequented by foreigners such as hotels, malls and restaurants." The PNM Government took objection to the advisory and blamed Mr. Panday and Senator Sadiq Baksh for making public statements in the United Kingdom and Trinidad and Tobago, which in their view, led the British Government to take circulating rumours more seriously than they deserved.

Both Baksh and Panday however insisted that the threats were real, and that the United Kingdom Government had their own sources of information. Both saw a connection between what happened during the election with respect to the Jamaat and the increase in gang related violent crime, kidnapping and Islamic radicalism in Trinidad and Tobago. To quote Baksh:

> We have an unprecedented spate of murders taking place; we have an unprecedented amount of kidnappings taking place, and the PNM is clearly responsible for that. They are encouraging terrorists in Trinidad and Tobago. The Jamaat was the prime enforcer of fear and terrorism that we saw displayed in San Fernando West, Ortoire/Mayaro, Barataria/San Juan and in Tunapuna on election day, and that is what I made absolutely clear during that interview. (*Express*, January 19, 2003)

Baksh argued that the advisory put out by British authorities advising its nationals against travelling to this country was done "because of the PNM's collusion with terrorists in Trinidad and Tobago and their inability to deal with crime, governance, create jobs and stop the kidnappings." Asked if he felt acts of terrorism could take place here, Baksh declared: "Under the PNM anything can happen, anything can happen" (ibid.).

Panday also repeated his claim that the PNM had firm links to the Jamaat al Muslimeen and that the latter was an al Qaeda asset. According to Panday, "it is well known that the Government was in association with those elements before the elections. Election day was fraught with terror. We don't have to tell anybody that... I have evidence with my own eyes of the terror tactics that were used for the election. The country is reaping what it sowed." Panday recalled that he had warned that if the PNM won by thuggery, it would have to rule by thuggery. "That is what is taking place in the country." (Express, January 21, 22, 2003 and Guardian, January 22, 2003). Panday also charged that the Jamaat al Muslimeen was involved in quarrying operations and that these operations provided cover for terrorist activities:

> The leaders of that same terrorist group have been given a quarry deep in the jungle where they can train terrorists and killers and kidnappers and robbers in secrecy. Since they own a quarry, they now not only have an excuse for importing dynamite and other explosives, but they have a nice secret place to test with impunity bombs that they themselves have made. This is payback time in Trinidad and Tobago for the muscle, the fear, the threat and terror that they inflicted upon supporters of the UNC during the election campaign and on election day (Express, February 10, 2003).

Moneys earned from the quarrying and other operations were said to be used for buying drugs, guns and cars.

Messrs. Baksh and Panday were however clearly exaggerating what was taking place in order to score political points. There was in fact no evidence that the Jamaat al Muslim was in fact a "terrorist" group with links to *al Qaeda*, in the sense in which that term should be properly understood. Terrorism is the systematic use, or threatened use, of violence to achieve symbolic political or ideological ends against victims or governments, and must be differentiated from petty thuggery designed to secure purely material ends (Headley 2002:8). The Jamaat al Muslimeen were in fact conventional enforcers of the type that are to be found in most inner cities. Mr. Manning did however provide the UNC with the ammunition which allowed critics to paint the PNM into a corner by meeting clandestinely with members of the Jamaat and other known underworld elements whom he promised involvement in the TT$200m Unemployment Relief Programme (URP) and the National Housing Authority Rehabilitation Programme in return for cooperation in maintaining peace in the inner city area of Port of Spain.[1]

Manning blamed Panday for besmirching the reputation of Trinidad and Tobago. He described Panday's behaviour "as one of the worst examples of irresponsibility" which he had seen in his whole career. Panday he said, had decided to be

> ...venomously vindictive, diabolically destructive, and throw all caution and common sense to the winds, while attempting to join his own defeat to the demise of our nation-state, if he can at all bring it about. Trinidad and Tobago was now witnessing the poisonous conduct of a loser who seems bent on slithering from political suicide to national fractride. The so-called fox has now become an embittered snake. For someone in Basdeo Panday's position to so casually brutalise this country, transmitting information he knows is baseless, senseless and purposeless, is to leave the rest of the good citizens – even his own supporters – hanging their heads in shame. No other Trinidad and Tobago politician, elected to the sacred role of representing a body of people, has ever

embarked on such an obscene campaign to bring harm to an entire country. (*Express*, January 22, 2002).

Despite the exaggerated criticism, the PNM's victory may nevertheless be deemed Pyrrhic since it was achieved at a potentially serious long-term social cost that need not have been incurred. As we have indicated above (p. 235) it was not unequivocally evident that the Jamaat provided the PNM with the critical margins which it needed to win the election. The Jamaat nevertheless believed that it did, and was able to extract its pound of fiscal flesh from the PNM. Following the election, the Jamaat strengthened its effective stranglehold on the Unemployment Relief Programme (URP) and National Housing Authority (NHA) reform programmes, and was able to secure a major share of the funds that are allocated to those programmes.

What is even more troubling is that the peace in the community that was supposed to have been a by-product of the truce between rival gangs that had been brokered by the Prime Minister prior to the election, fell apart amidst gun battles between those who once controlled the programmes on behalf of the UNC and the Jamaat al Muslimeen, as well as others who wanted a piece of the cake. One casualty of the turf war was Mark Guerra, the self-described "Don" of Sea Lots and John John communities in the inner city areas of Port of Spain. Guerra, who was executed on March 23, 2003, was the National Advisor to the Manager of the URP, a position which allowed him to assume the role of "saviour of the ghetto." He was the "caliph" who decided who worked on the projects or not, who were on "ghost" gangs, and how much the ghosts paid for the facilitation. He was regarded by many as a beneficent godfather, and a "good man." As the rival UNC linked "Don" explained, "who feeding the "hood" control the crime; these people will make the Government fall. Crime have a propeller now (*Express*, December 17, 2002. Cf. also note 11, *supra*, p. 244).

Prime Minister Manning was taken aback by the execution and had obviously not appreciated that by empowering people like Guerra, whom he described as a "community leader," he had taken one additional step, all be it unintentionally, to entrench the "garrison" phenomenon in Port of Spain, one that has now become an ugly feature on the political landscape of Jamaica and Guyana (Ryan 1999: 19-25). That decision could well have serious long-term consequences for urban politics in Trinidad and Tobago.[2]

Endnote

1. As journalist Anthony Fraser correctly observed; "Manning cannot dump in Panday's lap all responsibility for feeding ammunition to the British. He must absorb a large chunk of the blame for thinking that he could associate his party with the Muslimeen without giving Panday an offensive - even though it was the latter who first rehabilitated Abu Bakr and used his political services in the 1995 election after the Jamaat's 1990 act of terror on the people of Trinidad and Tobago. The media, too, without giving up the right to expose, to display on its front page and on its lead television and radio newscasts all the warts on the face of society, must acknowledge too that stories carried impact positively and negatively. Acknowledgment will lead to even greater responsibility and circumspection by the professionals of the newsroom" (*Guardian*, January 23, 2003).

2. It is worth nothing that when Manning, accompanied by Guerra, walked through the streets of Laventille in the weeks prior to the election, Guerra referred to him as "father" and also said that if the PNM did not win the October 7 election, there would be a serious revolution of "black against Indian dreads" (*Sunday Guardian*, April 16, 2003.

Chapter 13

RESOLVING THE DEADLOCK?

There will be a total lack of cooperation with this
illegitimate and corrupt regime.

- Basdeo Panday
Guardian, April 28, 2003

*T*he deadlock that characterized Trinidad and Tobago's
political system was "broken" on October 7, 2002. It
might however be more accurate to say that the
parliamentary deadlock was broken but that the more fundamental
problem of the perceived inequitable distribution of political power
remained unresolved. One assumes that the electoral deadlock that
was experienced in 2001 - 2002 will not recur in quite the same form.
That problem is fixable by the Elections and Boundaries Commission
by way of a recommendation to Parliament that the number of seats
should be altered to produce an uneven digit. Having 35 or 37 seats
does not however automatically guarantee that awkward situations
would never again occur, especially if regional, fragmented, or minor
parties enter the ring successfully, or unorthodox coalitions were to be
formed. One can still have a technical draw or a stalemate in a
parliament with an uneven number of representatives.

There are many areas in which deadlock continued to manifest
itself in the society. It obtained at the level of local government where
control of the regional and municipal corporations was equally divided
(7-7) between the two major parties. More fundamentally, it existed
demographically and sociologically. Gone were the days when the
Afro-Creole community enjoyed a political and social hegemony with

the Indo-Creole group constituting a numerical and sociological minority. Trinidad society was now at a conjuncture wherein the two major ethnic groups enjoyed a rough sort of parity, and could effectively checkmate each other. Overtime, that balance will change, and as it does, there is going to be conflict at all levels of the system. The nature and decibel level of the discourse that accompanies that conflict would at times lead one to conclude that the society is in a state of incipient collapse. What we would however be witnessing is the struggle of the post-independence order to emerge from the entrails of the dying creole social order. Social destruction is always a messy affair, even if at times it can be creative.

Constitutional change (in a non-literal sense) has also been taking place over the past few years, and more so since 1995 when the new Indo-political elite emerged on the political stage and was evidently not comfortable with the old Afro-Saxon social order. The styles of governance of the two elites were qualitatively different and expressed itself symbolically in conflicts between the Prime Minister and the President, between the Attorney General and the Chief Justice, between the Prime Minister and the Attorney General on the one hand and sections of the Fourth Estate on the other, and between the new ministers and sections of the Public Service. Mr. Panday openly declared that the creole regime, including the media, was out to destroy him, and that he would "do them in before they did him in." Mr. Manning, for his part, was clear in his mind that the differences in his governing style, and that of Mr. Panday and his colleagues, were fundamental. As he put it, "Panday and I are two different people. We come from a perspective that stems from integrity. We understand the administration of the public trust" (*Guardian,* April 22, 2002). Those alleged differences in characterisation remain contested, but the discourse was symptomatic of the underlying tension between the two regimes.

Deadlock did not only characterise the relationships which existed between the leading political personalities and the institutions they represented. *Stasis* was evident within the trade union movement, within the legal fraternity, and within the media, to note only a few of the arenas where conflict was endemic. Lloyd Best was fundamentally correct when he remarked that "the parliament of 2001 faithfully reflected the country that had for a long time been polarised into roughly equal parts. The issue was not a hung Parliament, but a hung country. It is no hyperbole to conclude that the apparent unraveling of 2002 can only be an illusion. The country might be sitting on a not so inactive volcano. It still has to fashion a true solution. This can only mean reform of the constitution in the sense of reorganizing the arrangements put in place for the purposes of colonial rule" (*Trinidad and Tobago Review*, December 2, 2002).

There are those who regard deadlock as a dreadful and dysfunctional thing which one must try to overcome at all costs, lest the volcano erupts. Others see it as an indication that the society in Trinidad is at last becoming politically mature, and that its social and institutional complexity are empowering, at least for some groups. Indeed, gridlock may in fact contribute to greater democratisation since it encourages broader and closer scrutiny of government business. Yet others argue that in situations of extreme conflict, gridlock is inevitable regardless of the model of governance unless it is overridden by naked force (see David Hinds, *Stabroek News*, March 27, 2002).

Those who abhor deadlock and the confusion that seems to attend it, long, in some cases with nostalgia, for an era when one group, whether formally in a political party or invisibly in the shadows, controlled and managed a relatively stable system autocratically, and called all the shots. That system was best exemplified by the crown colony system and its successors in the era of self-government and early independence. There was then a dominant epistemology and a related set of ideological assumptions and prescriptions about how the society should be ordered. That order was serially challenged over the years by radical blacks, Indian women, trade unions, non - Christians (black and Indian), and Tobagonians, all of whom felt that they were marginalised by the old established creole order. The old system was badly ruptured in 1970 and 1990, but the social dykes proved elastic enough to absorb the new seekers of inclusion, be they organised on the basis of class, gender, region or "social" race.

In doing so, however, the mechanisms through which the symbolic and material resources of the society were allocated became more complex and competitive. The political system however remained fused and archaic. The society had become more polycentric or multi-polar while the political system remained fundamentally centrist and unipolar. The Wooding Constitution Commission, which was appointed following the Black Power uprising of 1970, recognised the underlying problem, and tried to open up the system and make it more inclusive. Wooding's Report said clearly that "the Westminster model in its purest form as set out in our present constitution is not suitable to the Trinidad and Tobago society." William's vision was that of a majoritarian democrat, and he was savage in his attack on the commissioners whom he dismissed as persons intent on sabotaging the established PNM order. As Williams said of Wooding *et al*:

> They had an illogical obsession ... and proceeded to reduce the powers of Parliament to create confusion and to break up the centralisation of Parliament, Cabinet and the political party. (*Hansard,* December 13, 17, 1974)

The problems which Wooding *et al* identified and sought to deal with are still very much with us and have in fact become more marked. The Hyatali Constitutional Commission also grappled with the problem, but their report was superseded by the events of 1990 which delegitimised the NAR. Those exercises were however not wasted and should be revisited if only to help us decide what needs to be revisited and what does not need to be reinvented.

Both Commissions felt that part of the problem lay in the unfairness of the system of representation in the Parliament and the over concentration of power in the elected executive. In their view, structural readjustment of the political system required deconcentration of power at the executive level by having some of the powers of appointment which the Prime Minister enjoyed shared with the President whom it was assumed would be a "selector" at the "Test" level, and a neutral umpire when necessary. Breaking the deadlock would require a revisiting of the consociational/consensus model and the Westminster paradigm to determine which of them, if any, was more appropriate to our polyarchic context.

Trinidad and Tobago is now searching for a new architectural paradigm to resolve the deadlock, and a number of proposals have been put on the table. Some are simple and even simplistic while others are complex and visionary. Some are minimalist, while some involve major restructuring. Some are familiar, while others wear exotic disguises. We look at two of them, one proposed by Mr. Panday and the other by Lloyd Best.

Mr. Panday has insisted that constitutional reform had to be put on the national agenda, failing which, he would initiate a long bruising campaign involving non-violent civil disobedience and non-cooperation with the PNM government - no constitutional reform, no taxation. In terms of specifics for reform, Mr. Panday's suggestion is that the leader of the party which wins the largest share of the popular vote should be appointed executive president while the runner up should be appointed prime minister. "Both parties would be in power," according to Mr. Panday. When the suggestion was advanced, Mr. Panday probably assumed that the proposal would favour the Indo-Trinidadian community which until the 2002 election, had showed a higher rate of mobilisation than the Afro-Trinidadian population. That assumption was put in question in October 2002 when the PNM secured a higher proportion of the popular vote than the UNC.

The viability of that proposal would depend on how power was allocated between the President and Prime Minister and the extent to which power and influence were shared at the policy making level, both in committees and in the cabinet. The Guyana version of the model assigns the Prime Minister a very peripheral role. In the French model, the Prime Minister has an important role in the sphere of domestic politics while the President is dominant in the area of foreign policy. In Mr. Panday's model, the President would present his plans to parliament which would deal with them in a process of bargaining. "You would have to bargain, you have to talk, you would have to give and take. The new arrangement would help forge channels of unity [and would be] more than adversarial." Panday noted that if the UNC had won the 2001 election, the PNM would have been equally alienated. "Elections alone cannot solve the problem. We must have constitution reform as well, and it would not take a rocket scientist to say where we want to go." One suspects that Mr. Panday's exotic cohabitation model would enjoy little appeal in contemporary Trinidad and Tobago.

Best's proposal is an elaboration of one that was advanced in the 1970s and which came to be known as the "macco senate." The proposal is informed by the distinction which Best seeks to make between "government" and "politics" which he regards as being quite distinctive things. In our view, the two things are part of a continuum, a loop in the chain of governance. One is on the input side of the political equation while the other constitutes output, and the process continues.

Best's argues that Caribbean political systems are about government and not about politics and representation. As he contends, perhaps with some exaggeration, there has never been any representation of the population in the councils of Government in the Caribbean. In-so-far as there has been participation, it was controlled participation. In these systems, the Prime Minister is head of the cabinet, head of the administration, and chief of the legislature. He is not merely three in one and one in three, as CLR James argued. He is also the *de facto* king. Everyone is an aide to him, a veritable *crapaud.* "What we have is a system of government led by one man and run by one man."

In Best's scheme, constitution reform requires that we abandon the "all or nothing" neo-Westminster paradigm and replace it with an alternative arrangement which would allow the political forces in the country to be better represented, and to influence policy decisions in a meaningful way. "We want to be represented by real people in parliament, and people could only get there if they are in politics." Best argues that what we have in the Caribbean, with Trinidad being the extreme case, is government and no Parliament.

Since reforms must be familiar in order to be accepted and deemed legitimate, Best recommends that we keep what we have. "I propose we keep the House of Representative exactly as it is now with a maximum leader who is the Chief Executive like an American president." Everybody in that House would be put there by the Prime Minister or the Leader of the Opposition. This would be the House of Government that does not pretend to be a Parliament.

Best argues plausibly that when MPs are elected or rejected by the electorate, it is known that it is in effect the leader of the party that is being endorsed or rejected. His suggestion is that we require rival party leaders to publish a list with the names of the people whom they plan to appoint to head Ministries and other major public bodies so that the public would be able to compare the lists and make choices between or among them. The election will become a contest to determine which Chief Executive has the best people with him. The question that will have to be determined is "best" in terms of what?"

In Best's view, there was another advantage to be achieved by publishing such a list in advance of the election. *Crapauds* could well emerge from their integument. They would be able to negotiate the terms of their involvement prior to the election. "They could determine in advance how much independence they are going to be allowed if they were to agree to come in. The bargaining between them would come into the open… It would strengthen the country because he would have to put good people. It would also strengthen the people he puts because they can bargain with him." This proposed House of Executives or of Government would be elected on the basis of proportional representation. Parties would get shares of seats in relation to the share of the votes which they receive. Best claims that the essence of PR already exists, "although we don't know it."

The House of Government will be complemented by another House which will be elected on the basis of community interest for three, five, or seven years. This new house will include the corporate and vested interests of the land - the trade unions, business and professional associations, women, sportsmen etc. "It would be a huge assembly of interests from the community, each electing their people and changing them as they want so you get representation and politics…. Once you emancipate the people from the Executive, you are going to have real competition about who gets jobs and therefore you are going to get representation."

How workable is Best's corporatist scheme? Might it not lead to greater bureaucratisation in the proposed House of Government instead of greater autonomy? Will *crapauds* in fact become princes and princesses simply because their names are made public prior to the election? Will every dissident splinter group or mini association be entitled to membership in the new House of Parliament? And if so, in what proportion? How would these delegates be controlled, disciplined or recalled if they are seen to be acting contrary to the interests of their parent bodies? How will policy differences between the new House of Parliament and the House of Government be negotiated? Will the new house replicate the divisions in the society and eventually come to resemble the old House? What will be the dynamic between the two houses? Will new tabnernacle be old church writ large?

Best has proposed that the House of Parliament be given the *final* power to approve or reject legislation, and to ratify key appointments. As he writes, "debate in the House of Government is deliberately meant to focus on the relative merits of competing administrations as an output separate from the communication that the executive in its own House of Government would necessarily be making to the legislature, or House of Parliament for the purpose of having bills and motions passed" (*Express*, December 14, 20, 2002). But when the two Houses do not agree, as would frequently occur, how would differences or deadlock be resolved? Will the differences be negotiated in joint select committees? Best insists that "there can be no dilution whatever of the power of the Legislature and its attendant prerogatives."

Best admits that some of the positive benefits which he envisages will not obtain immediately, that it is likely that the new House of Parliament would not be very different from the old Senate, and that it could become dominated by the old ethnic and cultural considerations. He is however hopeful that over time the systems would morph into something that is positive, and that the various groups would get themselves properly organised and functioning to elect their delegates. He also recognises that where there is politics, there is inevitably cacophony and confusion, and that some formula would have to be instituted to "incorporate new interests or expel old ones on the basis of stipulated majorities" (*Express*, December 2002).

Best is however not deterred by details, all of which could be negotiated. The creation of the House is however deemed a compelling requirement. Such a creation would change the algebra of politics. "What you want to do is to impregnate the process with a dynamic that would carry it in the other direction. And it would be enough simply to have different types of elections and to have community interests there. It is very difficult for community interests simply to replicate the ethnic polarization that you have in the other House. There will be that tendency, but it would be circumscribed. And that would be the dynamic principle that makes it different over the long run."

Best admits that getting the proposal accepted and understood could take time, but counsels patience. "I can wait one hundred years, but I want to install the mechanism to make it possible some time in the future on the assumption that people are going to learn, and that people are intelligent and reasonable, and sensible, [at least] some of them. And if you get sufficient people like that - we don't know what the magic number is, 5%, 10%, 20%, then the civilization could save itself by its own exertions, and save it's Caribbean neighbours by example" (Ryan 2003a).

National and regional surveys indicate clearly that most people in the Caribbean are basically satisfied with the existing constitutional architecture, and only want minimalist change to get the system to work as it was meant to (Ryan 1999, 2003). Given this, one is not sanguine that Best's proposals would find favour with many in the electorate, at least not in the form that it is proposed. There might however be agreement in principle that there is need to unshackle the Senate by broadening the basis of representation, and that there is also need to change the balances so that the government does not have an automatic majority on routine legislation. One would also need to institutionalise a formula to resolve deadlock when it arises, as it inevitably will.

The constitutional proposals advanced by Best and Panday for breaking deadlock have one thing in common, *viz.,* they share a "vision" of the process of governance, though for reasons that might be quite different. Both reject the dominant majoritarism Westminster paradigm in preference for the vision of democracy which emphasizes proportionalism. Westminster fundamentalists, who are in a majority across the region, insist that concentrated policy making power is desirable in the interest of clear accountability to citizens in future elections, while the supporters of proportional representation prefer policy-making to be the outcome of a complex process of bargaining between winners and losers, and ins and outs. The one stresses the responsibility of incumbent elites, authorised by elections, to do things on behalf of voters, while the other emphasises the importance of continuous participation, i.e., permanent politics.

In the majoritarian perspective, elections are a one-stage device for selecting both elites and policies. Elites are given a mandate by voters for which they account when they seek an extension of their trusteeship. If they do not perform, incumbents (the "rascals") are thrown out. Westminsterphiles argue that if power is dispersed, responsibility may be difficult to pinpoint, and elections may bear only a tenuous relation to the formation of winning policy coalitions. In the dispersed power paradigm, elections play an indirect role in policy-making, since the winning coalition may change from issue to issue. In the consociational vision, the views of all and not just a bare majority or plurality, must be considered. The views of the minority must not be ignored by the majority. Power must thus be dispersed. Minorities or their representatives or agents must be able to protect themselves prospectively rather than only after the fact. Post-election bargaining is thus seen to be as important a stage of the democratic process as are elections.

The two stage system is seen to be particularly desirable where the issues are not clear-cut, and the citizens not homogeneous or united in their views and values such as is the case in countries like Trinidad and Tobago. Where the citizenry is divided and the issues complex and unpredictable in terms of likely outcomes, citizens necessarily prefer to have representatives who bargain for them on each separate issue and who resemble them symbolically. We should however note that good governance almost always involves a "trade-off." No constitutional or electoral system can deliver all that democrats would wish them to. All systems have flaws, both in terms of design, and in the way in which they operate.

In his study of elections as instruments of democracy, and using case material from several countries that practice either majoritarian or proportional systems, Bingham Powell Jr. came to the conclusion that the latter system was to be preferred. As he wrote:

> The persistent superiority of the proportional influence designs in linking the median citizen and the policymakers should give pause to those attracted by the idea of the decisive election as a direct tool for citizen control. The majoritarian vision assumes that identifiability, unchecked majorities, and clarity of responsibility will sustain governments expressing majority preferences not distant

from them. The frequent appearance of the latter underlines the question, mandates for what?

The general good congruence between the citizen median and the governments and policymakers in the proportional design systems should be reassuring to those worried about dependence on elite coalition formation or the instability of post-election governments. With surprising consistency, each proved compatible with good citizen-policymaker congruence. In these countries at this time, the proportional vision and its designs enjoyed a clear advantage over their majoritarian counterparts in using elections as instruments of democracy. It remains to be seen if new democratic designs and new circumstances will challenge these findings. (Powell 2000: 253-254)

Proportionate systems of representation, or Presidential systems, hybrid or otherwise, do not avoid deadlock. If anything, they make deadlock a more frequent occurrence. Analyses of the political process in Latin America reveal that deadlock and political calcification are a recurrent problem, which in many cases are only resolved by violent street confrontations (Stepan and Skatch 1993) such as we witnessed in Venezuela in 2001-2003 We also note the case of the United States in 2000 where the intervention of the Federal Supreme Court became necessary to resolve electoral deadlock. Courts at the state level also often intervene to sort out conflicts arising from sclerosis and at the state level. Fifteen US states, New York among them, have Republicans in control of one house and Democrats in control of the other. At the federal level, only two seats now separate the parties. Indeed, if we undertook a survey of systems, we would see that political gridlock is the norm rather than the exception, and that resolution of deadlock, when it takes place, is never permanent but lasts until the next crisis erupts. Power sharing arrangements which are now part of the tool box of the good governance movement rarely last long as the recent cases of Israel, Northern Ireland, Italy, Austria and the Netherlands reveal. In sum, deadlock is the normal or permanent condition rather than one that is exceptional. We might need to redefine exactly what constitutes a constitutional crisis.

Power Sharing in the Caribbean

There are many who believe that some form of "power sharing" or "shared governance" is the only way to deal with the deadlock that currently characterises plural societies such as Guyana and Trinidad an Tobago.

One agrees in principle with that assertion. Attempts to broker political pieces in such societies must however take heed of the fact that both are deeply traumatised societies in which the two major ethnic groups each have their chosen rituals, taboos, traumas and hurts (real, invented and imagined) which mark and sustain their identity as a group, the "we ness" and "they ness" which characterises their behaviour. These feelings of shared belongingness and of being beseiged, were nurtured over many years of silent and open conflicts and fends in and around the plantations and villages, and are reactivated during periods prior to and following elections, and during ethnic festivals. Any attempt to build political bridges by the implantation of super-structural devices such as dialogue or power sharing must recognise the historical, social and psychological contents in which these attitudes were developed. To be effective, social reconstruction must accompany efforts at political reconstruction, if not precede them. Power sharing cannot work in a vacuum.

In traumatised societies, calls for power sharing and the empowerment of out groups are seen by the group or regime which is being asked to make the greater number of concessions or sacrifices as a prescription not only for material loss and deprivation, but for symbolic loss as well. Power is conceptualised as a zero-sum commodity and calls for power sharing are seen as a threat to the ruling political and social elite's control over the commanding heights of the state apparatus, and also as a recipe for the loss of psychic income and social face, especially if the new partner to the proposed shared arrangement is seen as being socially challenged or to have moral values that are more "flexible" than those claimed by the erstwhile hegemon. If one party thinks of itself as the party of god or virtue, and the other as ethically or religiously challenged, fears of contamination arise. The arrangement may either not last or remain fragile.

Power sharing seems to work best with groups which have shared core values and past associations, and equally important, where the relationship between them is asymmetrical. Where the parties are roughly equal in terms of power, or one is seen as a threat to the political survival of the other, the chances of success are less than would be the case where one party is clearly dominant, but needs the support of the other as a junior partner. Power sharing also seems to work best in societies where parties, though distinct, see themselves as part of a mosaic which must work together to get public goals achieved. The Dutch talk about the "polder" model, East African villagers talk about "harambee," and Tobagonians talk about "lend hand." In certain political systems, diversity is seen as legitimate; people are encouraged to be what they are and hold the views they have, but are also expected to cooperate with others to get certain basic things done. Parties in these systems are also mature enough to accept the discipline of coalition. Caribbean politics are however not driven by a search for the "general will" or for consensus, but by the notion that the winner takes all.

Another problem with the power sharing concept in the Caribbean is that the *word* itself poses ideological problems for many. Desmond Hoyte, for example described the word as a "shibboleth," something without any precise meaning. His complaint, and that of others, was that people use the term but do not stop to give it any precise definition or think it through thoroughly. How does one give the concept "traction" in a society where civil society is weak, ethnicised, and not easily mobilised, and where the political culture does not conduce towards consensual problem solving and coalition building? How does power sharing work in societies where leaders believe that they must present themselves to themselves, their followers, and to each other as "strongmen," cocks of the political gayelle?

Part of the problem is that Caribbean leaders have been programmed to see themselves as sabre rattling maximum figures. Politics is seen as an activity wherein macho men "cock" their rivals and monopolise the political stage. Power sharing also becomes a problem because the state and the spoils and patronage that are derived therefrom are considered the ultimate prize of politics, not to be shared with any competitor. Only one combatant can wear the golden crown. While power sharing might thus be an antidote to the deep feelings of ethnic insecurity and deprivation, the prevailing tension is much too high to accommodate any such entente. What is ideologically necessary might not now be politically possible. The longest journey however begins with small steps which clearly need to be taken in order to build the confidence and trust without which no regime of shared governance, however desirable, would survive.

Epilogue

MAXIMUM LEADERSHIP IN TRINIDAD AND TOBAGO: FROM WILLIAMS TO PANDAY

*T*he Caribbean landscape has witnessed the rise and fall of many *caudillos* or maximum leaders. Over the years, the passing parade has included the likes of Toussaint l'Ouverture, Juan Bosch, Fidel Castro, Raphael Trujillo, Francois Duvalier and Joaquin Balaguer. In the English speaking Caribbean, names such as Alexander Bustamante, Norman and Michael Manley, Eric Williams, V.C. Bird, Eric Gairy, Edward Le Blanc, Forbes Burnham, Robert Bradshaw, Ebeneza Joshua, Errol Barrow, John Compton and Cheddi Jagan, come readily to mind. All have had to stave off challenges to their positions of dominance mounted by younger aspirants for office who believed that the old "heroes" had outlived their political usefulness. The phenomenon of the maximum leader who is considered or who considers himself the "saviour" of his people and to be beyond political challenge, has been the focus of a great deal of debate within the Caribbean and other emergent states, old and new (Allahar 2001). All the mass parties which have appeared on the Caribbean landscape in the latter half of the 20th century were led by these flamboyant characters, most of whom have since gone to the great beyond.

In Trinidad and Tobago, the People's National Movement (PNM) and the United National Congress (UNC) are led by men who believe that they have a destiny to mould. Both men regard any challenge to their leadership as an unthinkable apostasy. One recalls PNM Political Leader Patrick Manning describing himself in 1994 as the "father of the nation," and saying that the "darkest day" of his life was that on which he was challenged for the leadership. That was not supposed to be done by members of the church that Dr. Eric Williams, the former Political Leader of the PNM and Prime Minister of Trinidad and Tobago had built, challenges by ANR Robinson in 1970 and Karl Hudson Phillips in 1981 notwithstanding (Ryan 1972, 1989). What, asked Manning, was he to do if he gave up political leadership as many were demanding when he lost the elections of 1995? Politics was his sole vocation. In the case of Basdeo Panday, political leader of the UNC, he had the historic role of being the first person in Trinidad and Tobago of Indian descent to be elected to the office of Prime Minister, an achievement which gave him heroic and guru status among Indo-Trinidadians. Challenging him was seen as an act of political harikari and ungratefulness.

The conflict between three former Members of Parliament belonging to the United National Congress (UNC), Messrs. Ramesh Maharaj, Trevor Sudama and Ralph Maraj, and Panday which took place in Trinidad and Tobago throughout the latter half of 2001, and which culminated in their expulsion from the party and their decision to form an alternative party to contest the general elections of December 11, 2001 was an Indo-Caribbean version of an age old phenomenon related to the dynamics of leadership change in Caribbean society. The "gang of three" who broke away from the UNC and established Team Unity expressed frustration with Mr. Panday's neo-traditional leadership style. Complained Trevor Sudama:

> We have come too far [along] the road of democracy to turn back now. We've come too far with maximum leadership and one-man rule. The leader must operate within the rules and listen to the people. If you cannot respect democracy in the party, how can you respect it in the Government? ... I am committed to supporting the leader on the basis of the principles that he disposes. If there is any semblance of betrayal to those principles, then it is my duty to question them regardless of the consequences. (*Guardian*, September 2, 2002)

Mr. Sudama felt that Panday was trying to imitate Dr. Eric Williams. According to Sudama, "there is no doubt about it. He is trying to emulate Dr. Williams and is doing so consciously." Sudama observed that "Panday has a very strong personality, and it is easy [for him] to cross the line and become an autocratic leader. If you are not willing to abide by the rules when you get state power, you can easily cross the line" (*Express*, August 5, 2001).

Ralph Maraj likewise fussed about Mr. Panday's leadership style and the dominance which he exercised over the Cabinet. As he averred, "we need to move away from the maximum leader syndrome that has suffocated the politics of Trinidad and Tobago for so many years. And when maximum leadership suffocates politics, talent is wasted." Maraj, who also suffered at the hands of Patrick Manning when he was a member of the PNM Cabinet of 1991-1995, remarked that it was time to

> …move away from [a system] where people vote every five years and we revert to a kind of tyranny, the tyranny of the Cabinet over the Parliament, for example, and the tyranny that exists sometimes within a Cabinet situation, where the views of one individual, whether right or wrong, could prevail. (*Sunday Guardian*, August 26, 2001)

Sudama agreed, noting that once it was known what the leader's preferences were, one either went along or resigned, an act which was not always easy to undertake, especially when the numerical balance in Parliament was close as was the case between 1991 and 2001. In such circumstances, community pressure served to keep one in line. Needless to say, many Ministers also thought twice about giving up the salaries and the perks of office which were not available to them once they left the Cabinet. One had to meet commitments and expectations.

Part of the problem is that Caribbean prime ministers are neo-tribal "heroes" whom supporters applaud and rally behind regardless of what others, including the detribalised middle class, think of them. As Calypsonian the Mighty Sparrow once said to critics of Dr. Williams in his composition, *William The Conqueror*, "Leave the damn doctor.

He ain't trouble all you. Leave the dam doctor, what he do he well do." The Prime Minister was seen to be exempt from the morality that would apply to mere mortals. The more bizarre, outrageous, corrupt, immoral or downright stupid and delusional his behaviour, the more canonized he was by his flock, many of whom believed he could do no wrong, providing of course that he "performs" and keeps their bread buttered. Another dimension of the problem is that civil society is weak and fragmented ethnically, and thus unable to speak coherently in a manner that would compel wayward leaders to act responsibly.

Maximum Leadership Panday Style

Albert Gomes, who as Chief Minister, dominated politics in Trinidad in the 1950-1956 era, once declared "I am the Government of Trinidad and Tobago." Eric Williams, who succeeded him, was likewise reported as having said, "when I speak, no dog must bark, and when I say cometh, you cometh, and when I say goeth, you goeth." Basdeo Panday, who one wag described as "Williams in a dhoti," declared that "no one will attack my government and remain unscathed." "No political leader will allow a Judas to remain on board" (*Guardian*, October 22, 2001). When challenged in 2001, Panday loudly complained that there were traitors on board his political ship. He however noted that political duplicity was a phenomenon with which his predecessors in office also had to deal, and that unlike what happened in Communist countries where people were shot or detained for challenging leaders, the "lil cussout" which was taking place within the UNC was a non-violent and "normal part of the dialectic of the democratic process. Once people competed for power, there was bound to be conflict." Panday conceded that it was "natural for people to aspire to leadership." He however warned those who challenged him that they were "playing with fire."

A variety of terms have been used by social scientists to define and explain the leadership style displayed by Panday. The most widely used (and abused) term is that of "charisma," which was introduced into Western social science by Max Weber (1968) who had the following to say about it:

> Charismatic authority rests on the effectual and personal devotion of the follower to the lord and his gifts of grace (charisma). It comprises especially magical abilities, revelations of heroism, power of the mind and of speech. The eternally new, the non-routine, the unheard of and the emotional rapture from it are sources of personal devotion. The purest types are the rule of the prophet, the warrior hero, the great demagogue. (cited in Truzzi 1971: 175-176)

Charismatic type domination has no ethical content. Hitler, in Weber's thought, would be as charismatic as Gandhi (Giddens 1972). Allegiance and obedience are given or expected to be given to the leader as a person rather than to the formal institutions he leads. He is seen as being the beneficial owner of whatever institutions exist as well as the financial resources (booty) which flow to and from them. He is free to do with the resources whatever pleases him or suits his interest. Spontaneity, creativity, non-routine, and seemingly irrational behaviour are also characteristic. Such leaders feel that they are not bound by rules or by tradition. As Jesus (who was the quintessential charismatic revolutionary) reportedly said, "It is written, but I say unto you." The charismatic leader regards himself as the political "father" (or "uncle")[1] through whom all must pass if they want a share of the political kingdom. This type of leader is thus intolerant of challengers since, in his view, there can only be one hero who enjoys the full confidence of the community. Only he could be right. The challenger must therefore be made to genuflect. Coercion, ostracism, or some other form of deprivation might have to be used to engineer this result.

Followers also have deep social and emotional needs and charismatise and empower leaders. The leader becomes a veritable "beast of burden" who embodies the hopes, fears, anxieties or aspirations of a people who feel dishonoured or alienated. The need for a saviour is particularly felt in "times of trouble" when a national, ethnic or economic crisis strikes or when the moorings of the old society are being challenged or seen to be obsolete and newer ones are blowing in the winds, so to speak, and seek a vehicle to give them concrete expression or validation.

Needless to say, charismatic leadership, by definition, is unstable and generates a great deal of insecurity amongst followers and cronies who feel an acute need to know who the leader's successor is likely to be, whether or not they themselves are ambitious to succeed. This is particularly so when the leader's charismatic integrity begins to decline and he seems about to lose the "mandate of heaven." Disciples and praise singers need to know that the prebends, privileges, prerogatives and pelf which they have acquired are secure. Charismatic administration and justice dispensed by the sage must thus be replaced by the rule of law and precedent. Arbitrariness must be curtailed. Taxes and gifts given to or collected by the leader must be accounted for. In sum, followers seek to force the leader to enact a "magna carta," and to transform him into a type of routinised leader with whom they feel more secure. All of these themes were in evidence in the struggle waged by the leaders of Team Unity against Panday in 2001.

But how genuinely charismatic are the leaders whom we label as such. Weber claims that the "true" charismatic leader "quite deliberately shuns the possession of money and pecuniary income." He is disdainful of economic gain and prefers to be supported by community gifts as he carries out his spiritual duty or mission (Allahar 2001:7).[2] The late Martiniquan psychiatrist, Frantz Fanon, however charged that most "third world" leaders are not genuinely charismatic. They were naught but "chairmen of the board of a society of impatient profiteers." Sir Arthur Lewis (1965) dismissed those he saw in Africa as "loud mouthed demagogues" who paraded as democrats and as successors to tribal chieftains (Osagyefos), teachers (Mwalimu), or even secular successors to Christ.

Nkrumah, for example, had a photograph taken of him with a picture of Jesus in the background saying to him "well done thou good and faithful servant" or "seek ye the political Kingdom and all else will be added unto you." There is the suggestion that Weber's concept of "office charisma" may be an appropriate label for what obtained in the Caribbean context where prime ministers were invested or invested themselves with the legitimacy that was associated with office holding by white colonial Governors who were held in awe. Their "office charisma" rubbed off on their successors. As Allahar (2001:10) observed:

> ...the fact that those offices were formerly held by white colonials gave them a certain esteem and elevated status in the minds of locals and their leader. It is understandable that in the estimation of the ordinary people, those locals who came to replace the colonials were regarded as heroes, liberators and even saviours.

Neemakharamism

In Trinidad and Tobago, the charisma principle was "Indianized" and reinforced within the Hindu community by the concept of *neemakharamism*. This concept gained a great deal of currency in the political discourse that followed Prime Minister Robinson's expulsion in 1989 of Basdeo Panday and other members of the former United Labour Front (ULF) from the cabinet which had taken office following the sweeping victory of the National Alliance in 1986 (Ryan 1989).[3] Those former members of the ULF who opted to remain in the NAR government were accused by Panday of having ridden the backs of the Indian community and its leader in order to secure election to office, and had shown their ingratitude by not joining him in exile. The term has since been mainstreamed and is consistently used to denigrate any individual who dared to oppose Mr. Panday. The word is emotionally loaded and regarded by many as the ultimate term of political abuse or insult within the Hindu community.

The term was of course not invented by Panday. In fact it has been in use within Hindu communities in Trinidad and Guyana to denote anyone who received patronage from a superior (usually a member of the family) and who failed to reciprocate. The concept is of Indian provenience and its literal meaning in Hindi is the betrayer of he who provides "namak" or "salt." The word was used by Morton Klass in his discussion of politics in the village of "Amity" during the 1956 general election. Klass noted that both the PNM candidate and the candidate who represented the Democratic Labour Party (DLP), a progenitor of the UNC, had strong "praja" feelings of obligation. The PNM candidate, who was also Indian, had done a lot for the villagers. His rival was the standard bearer of the DLP which was led by Bhadase Sagan Maraj who was not only respected for his wealth, but was hailed as the "Chief" who had advanced the status of the entire group. Since for most men to decide to vote for either candidate was to be a *neemakharam* to the other, it was not an easy decision to make (Klass 1961:223).[4]

Steven Kangal claims that the term is of "sacred" origin and was used to describe those who violated the life long bond that ought to exist between religious gurus and their *chelas* or devotees. It has however since become secularised and debased. According to Kangal, "the importation of this concept into the political arena to foster and promote self-serving and vindictive political agendas constitutes a flagrant abuse and violation of the sacred *guru/chela* bond and interface that are so fundamental to the tenets and doctrines of Hinduism (*Newsday*, December 2001). Kangal notes that the Hindu *guru* earns and expects life-long devotion and submission from his *chela* or devotee, symbolised by the latter's open display of public prostration. He claims that Panday expected those who crossed him to genuflect to him as an indication of their submission, as ULF/NAR parliamentarian Kelvin Ramnath did by touching Panday's feet (*gorlage*) as part of the penalty which he paid for crossing Panday in 1991. Panday, he noted called on Sudama to do likewise. He was told to apologise for his treachery or "face oblivion for the rest of your life" (*Newsday*, November 28, 2001).

Sudama refused to apologise, and counter accused Panday of being a "*Maha Neemakharam*" (a great betrayer).[5] Maharaj likewise refused to apologise. Professing to have been hurt by Panday's accusations, Maharaj denied that he was a *neemakharam*, and reminded Panday that when he was kicked out of the cabinet by ANR Robinson in 1988 and was impecunious, he had provided him with a rent free office in his chambers, secretarial services, court cases to handle as well as spending money since he had little of his own. He also reminded Panday that he had raised funds and provided legal expertise which, according to Maharaj, kept Mr. Panday out of jail following his arrest in 1995 on charges of having sexually assaulted two female employees in the offices of the All Trinidad Sugar Estates and Factory Workers Trade Union. Maharaj clearly hinted that Panday was guilty in the matter, and that were it not for Maharaj's efforts, he would have ended up in jail. Far from being an ingrate, Maharaj felt he had shown respect and devotion to Panday, his beloved *guru*. Maharaj tearfully noted that

> ....nobody loved Mr. Panday more than me. Nobody has been closer to Mr. Panday than me. This has been the most agonising experience in my life. The Prime Minister is a person I have built a strong attachment to over the years. We have both been lawyers in practice together; we have been in political struggle together from about 1979. I have respect for him as my leader.

Kangal considered Panday's use of the term *neemakharam* an indication of the "backward state of Indo-politics." He also claimed that there is no equivalent term within the Afro-creole community and that the PNM, which has had its share of dissidents and "millstones," never used terms of imprecation to describe them.[6] Kangal argued that Panday's abuse of the term was intended to bolster his claim to charismatic or guru status. As he complained:

> Charismatic leaders deify and *gurufy* their image, manipulate and enslave their supporters, personalise the politics and exact blind, submissive and chela-like adulations and political loyalties from the tribe. On what grounds are Ramesh, Trevor and Ralph branded as *Maha-Neemakharams* to be banished to *Banwas* (wilderness)? (*Newsday*, December 8, 2001)

The results of the 2001 election made it clear that *neemakharamism* was of various types. For many, voting PNM was a more heinous form of *neemakharamism* than having the leader violate their party's "core" founding principles. The latter was forgivable; the former was not. The rationale used by many was that they preferred to live under "Panday corruption" than "Manning corruption." As Maraj lamented;

> For many, party loyalty was more important than taking a stand on corruption. The sad thing about the issue of corruption is that so many people don't care. There are possibly hundreds of thousands of people in Trinidad and Tobago who care not one jot about corruption. For these people, party loyalty comes before everything else. I am reminded of a line from Shakespeare's Julius Caesar which says that if Caesar had stabbed their mothers, the people would still have adored and supported him. (*Newsday*, November 4, 2001)

Maraj complained that Indians cursed and were otherwise cruel to him on the campaign trail when he inveighed against corruption.

Criticisms of Panday became louder and more direct following his technical defeat in December 2001. A stinging critique of Panday came from the pen of Mukesh Babooram whose winning composition at the 2002 *Pichakaree* composition, "Back to the Opposition," lampooned Panday's claims to charismatic authority.[7] Babooram accused Panday of having "charhawayed" (betrayed) the sugar workers and his party supporters in pursuit of his own personal goals and those of his new friends, and of insisting that those who crossed him and wanted restitution had to bow down and "soorhaway" (appease) him. As Babooram warned Indians, "never take a bound coolie and make him a dignitary."

Lloyd Best and Indian "Doctor Politics"

An interesting analysis of the phenomenon of maximum leadership in the Caribbean, and of Panday's leadership style in particular, was forthcoming from the pen of Lloyd Best who first coined the phrase "doctor politics" to describe academics who sought political office. Best later broadened the concept to include maximum leaders generally. Best likened the people of the Caribbean to the Israelite tribes who in their despair and "epistemic dispossession," turned to the magical hope of the Messiah for delivery. "That is the psychology behind what we have called "Doctor Politics" - the politics of the lame and the dispossessed, of those who have been intimidated and discouraged into the conviction that they could never hope to help themselves and must depend on the Ministry of an omnipotent Redeemer" (*Tapia*, November 16, 1969). Maximum prophetic leadership, like charismatic leadership generally, was one of mutuality. The dependency of the flock brought the shepherd into being and sustained him:

> Such expectations always throw up the men to meet them; and in such a climate, the best-intentioned leadership is always tempted to take a prophetic turn. Leadership itself is perverted by the passive salvationism of the people; in place of the leader, we get the Prophet, and the fundamental ascription of the Prophet's role is that of infallibility. The process involved is a circular and cumulative one; and the delusions of follower and Prophet feed and magnify each other, with cumulatively disastrous consequences. *(ibid.)*

Best observed that Westminster created institutions required participatory behaviour, but that the political process in the Caribbean remained akin to that of the crown colony regime. In his view, Williams, Panday, and other Caribbean leaders were a Governor Picton writ large. As Best observed:

> Our political practice presumes a messiah and a crowd, a man with power necessary to keep other men in order. In our voyage from Picton to Panday, we've sought in vain to displace governors who derive their authority from above and outside by leaders whose legitimacy is supplied from below and inside. And yet, personal power has remained effectively unbridled. The result is continued and continuing excess.

Best argued that the law of politics in the Caribbean is that "there is only space for the single politician and leader; so long as he is in the saddle, every other contender or candidate is required to hunker down as supporting cast. If you want to be top and to enjoy celebrity, take your bundle leave and go. Form your own party. That is how we got Bustamante when Manley started the PNP. It is how we got Burnham, perhaps even Barrow. That too is how we got Robinson."

Best was as sharply critical of Panday as he had been of Dr. Williams whom he accused of leaving the PNM and the UNC like political morgues. He also felt that Panday was seeking to be the Williams of the 21st century. "This was however impossible because Trinidad and Tobago is not going to allow it.... He does not own the party. He is just another member of the party," a judgement that few would have agreed with at the time. Continued Best as he surveyed the twists and turns which Panday made with respect to the UNC, "Panday wants to run the party and Government like a one-man show, so he decides that there must be inclusion, and he wants to turn the party on and off as he likes it. That era is over; people are emerging from the political morgues of both parties" (*Express,* October 22, 2001).

Best saw Panday as the prototype of the charismatic maximum leader. As he wrote:

> Panday's *persona* and method relied neither on organization or ideas; they conformed almost ideally to the messianic prescription of hero and crowd, necessarily buttressed by parasitic oligarchy. The issue of the Leader's stewardship has always been at what precise moment and by what precise devices would that outmoded way of proceeding come up against the ethos of a free people – with its stress on democratic participation based on individual, group and community autonomy. (*Trinidad and Tobago Review,* April 1, 2001)

Best observed that the response of the Indian community to the prophetic leader was in the main to follow automatically and to "ask no awkward questions, for the time being, at least." Best was however correct when he noted that neither of the two leaders was a genuine tyrant. They were "authoritarian democrats":

> We must not fall into the error of confounding the governor figure that Williams was and that Panday has been successor to, and of which Manning and Robinson have been carbon copies of, with a Hitler, a Franco or a Mussolini (*Express*, February 2, 2002).

Best notes that whereas dominant leaders in Europe needed to create a vast police state to keep themselves enrenched in power, this was not required in the Caribbean:

> In Europe a would-be dictator needs to quell a great multiplicity of forces before he can consider himself installed. Here, Duvalier, Trujillo, Gomez, Bastista, Machado and Marco Perez were pushing an almost open door. In the Caribbean, central domination is a way of life. Only in Cuba and Barbados perhaps, are the elements of a ruling class confident of being inheritors of the landscape, governors of the dew. James was the first in the English speaking WI to raise the alarm, not about an individual with whom he disagreed and had plumbed to the very depths, but about a system problem much larger than the person.
>
> Doctor Politics is not dictatorship, neither creeping nor galloping. Maximum leadership is as integral to authoritarian democracy as is parasitic oligarhy. It enjoys widespread popular if still ambivalent support, even when, as in present-day Cuba, it is not facilitated by an external state of siege. Its irresistible appeal is to the lame and the weak, especially the educated who enjoy much technical skill, can boast excellent performance in imperial school ... but have been rendered utterly impotent by endemic exile and epistemic dispossession and are therefore in Babylon forever, waiting for deliverance, be it President's pronouncement, constitution reform, Leaders' agreement, or act of God. (*ibid.*)

Interestingly, Best was of the view that Panday, the Indo-Trinidadian maximum leader, had given birth to an Afro-Trinidadian alternative maximum leader, just as Dr. Williams had brought Dr. Rudranath Capildeo into being as the Indian answer to him in 1962 (Ryan 1972). That individual was not the current Political Leader of the PNM, Mr. Patrick Manning, who was not seen by many as having the status of a maximum leader, try as he might to project himself as the "father" or the "shepherd" of the nation chosen by God, but the President, ANR Robinson, whom many Indians saw not as a neutral Head of State, but as the partisan leader of the Afro-Trinidadian community whose agenda was to bring down the Panday regime which he had helped to enthrone in 1995 when the elections of that year yielded a 17-17 tie and Robinson's two seats in Tobago were used to give Mr. Panday a working majority (Ryan 1996). As Best opined:

> The paradox here is that Panday's spirited revival of the Doctor Politics of Williams is what lent legitimacy to his old rival in the role. The UNC Leader's way is through confident improvisation. Soon he was assaulting expectations simply by the change of procedure without actually changing either law or regulation. The public duly saw a new role for Robinson as alternative maximum leader. Many were soon glad they had not succeeded in blocking a practising politician from being elected as President. The repeated standoffs of the last 30 months attest to the ensuing contestation. *(ibid)*

Best argued that Panday had helped to enhance Robinson's stature as a maximum leader:

> Robinson's place in the pantheon is every bit as secure as that of Williams. Just when it mattered, in the age of sovereign independence and democratic participation, and in spite of needing himself to be an alternate maximum leader, he did find the way effectively to torpedo authoritarian democracy, Doctor Politics, central domination, personal power and one-man rule. His device

was simply to invoke the power of deliberation and delay
(*Express* April 6, 2001).

This transformation of the role of non-ceremonial head to one
which has active political clout was seen to Best to be a "Caribbean
revolution without violence" (*Express,* April 6, 2001).

Best was correct when he noted that Robinson's political method
of proceeding was radically different from that which was typical of
the flamboyant leaders who had adorned the Caribbean political
landscape. His style was not to be garrulous, but to use the power of
his office to delay and dither, and occasionally to use it as a bully pulpit
to warn the country about "creeping dictatorship" or about the absence
of "moral and spiritual values." "Through his method of galay,
deliberation, dithering and delay, President Robinson has emerged not
only as the man in the middle, but also as the most charismatic *persona*
of this revolutionary age of sovereign independence and democratic
participation" (*Express,* April 9, 2002). While Robinson did emerge as
a foil to Panday, few would however concede him genuine charismatic
status. He was a legal-rational instrument of those Afro-creoles who
were looking for someone to checkmate Panday.

Despite his encomiums about Robinson, whom he puzzlingly
described as "the most charismatic persona of this revolutionary age
of sovereign independence and democratic participation," Best believed
that his intervention had served to accelerate the delegitimisation of
maximum leadership:

> In spite of himself, the President has driven the final nail in
> the coffin of personal power, central domination, one-man
> rule, and authoritarian democracy.... Maximum leadership
> has self-destructed as a class, breed and genre. (*Express,* April
> 9, 2001)

These leaders, who were all overwhelmed by *hubris,* "have now
gone down with Williams, destroyed by the accumulation of experience,

event and episode" (*ibid*). But is charismatic leadership indeed dead, waiting only to be churched? We shall return to this question.

Evaluating Mr. Panday's Leadership

Maximum leaders often cultivate an "image" and identify themselves with a major project that allows them to appear to transcend petty differences within the parties or nations which they lead. One is reminded of the Hegelian aphorism that "political genius consists of identifying oneself with a principle." National Unity and ethnic and social inclusion were the *mantras* chanted by Panday. Mr. Panday sought to grab the high ground in this battle for inclusion, and argued that the aim of his PNM and Team Unity rivals was to keep the UNC bivouacked in Caroni, Naparima and Oropouche. Panday's declared long-term political ambition was to mobilise his political troops and take them across the Caroni plains, encircle the PNM in the East West Corridor, and eventually drive it into the Gulf of Paria there to rendezvous with its founder, Dr. Eric Williams. He however dressed up his goal in noble nation building terms. As he told his followers, the goal of unity and inclusion was so important to him that he "would rather lose the government and the Prime Ministership, and pack up and go home rather than give up the struggle."

Many however believe that notwithstanding his unity narratives, Mr. Panday was a hypocritical closet racist who did not genuinely care for the grass roots of either race, claims to the contrary notwithstanding. But there is no gainsaying the fact that his politics over the years, whether in opposition or in office, revealed him as one who was committed, even if ritualistically, to the politics of ethnic and class inclusion. Some will no doubt say that he was a political chameleon who knew what one had to say and do if one had to win and hold power in contemporary Trinidad and Tobago. One had to straddle many fences. Panday also knew by dint of hard experience that it was even more important for a party which had its centre of gravity in the "groves" and the "plantations" to genuflect to the communities that surround the Port and the hills that overlook it if it was to succeed in securing the social legitimacy which it needed to become "creole" (in a generic sense) and part of the mainstream. That was an inevitable dimension of the politics of transition. As Lloyd Best well puts it, "his main drive towards dilution of the essentially Indo party was more practical than pragmatic. How would he break the deadlock if he remained in his central Trinidad cocoon? National Unity, therefore, was no mere propaganda ruse or ideological indulgence" (*Trinidad and Tobago Review*, September 2, 2002).

One can thus argue that Panday's personality and his private views and prejudices on the question of race were of secondary importance. Panday, it could be argued, recognised the need for a politics of national unity and inclusion, and his "genius" as a leader lay in the fact that he acted in accordance with the role that he believed history had carved out for him. Had he chosen to go against the tide, he would have remained a "Caroni Prime Minister," marooned on the southern side of the banks of the river that runs through that county. His "freedom" derived from his recognition of necessity. Panday must thus be given credit for helping the society to manage a soft landing on the ethnic issue when he first came to power in December 1995. Had he been triumphal, there is no telling what might have happened. Panday's other gift was his ability to "deal," to "zigzag" and to be flexible. As he philosophized, "in politics, one cannot be rigid and unbending. There must always be compromise because you have to deal with all kinds of people" (*Guardian*, May 8, 2002).

Panday was however a dismal failure on several other counts. He bragged that his regime out-performed every other that we have had since Independence. And it is true that under the Panday administration, one saw some improvement in the quality of the physical infrastructure. Roads were paved, more water flowed in the pipes than was the case in 1995; there were more new schools, more sports stadia, a new Airport, a new energy plant, a desalinisation plant, and much else. As important as these were, much of it was made possible by economic circumstances which the PNM had helped to put in place and which the UNC did nothing to create. The surpluses were there and they spent them, wasting and stealing much of it in the process. One agrees fully with

Lloyd Best when he observed that "the cackle about 'performance' adds up to no more than the good fortune of enhanced surpluses from the offshore to be distributed lavishly onshore while the opportunity lasts." Where surpluses did not exist, the option pursued by the UNC was to lock the country into high levels of indebtedness.[8] Much that was borrowed was stolen or wasted.[9]

What Panday also failed to do was to improve the quality of governance in the country, or to add value to the stock of social capital. His legacy on the good governance criterion was completely negative. Almost from the very beginning of his ministry, he found it difficult to make the transition from political pugilist to statesman, the use of jackets and tie notwithstanding. He just did not wear the mantle of Prime Minister well. He played himself to the hilt, insulting the peoples collective intelligence in the process. The result was persistent bitterness in the public theatre. The bile flowed almost uninterruptedly. The attack on the institutions and processes of good governance was sustained. There were vicious attacks on the media, on the judiciary, the President, on individuals in civil society with whom he did not agree and who were deemed to be "enemies" to be done in preemptively, on political rivals whom he called "jackasses," "corbeaux, and "satanic elements," and much else.[10] The Speakership was corrupted as was the office of Prime Minister which was used as part of a game of musical chairs or revolving doors to exclude and embarrass his Attorney General. The office of Government appointed senator was also devalued by the excess to which it was exposed.[11] Panday also enunciated a chilling credo as to what he believed the Westminster system allowed or indeed mandated. As he said in response to criticisms, "in politics, you do what you must in order to win in the struggle for power. You either do or die. There are no points for coming second. Glory belongs only to the winner. That is the nature of our political system."

Corruption and state plunder also became the defining characteristic of the regime. While some ministers heroically held their noses above the water line, the stench that emerged from the state rooms eventually enveloped all, guilty or innocent. All were tarnished by tales or rumours of public wrong doing. Polling data indicated that close to half of the population drew its own conclusions as to why the Prime Minister was unable to detach himself from the pack as it fed frenziedly at the public trough.[12] It was as if the *epigoni* felt that if the pundit was not squeamish about sin, or did not admit to the validity of the concept, why should they?

Mr. Panday apologised for the behaviour of some of his colleagues whom he said had revealed that they were not electable. For a long while he did not see it fit to apologise for his own public misbehaviour which embarrassed citizens in general and Indo-Trinidadian citizens in particular, even though, as we have seen, only a few dared to pierce the loud silence of the tribe to articulate their displeasure, fearful perhaps that in doing so, they might be deemed disloyal *Maha Neemakharams* or votaries of the demonised or untouchable PNM. Mr. Panday and other UNC front liners later admitted that they made an "error" in not paying more attention to the corruption issue. Panday also apologised to the media for his boorish behaviour which he blamed on his "aggressive nature." "If I was rude and aggressive, I am sorry. Some people are made up like that. They're just aggressive. That is who and what I am. It is my nature, but I assure you, it is a pleasant kind of aggressiveness" (*Guardian,* May 8, 2002).

Given the demographic characteristics and political cultures of Trinidad and Tobago society, Mr. Panday did not lose the 2001 election; neither did he win it. The result as we have seen, was an 18-18 tie. It was however clear that he had lost much of the popular legitimacy which he previously enjoyed. Those who continued to support him did so either instrumentally - these were mainly people who lived "off" politics materially or psychically - or because they believed that the security of the tribe was paramount, notwithstanding the behaviour of its political leader. Though compromised by the events of 2001-2002, Panday remained the reigning communal hero who would prevail over his challengers inside and outside the UNC since a majority in the Indian community still feel that there was no one in the party who could lead it successfully. The UNC will however be quite a different kind of institution after Panday is either disgraced or eventually retires.[13] In sum, what happened to the PNM in the post-Williams era will also befall the UNC.

Panday is anxious to avoid having to leave the political stage in disgrace. A desire for political martyrdom often characterises the behaviour of charismatic or would be charismatic leaders. Sacrifices, such as going to jail for the "crime' of confronting a superior political enemy, is often viewed as a useful strategy for creating emotional bonds between leader and followers. Nehru, Gandhi, and Kwame Nkrumah challenged the might of the British Raj and reaped huge political dividends from doing so. Panday was anxious to mimic their odyssey. Like Kwame Nkrumah who led the Convention Peoples Party to victory in the Gold Coast in 1951, Panday clearly sought to refurbish his tarnished image by courting a prison sentence. He in fact advised his followers to leave him in jail if the PNM conspired to have him imprisoned. As he told them, "my cell is reserved from me…. If they [jail me], this is the first time someone in Trinidad and Tobago is going to win an election from inside the jail." Panday reminded his audience that he had faced the 1995 general election with charges of committing sexual offences hanging over him (*Express*, June 13, 2002). Panday was clearly seeking to reconnect with the Indian heartland, and becoming a "prison graduate" seemed to be one of his strategies for effecting the goal of martyrdom.

Panday: Williams in a Dhoti?

Comparisons have often been made between Eric Williams and Basdeo Panday, and the latter has been described by critics as "Eric Williams in a dhoti." One is not clear what is meant by this expression and whether it was meant to be taken seriously. Admirers of both Williams and Panday find the description odious, though for different reasons. Indo-Trinidadians assert that in terms of the leadership-followership relationship, Williams' interface with the Afro-creole community was no different from Panday's with the Indian community, and that there was as much silence, deference, and mindless support of the one as there is of the other. It is also asserted that both men believed they were little kings or gods who owned the parties they founded and felt that it was out of order for any "traitorous deputy" to challenge them. The accusation is also made that Williams presided over grand corruption in the PNM, and that in this regard he and Panday were different sides of the same coin. Likewise, it is said that both started out as radicals and ended up capitulating to the parasitic oligarchy. How true are these assertions? No doubt there are many competing "truths."

Even though both men were characterised as political doctors and maximum leaders, and they do have many characteristics in common, there is also much that distinguishes them in terms of their political style and policy preferences. Here we are concerned only with matters of style. One obvious difference is that Williams was a scholar politician and a philosopher king while Panday is a professional politician *par excellence,* one of the most colourful in the contemporary Caribbean. Williams the politician was an extension of Williams the historian who used the political platform and his knowledge of Caribbean history as an instrument for furthering the emancipation of the people who were the offspring of the enslaved and the indentured. Williams wrote *The Negro in the Caribbean,* and spoke at length about the inequities of slavery and the massa system, but he was not, as some allege, unmindful of the children of indenture. Williams in fact advised his primary constituents, the Afro-creoles, that "every step in the education of Indians is a step in the production of that well-informed body of citizens on which West Indian democracy depends; every Indian admitted to the professions and the Civil Service is a further victory in the cause of that full participation of local men in the administration of the British West Indies without which self-government is a delusion" (*Guardian,* January 28, 1955).

As a politician, Williams was economical with the use of coercion to deter opposition though he was not above doing so when challenged, as he repeatedly was, by radical intellectuals, unionists, calypsonians and the media. Williams' style was to rely on ridicule, "picong" and the clever riposte. "Let the jackass bray", he would say to the critical calypsonian. He also sought to deflate the opposition by asking "Change from what to what"? "You do not change the successful for the unsuccessful, you do not change winners for losers". Such was his olympian confidence that he often ignored his critics. Not for him the threat that "no one who attacked his government would remain unscathed."

To be sure, states of emergency were declared and repressive legislation placed on the statute books, (the Public Order Bill; the Industrial Stabilisation Bill, the Firearms Ordinance, the Summary Offenses Ordinance, undated letters of resignation, a ban on subversive literature etc.), but one could still agree with Williams that under his leadership, Trinidad and Tobago was one of the "most relaxed democracies in the Third World. Discussion was free as was the press. No one is locked up for attacking the government" (*Guardian,* October 9, 1978). The society was never militarised as Burnham or Manley sought to do in the case of Guyana and Jamaica. The other side of the coin was that Williams refused to follow the path chosen by Lee Kuan Yew who imposed a regime of discipline on Singapore. As he shrugged, "if freedom means irresponsibility, too bad" (Ryan 1989:226). He preferred to have Trinidad characterised as a society with a "carnival mentality" rather than as one in which freedom was extinguished in the pursuit of order and industrial development.

While Williams did use abusive language to intimidate his critics when he got "blasted vex" - "who don't like it, get to hell outa here", (or "go and clean toilets in the Bronx") - few ever felt that if they challenged him openly, they would be physically injured by an agent of the state or some unofficial enforcer who felt that he had to rid his master of some "meddlesome" intellectual, unionist, or media magnate. Williams, unlike Panday, never said that "in politics, you do what you must in order to win in the struggle for power. You either do or die. You do in your enemy before he does you in." He did not, for example, deem this author (who was a persistent critic) an "enemy" when he openly told him in a 1976 column (*Express,* May 30, 1976) that he was "the principal fetter on the continued progress of the nation. No one takes you seriously any more, not even your closest colleagues. The country needs to take a good hard searching look at itself, one that is not mediated by the distracting prism of your leadership. As an historian, you must recall Oliver Cromwell's rebuke to the Long Parliament as he dismissed it from power: 'You have sat too long here for any good you have been doing. Depart, I say, and let us have done with you! In the name of God, go!'" The most I recall him doing was to dismiss me as a "scribe" (Ryan 1989: 12-15).

Williams also chastised Karl Hudson Phillips, Vice Chairman of the PNM, for making the statement that power was a resource which, if not used, one would lose, or that "politics was a game of total warfare, of control of people's minds." Williams told Hudson-Phillips that he could not associate himself with any of those ideas. "The responsibility of the PNM is overwhelmingly to assure the country, irrespective of party, that it is competent to rule without making the citizens feel insecure in respect of the abuse of power." Williams told the Vice Chairman who was then organising a campaign to run for the Chairmanship of the PNM, that "[my] understanding of the larger and ultimate goal was more philosophical and less superficial than [yours]. If the party opts for your ideas, so be it. They will have to lie on the bed they make" (*ibid.*).

It is instructive to compare the manner in which Williams dealt with the challenges to his leadership posed by Robinson and Hudson-Phillips, and the way in which Panday dealt with Maharaj, Sudama and Maraj. While there was much that seemed to be similar in those two episodes, Williams treated the challengers with far more "couth" than Panday was able to display. While both challengers told their leader, "who vex, vex," Williams never suggested that those who challenged him were "playing with fire" or might have to "live in the sky." Williams in fact let Hudson-Phillips know that challenging him was not a crime. As he told him, "there is no law against challenging me, and it has become conventional within and outside the party [to do so]" (*ibid.:* 14). Panday likewise accepted challenges and "cuss outs" as normal in democratic politics. One however senses that he was less tolerant and philosophical about it than was Williams. One might argue that Williams could afford to be philosophical since he did not have to face meaningful competition form the Democratic Labour Party (DLP) or the United Labour Front (ULF). But Williams did in fact regard both as serious political threats. He always feared that a radical coalition of Afro-and Indo-Trinidadians could overthrow the PNM.

Panday was equally economical with the use of political force. He was however fortunate that his regime was never systemically challenged as was the case with either Williams, Chambers or Robinson. By 1995, the times had changed. The unions had been tamed and were in retreat. No radical Indo-Trinidadian intellectuals (Raffique Shah excepted) ever confronted Panday the way Williams was challenged by both Afro-Trinidadians and Indo-Trinidadians, often acting together. Whereas oil and sugar were often mixed and used as weapon to hobble Williams and the PNM, Panday never had to face such a combination, not even in a solidarity march on Labour Day. When he was threatened by teachers, public servants or telephone workers with strike or boycott action, Indian workers seemed diffident and reluctant to embarrass Panday and the UNC. One did not want to be branded a *neemakharam*. Race triumphed over class, the reverse of what Panday used to claim would happen in his days as an opposition leader.

In our judgement, it is neither politically correct, nor correct in any way to describe Panday as "Williams in a dhoti". The phrase does not do justice to either personality. There is little question that Panday borrowed freely from Williams' repertoire, but so did Robinson, Chambers and Manning. Williams was the model which they all sought to copy whether consciously or unconsciously. None has been able to match the master. None should in fact seek to do so since the times and circumstances which helped to shape the Williams style have gone forever.

The "Death" of Doctor Politics

Is maximum or charismatic leadership obsolete in Trinidad and Tobago or in the Caribbean as is now widely assumed? Are we living in a "post-heroic," post-charismatic age? Is "Doctor Politics" really dead as radical intellectuals and middle class elements have long been proclaiming, or is this an assertion of what they believe ought to occur in the age of globalisation and good governance? In sum, is the death announcement analysis or advocacy? The assumption that the old leadership paradigm has shifted is based on the assumption that a majority of the Caribbean people are no longer among the politically "lame and halt" looking for a secular messiah, and that they are now ready and able to take up their beds and walk down the road to freedom. In this act of self assertion, the newly empowered masses, assisted by the electronic and transportation revolutions which have exposed their leaders to the relentless glare of the video camera, are said to have consigned would be maximum leaders to the political cemetery. Talk shows, the print media, and 24 hour TV have served to demystify the world, and to expose the fact that contemporary Caribbean emperors have no clothes, let alone underclothes.

Maximum leadership generally thrives best in pastoral or peasant societies or in communities with political and social structures which isolate the masses from the centres of social and economic power and which nurture attitudes of alienation. In such societies, shepherd type leaders appear, crock in hand, offering to take the multitude across the desert into the New Jerusalem, using class, race, religion, language and historical myths of origin or calling as principles around which the crowd is rallied or mobilised. While the goals remain unfilled, the bond between leader and following remains substantially intact unless displaced by a new and successful challenger who either redefines the goal, or displays a superior capacity to achieve the old one. If and when the goal is substantially achieved, the process of routinisation and rationalisation begins to take place as erstwhile followers feel that the need for unity and discipline in the face of the historic enemy or "other" is no longer as acute as it once was.

We have seen some of these things occur in the Caribbean. In the case of Trinidad and Tobago, the children of Williams and the PNM rose up in 1970 and thereafter took charge of their own destiny. The radicals took to the streets and the hills in protest, while the new middle class occupied the offices that had been opened to them as they left the schools and university which the PNM had built. While the process of graduation is not complete, many no longer believe that politics can deliver the kingdoms which they were led to believe lay beyond the mountain top. On reaching the top, they found that there was nothing there, a perception which partially explains their apparent disenchantment with politics.

The graduation process within the Indian community was later in coming. The first generation which had been educated in Christian schools sought to become cosmopolitans and generally tolerated their social and political marginalisation. Those who came later via the Hindu and Islamic schools, and those built by the state, took their places in the interstices of the public and private sectors. Feeling themselves a sociological minority and a pariah group even as they progressively became dominant in both sectors, they rallied behind Panday once it appeared that the UNC constituted a viable ethnic beast of burden which would enable them to achieve social, economic and political empowerment and enrichment. Some are of the view that the community has now graduated, and no longer needs a salvationist leader such as Panday. In their view, he has fulfilled his historical purpose. The majority however still believes that six years in office is not nearly sufficient, and that there is still need for much to be done to consolidate the victories which were "won" in 1995 and 2000.

This feeling that the revolution is unfinished and that it is still reversible is entertained by elements within the middle class and the *nouveaux riche,* but even more firmly among rurally based Indians especially the elderly. Both groups still feel dispossessed and claim that the socio-cultural deficits that the community accumulated over the wilderness years have not yet been erased. They in fact accuse Panday of having paid insufficient attention to their needs and of taking his base for granted as he pursued the chimera of national unity and ethnic inclusion.

While some abandoned the erstwhile hero, a majority saw no alternative instrument on the horizon, and hoped that he would have successfully led a chastened UNC to victory in the 2002 election. They however knew that Panday had a short shelf life, and that another figure would have to be cast and constructed in due course to solidify the gains that have so far been achieved, and which it feared would be reversed by a vengeful PNM. In the meantime, they were prepared to continue "riding with Bas." In a curious way, Manning and Ramesh Maharaj have helped to keep Panday on political life support, the former by the many unforced policy errors which he made following the results of the 2002 election and the latter by giving him an excuse to remain leader of the party to avoid its capture.

Given the fact that Trinidad society is riven down the middle and that both ethnic groups feel threatened and insecure, it is unlikely that the disposition to look longingly for a heroic leader would completely disappear. Significant sections of both groups feel ashamed and embarrassed by their current leaders who have shown themselves to be either greedy or politically clumsy, and are looking for an alternative whom they respect and with whom they can vicariously identify. A significant number however still regard the two national "stick fighters" as their national shepherd, and justify their choice primarily on the basis of race and/or religion.

Classical maximum charismatic leadership might well be dead or pre-collapsed in the Caribbean and it may well be that the search is on for a more instrumental type leader.[14] One however suspects that the messianic impulse still has life in it yet, and that substantial elements in both groups are still in a "cargo cult" mode "looking for Godot." The leaders, for their part, also continue to milk that impulse for whatever it is worth by either seeking, or sheepishly accepting religious or cultural "oil downs" and credentials. The charismatic radius may have grown narrower, and the emotional link between leader and follower weaker.

It has however not yet contracted to insignificance, and will not do so until the ethnic struggle for control of the state is transcended by other kinds of interest cleavages, assuming of course that it can ever fully be in societies such as ours.

Endnotes

1.   In Tobago, Panday referred to himself as "Uncle Bas." Williams and Gairy were also "Uncle Eric" and "Uncle Gairy" respectively. Manley was "Joshua" with his "rod of correction," while Duvalier was "Papa Doc."

2.   We note that Weber talks about "pure" or "genuine" charisma, but also of "heredity charisma," charisma of primogeniture," "charismatic king-ship," "office charisma" and "routinised charisma" (Allahar 2001: 6).

3.   Panday described that expulsion as "my darkest moment in politics." "I thought of giving up. I thought I had reached the end of the line. There was no where to go. The dream of unity seemed to be crumbling" (*Express*, April 9, 2002).

4.   Klass also refers to the *praja* relationship which he said is found in parts of India. As he explained: What is involved is a reciprocity of obligation, but in a highly patterned way. One person in the relationship is the "superior," and has the responsibility of guiding, advising, and assisting the "inferior" and his family. The "inferior" must obey his "superior," and perform labor for him, asked or unasked. The villagers have this sense of being *praja* to East Indian political leaders because of services rendered to the village, to the individual, or to the East Indian group as a whole. Any *praja* relationship may dissolve if one side fails to reciprocate properly (*ibid.*: 236).

The "praja" relationship closely resembles the *jajmani* relationship which one finds in many parts of the Indian countryside (Milner 1994).

5.   In May 2002, Panday held out an olive branch to Sudama, no doubt because he felt the need to unify the UNC in time for

elections that were due later that year. According to Panday, "in politics anything is possible, and we are always open to suggestions. In politics, one cannot be rigid and unbending. There must always be compromise because you have to deal with all kinds of people. Kelvin Ramnath alienated himself from the party and is now back. There is always the possibility of [Sudama's return]" (*Guardian*, May 8, 2002). Sudama expressed disinterest since the matter of corruption over which he left the party had not been addressed. As he declared:

> I left the UNC mainly because of the treatment in the party of the corruption allegations and because Panday wasn't dealing seriously with it. Everyone (in UNC) was becoming tarnished with the allegations and I was offended by this. Up to now I haven't seen any action on this. We've even heard UNC's Gerald Yetming complain recently that he felt Panday had erred in handling certain things. Recently we also had the police charge a former UNC Finance Minister and UNC financier, and if the police charge people, one assumes they have some evidence to do so. So the situation remains the same. (*Guardian*, May 9, 2002)

6. We however recall that on Good Friday 1997, the MP for Arima, Rupert Griffith, was called a Judas for having switched to the UNC in 1996, and that his effigy was beaten as a "bobolee" and a "coffin" bearing his "remains" dragged through the streets of Arima.

7. Pichakaree might be described as a Hindu version of the Trinidad calypso sung in a mixture of English and Hindi (cf. Ryan 1999a). The text of the song is as follows:

I was once the Raja
You were the Rani
We were like majesty
All over TnT
Liming and we dining
With we brand new friends
Recently we purchased
Two Mercedes Benz
I was always boasting
I is prime minister
So long as Mr. Patrick
Is Opposition Leader
Since I started boasting
Now six years later
Is the same Mr. Patrick
Who riding dem motorcar

CHORUS

Gyul pack up you bundle le we go
Mr. Patrick now running the show

Six years I in power
Running ah government
To go back opposition
That is embarrassment
But ah know how you like Port of Spain
But soon we may come back again
We going Pichakaaree
And throw up some gold
And when we get back power
You go go back in Carnival
You go go back in Carnival

As a union leader
And a politician
I feel like bhagwam bless we
With plenty gyan
I had so much shakti
I feel I could fight ah lion
Some say I get sarapay
With too much abhiman
I doh want successor

Not in this janam
I go give them pressure
And call them nemakharam
If dey want to come back
From the cemetery
Do like Kelvin Ramnath
Bow down and soorhaway me

As former PM
To show I was tough on crime
Ah char-ha-way Dole Chadee
Eight Indians at one time
All dem Indian people
Who built the UNC
Ah char-ha-way everybody
This party belong to me
To hell with dem sugar workers
Who begging for gratuity
When I was in power
Ah almost char-ha-way Caroni
And you know my memory
I doh forget easily
After the Pichakaaree
Ah go char-ha-way Ravi ji
The people were so happy
For ah Indian Prime Minister
They thought I would uplift them
In Indian culture
They know I would be busy
So they expected my patni
To see she in a sari
For Holi Shivrathi
They thought it would be very easy
To get paisa for chutney
Look how I had dem begging
To get paisa for Pichakaaree
Go and tell the country
To take advice from my agee
Never take ah bound coolie
And make them a dignitary.

8. The public debt grew by 50 percent between 1995 and 2001. A great deal of money was borrowed by state companies to finance the paving of roads, the construction of the airport and various infrastructure projects. Substantial amounts had not been catered for in the annual Budget.

9. Eight persons were arrested and charged for a variety of offences related to the improper and corrupt handling of moneys used for the construction of the Airport. Thirty million ($30m) dollars was also used to build a school in Biche that has not yet been opened. The school was built on a site that was given to subsidence and emission of subterranean gases.

10. Panday declared that his "enemy list" was drawn from high society. The list included the Chief Justice, the President of the Republic, the Chairman of the CCN media group, economist Lloyd Best and the author. With respect to the author, Panday indicated that "I have no hatred, no bitterness, no anger, no grief, no envy. Is just that I out to destroy him." With respect to the *Express*, Panday said one could send them flowers, but there was a time to do so, "when you bury them." When asked whether he wished to make peace with his enemies, Panday said he was prepared to do so at any time. But "while you are suing for peace, you must prepare for war" *(Express*, March 25, 2000). He was of the view that in politics, one must ensure that one's enemies "were done in before they had a chance to do you in."

11. Following the 2000 elections, Panday advised the President to appoint seven persons who were defeated to the Senate and to install them as junior ministers. The President initially refused, but reluctantly gave way.

12. A St. Augustine Research Associates (SARA) poll done in November 2001 revealed that 49, 69 and 29 percent of the general, Afro and Indo population respectively, believed that Mr. Panday was involved in corruption, Panday deemed the poll "libelous."

13. Panday said he would give up politics and retire at the age of 70, an age which he attains in May 2003. He indicated a wish to write a book in his retirement. "I have been in politics since 1965 and I know what has gone on" (*Guardian,* May 8, 2002). He however made it clear that he did not plan to give up the leadership of the UNC soon.

14. The phenomenon is very alive in Latin America as recent events in Brazil and Venezuela indicate.

Appendix

In February 2003, Mr. Robinson raised eyebrows when he remarked in an after dinner speech given in honour of the PNM cabinet that "we began on the same side, but soon found ourselves on the opposite side, and we continued on opposite sides for some time, but the fact of the matter is that we are on the same side again. I am sure it is a divinity that has produced Mr. Manning and myself now sitting side by side" (*Express*, February 21, 2003). Mr. Manning reciprocated Mr. Robinson's remark, declaring that "when the history of Trinidad and Tobago is examined, your periods of governance and your period in public life of the country, the period [*sic*] late 2001 when we found ourselves in an 18-18 situation, the way that period was handled in my respectful view will be recorded as your finest hour (*Express*, February 22, 2003). Some saw this as proof that Mr Robinson had returned to the PNM tribe and that he had displayed his "true colours" when he appointed Manning to be Prime Minister. (*Sunday Guardian*, March 2, 2003.) This was also seen as proof that the two men had conspired to out maneuver Mr. Panday.

Judgements on Robinson's career as President have been mixed. Some insist that he was a PNM partisan and hostile to Mr Panday. Some deny this and say that he acted courageously and in keeping with his declared concern for high moral standards of governance, at least as he understood them. The manner in which Panday dealt with appointments to and removals from the Senate, the cavalier manner in which he appointed unelected persons to act as Prime Minister during his various absences (seemingly in a game of musical chairs) clearly bothered Mr. Robinson, who believed that a "constitution is more than a legal document, [and] acknowledges the supremacy of God." As he also complained, "there were those who said I should act as a rubber stamp and as though I did not have a brain (*Guardian*, February 14, 2003).

Robinson did not accept the view that his role was to comply mechanically with what the Constitution prescribed without taking political morality into account, the "lore" as opposed to the "laws." There were however those who believed that the responsibility of the President was to act in accordance with the black letter provisions of the Constitution whatever his private views might be. As one jurist argued: "The Constitution has to be interpreted in terms of certain principles of democracy and fundamental rights, but there is no morality like the Ten Commandments. A person who is corrupt is as entitled as a saint to hold the Prime Minister's Office if he wins the most seats" (*Guardian*, February 14, 2003).

One recalls that Mr. Robinson's elevation to the Presidency was accompanied by a chorus of controversy. Many PNM supporters believed that a deal involving the Presidency was made with Mr. Panday in 1995 when Mr. Robinson decided to break the 17-17 deadlock by throwing his political weight behind the UNC. I have investigated this claim, and no evidence has been forthcoming to support it, but suspicions remain strong among PNM and NAR supporters. The latter believed that Mr. Robinson sold out the party and Tobago for a mess of status pottage. The charge was that he had exchanged the crown jewels for the plumage of the crown.

Ironically, many who distrusted Mr. Robinson then, and who recalled his celebrated break with the PNM in 1970, came to regard him as their man on a white horse. The view of the Afro-creole community was that the prodigal son had betrayed the tribe out of spite but had come back to redeem it.

Lloyd Best was of the view that Robinson's attempt to transform the role of non-ceremonial head to one which had active political clout was a "Caribbean revolution without violence" (*Express*, April 16, 2001). There were indeed several occasions when Mr. Robinson's actions raised serious constitutional questions which, potentially had "revolutionary" implications. These included the question as to whether he had the power to appoint a Commission of Inquiry on his own motion, the question as to whether he had the power to recall a commissioner of the EBC with whom he was displeased, the question as to whether he had the power to refuse to appoint 7 defeated candidates to the Senate and to junior ministerial office, and whether he had the power to refuse the request of a Prime Minister to dissolve Parliament or the power to appoint Mr. Manning to the Prime Ministership in place of Mr. Panday who had not "lost" the election.

In the first three instances, Mr. Robinson clearly did not have the power to do what he wished to do, or was being asked to do. It is also clear that the President did the politically, if not the legally, correct thing when he raised objections to what Mr. Panday sought to do in respect of the 7 defeated candidates. He used the power of delay to force Mr. Panday and the country to think again. As Best would say, it was the "right mistake." I also believe that he made the right decision as to whom to appoint as Prime Minister after the 18-18 tie, just as he had done in 1995 when he shoe horned Mr. Panday into the Prime Minister's chair. Many criticised what he did in 1995, but supporting the UNC was the politically and historically correct thing to do. The Indian community had been politically marginalised for much too long, and it was time for the UNC to be allowed a turn at the crease. It was a disastrous innings, but Robinson could not have anticipated that Mr. Panday would do or permit to be done some of the things which occurred during his stint as Prime Minister. On becoming President, Mr. Robinson was given a chance to reverse his "mistake," took it, and in the process earned the gratitude of a substantial section of the population who now claim that it was his "finest hour."

UNC supporters of course have a different view of Robinson's ministry. While they applauded him in 1995, they were eager to crucify him in December 2001. I do not share the view that his decision in 2002 was primarily driven by spite and racial animus though one understands why some would so conclude.

The question of motive is always difficult to determine, especially when complex decisions are being deconstructed. More often than not, critical decisions are driven by a complex of motives that are not easy to disentangle. All that one can conclude at this juncture is that Robinson was an instrument of history, the proverbial midwife who helped to give birth to an embryonic political regime which was struggling to emerge out of the bosom of the old PNM dominated society. By December 2001, that new regime had shown that it was not yet capable of providing the quality of governance which many had expected or hoped for, and had to be changed. As was the case with Manning in 1995, Panday asked the electorate for a renewal of his mandate, and did not quite get it. The result was as ambiguous in 2001 as it had been in 1995. In 2001, Robinson felt that the historical spirit "compelled" him to select the PNM. He did what was politically necessary. The question as to whether spite was operative is irrelevant.

Only time will tell whether Mr. Robinson's tenure as President permanently revolutionised the office as has been claimed. The 1997-2002 era was a politically turbulent one, and Mr. Robinson's stature and experience allowed him to play a creative role. The man and the times coincided. Professor Vernon Bogdanor once observed that "precedents and conventions do not exist in a vacuum. Rather, they reflect the facts of political power. No alternation in conventions is likely until the existing ones have been shown to be no longer applicable and therefore exhausted." Bogdanor was also correct when he observed that an extremely "messy" situation usually exists in the intervening period. Differing conceptions as to what is correct reflect a conflict between the order that is dying and one that is struggling to be born.

References

Allahar, Anton. ed. 2001. *Caribbean Charisma*. Kingston, Jamaica: Ian Randle.

Alleyne, Dodderidge. 1999. "Oran Reminiscences." *Caribbean Issues* 7(11) (March).

Best, L., and Allan Harris 1991. *A Party Politics for Trinidad and Tobago*. Trinidad and Tobago:Tapia House.

Bogdanor, Vernon. 1995. *The Monarchy and the Constitution*. Oxford: Clarendon.

Deyalsingh, Lennox (Chairman). 2002. *Report of the Commission of Enquiry Into the Functioning of the Elections and Boundaries Commission*. Mimeo.

Ghany, H. 2000. "Constitutional Interpretation and Presidential Powers: The Case of Trinidad and Tobago." *Caribbean Dialogue* 6(3&4) (December).

Giddens, Anthony. 1972. *Politics and Sociology in the Thought of Max Weber*. U.K.: The Macmillan Press.

Gonsalves, Ralph. 2001. *Are Caribbean Prime Ministers Too Powerful?* Paper Presented to Conference on Constitutional Reform in the Caribbean, Barbados, January 21, 2001.

Grant, Ruth. 2002. *Ethics and Politics: Institutional Solutions and Their Limits*. Central Bank of Trinidad and Tobago.

Headley, Bernard. 2002. *The Social and Political Construction of the Drug Menace in Jamaica*. Paper presented at the 3rd Annual SALISES Conference, UWI, Mona, Jamaica.

Klass, Morton. 1961. *East Indians in Trinidad.* New York: Columbia University Press.

Lewis, Arthur. 1965. *Politics in West Africa.* Oxford University Press.

Lipset, Seymour Martin. 1996. *American Exceptionalism.* New York: Norton.

Maingot, Anthony. 1996. "Haiti: Four Old and Two New Hypotheses." In *Constructing Democratic Governance: Latin America and the Caribbean in the 1990s,* edited by Jorge Dominguez and Abraham Lowenthal. Johns Hopkins.

Milner, Murray. 1994. *Status and Sacredness: A General Theory of Status Relations and an Analysis of Indian Culture.* Oxford University Press.

Powell, G. Bingham Jr. 2000. *Elections as Instruments of Democracy.* New Haven: Yale University Press.

Pulzer, Peter. 1967. *Political Representation and Elections in Britain.* London, Allen and Unwin.

Ryan, Selwyn. 2003. *Levels of Satisfaction with Governance in the Eastern Caribbean and in Guyana and Trinidad and Tobago.* Paper presented at a UNDP Conference of Donors, Runaway Bay, Jamaica, November 13, 2002.

_____.2003a. *Independent Thought and Caribbean Freedom: Essays in Honour of Lloyd Best.* (Forthcoming).

_____. 2001. *The Judiciary and Governance in the Caribbean.* The University of the West Indies, St. Augustine, Trinidad: ISES.

_____. 1999a. *The Jhandi and The Cross.* The University of the West Indies, St. Augustine, Trinidad: ISER.

Ryan, Selwyn. 1999. *Winner Takes All: The Westminster Experience in the Caribbean.* The University of the West Indies, St. Augustine, Trinidad: ISER.

_____. 1996. *Pathways to Power Indians and the Struggle for National Unity in Trinidad and Tobago.* The University of the West Indies, St. Augustine, Trinidad: ISER.

_____. 1995. *The Black Power Revolution 1970: A Retrospective.* UWI, St. Augustine, Trinidad and Tobago: ISER.

Ryan, S., and J. LaGuerre. 1994. *Ethnicity and Employment Practices in the Public Sector.* The University of the West Indies, St. Augustine, Trinidad: Centre for Ethnic Studies.

Ryan, Selwyn. 1991. *The Muslimeen Grab for Power: Race, Religion and Resolution in Trinidad and Tobago.* Trinidad and Tobago: Inprint Caribbean.

_____. 1989a. *Revolution and Reaction: Parties and Politics in Trinidad and Tobago.* University of the West Indies, St. Augustine, Trinidad: I.S.E.R.

_____1989. *The Disillusioned Electorate: The Politics of Sucession in Trinidad and Tobago:* Imprint Publications.

_____. 1972. *Race and Nationalism in Trinidad and Tobago.* University of Toronto Press.

Samaroo, Siewah, and Roodal Moonilal, eds. 1991. *Basdeo Panday: An Enigma Answered.* Curepe: Chakra Publishing House.

Stepan, Alfred, and Cindy Skatch. 1993. "Constitutional Frameworks and Political Consolidation: Parliamentarism *vs* Presidentialism." *World Politics*, 46 (October).

Weber, Max. 1971. "The Three Types of Legitimate Rule." In *Sociology: The Classic Statements*, edited by Marcello Truzzi. New York: Random House.

Index

Other Books by Selwyn Ryan

1972 - *Race and Nationalism in Trinidad and Tobago: A Study of Decolonization in a Multiracial Society*

1979 - *The Confused Electorate: A Study of Political Attitudes and Opinions in Trinidad and Tobago* with Selwyn Ryan, Eddie Green and Jack Harewood

1988 - *Trinidad and Tobago: The Independence Experience 1962-1987* edited with the assistance of Gloria Gordon

1989 - *Revolution and Reaction: Parties and Politics in Trinidad and Tobago 1970-1981*

1989 - *The Disillusioned Electorate: The Politics of Succession in Trinidad and Tobago*

1990 - *The Life and Times of Ray Edwin Dieffenthaller*

1990 - *The Pursuit of Honour: The Life and Times of H.O.B. Wooding*

1991 - *Social and Occupational Stratification in Contemporary Trinidad and Tobago* (edited)

1991 - *The Muslimeen Grab for Power: Race, Religion and Resolution in Trinidad and Tobago*

1991 - *Male Attitudes Towards Family Planning and Gender Equity in Grenada*, IPPF, New York.

1992 - *Issues and Problems in Caribbean Public Administration* edited with Deryck Brown

1992 - *Sharks and Sardines: Blacks In Business in Trinidad and Tobago* with Lou Anne Barclay

1994 - *Entrepreneurship in the Caribbean: Culture, Structure, Conjuncture* edited with Taimoon Stewart

1994 - *Ethnicity and Employment Practices in the Public Sector* with J. LaGuerre

1995 - *The Black Power Revolution 1970: A Retrospective* with Taimoon Stewart and Roy McCree

1996 - *Pathways to Power: Indians and the Struggle for National Unity in Trinidad and Tobago*

1997 - *Behind the Bridge: Poverty Politics and Patronage in Laventille, Trinidad* with Roy McCree and Godfrey St. Bernard.

1999 - *Winner Takes All: The West Minster Experience in the Caribbean*

1999 - *The Jhandi & The Cross: The Clash of Cultures in Post-Creole Trinidad and Tobago*

2001 - *The Judiciary and Governance in the Caribbean*

2002 - *Governance in the Caribbean* with Anne Marie Bissessar

2003 - *Independent Thought and Caribbean Freedom: Essays in Honour of Lloyd Best* (edited)